D1179640

MINDING CREATION

T&T Clark Studies in Systematic Theology

Edited by
Ian A. McFarland
Ivor Davidson
Philip G. Ziegler
John Webster[†]

Volume 37

MINDING CREATION

Theological Panpsychism and the Doctrine of Creation

Joanna Leidenhag

LONDON • NEW YORK • OXFORD • NEW DELHI • SYDNEY

T&T CLARK
Bloomsbury Publishing Plc
50 Bedford Square, London, WC1B 3DP, UK
1385 Broadway, New York, NY 10018, USA

BLOOMSBURY, T&T CLARK and the T&T Clark logo are trademarks of
Bloomsbury Publishing Plc

First published in Great Britain 2021

ISBN: HB: 978-0-5676-9621-2
ePDF: 978-0-5676-9622-9
eBook: 978-0-5676-9624-3

Series: T&T Clark Studies in Systematic Theology, volume 37

Typeset by Newgen KnowledgeWorks Pvt. Ltd., Chennai, India

To find out more about our authors and books visit www.bloomsbury.com
and sign up for our newsletters.

For Mikael Leidenhag

CONTENTS

ACKNOWLEDGEMENTS

Someone once told me that a book is never truly finished, but merely published when the author decides that the debates she's been having with friends and colleagues are worth sharing more widely. Acknowledgement sections are a useful way to thank the various conversation partners who have developed the ideas found in this book, and others who have helped me share this conversation more widely.

This research began and remains primarily a conversation I am having with Dr Mikael Leidenhag. Without these conversations and without his love this research would not have been possible. He must receive the first statement of gratitude. It is to Mikael that this book is dedicated.

I would like to thank my doctoral supervisors, Prof. David A. S. Fergusson and Prof. Mark Harris, and the wider postgraduate community at the University of Edinburgh. In particular, thanks go to Nomi Pritz-Bennett, Sarah Lane Ritchie, Andrew Johnson and Clement Chen, who sustained this conversation over three years. Prof. Fergusson deserves special mention for permitting and even encouraging me to follow the research into the bizarre topic of panpsychist philosophy, for reading numerous drafts of these chapters and for casting his pearls of wisdom before me. I owe a debt of thanks to the growing community of analytic theologians, which has encouraged me and taught me to think carefully through how issues in analytic philosophy might be used as a resource for Christian theology. In particular, I would like to thank R. T. Mullins, Oliver D. Crisp, Alan J. Torrance, Andrew B. Torrance, Jonathan C. Rutledge, Joshua Cockayne, David Worsley, Tim and Faith Pawl and many others whose work has inspired me.

Many thanks to the Scottish Graduate School of Arts and Humanities, which funded this research. Thanks also to the John Templeton Foundation whose Science-Engaged Theology grant currently employs me at the University of St Andrews and allowed me to turn this dissertation into a monograph. Many thanks to Ian A. McFarland and David Grumett for examining this research in a way that offered me both big probing questions and detailed corrections. Thank you to Anna Turton and her colleagues at T&T Clark for all their hard work in preparing this text for publication.

Finally, my deepest gratitude and love goes to my family. Harry, Alison, Colin, Margaret, Timothy Macdonald and Hillary Coote each instilled in me the importance of education, fostered in me a love for learning and intellectual debate and refused to let learning disabilities hold me back. They always saw the person I could become and loved the person I am. Most importantly, they shared with me the love and grace of our Lord Jesus Christ and encouraged me to question that faith with hard thinking. It is an honour and privilege to be a member of this family.

INTRODUCTION

The doctrine of creation in Christian theology is not primarily a statement about how or when the universe began. Rather it is an articulation of, first, how everything that is not God (the creation) relates to God (the Creator) and, second, how different creatures relate to one another. How this universe relates to God depends in part upon what type of universe this is, and so the doctrine of creation is always in dialogue with the natural sciences and philosophy. Within these disciplines there is a growing consensus that recent attempts to describe reality in exhaustively physical categories are insufficient in light of the mysterious reality of human consciousness. As such, any theory that separates humanity off from the rest of creation in such absolute ontological terms is unlikely to prove beneficial to the quest for greater understanding of either ourselves or the world.

Questions regarding the place of the human soul or mind within God's creation have always been a central part of Christian theology. However, the Christian tradition puts forth no one single view regarding the mind such that a variety of possibilities continue to be explored and weighed today. In keeping with this tradition of debate, this book investigates how the philosophy of panpsychism might benefit the doctrine of creation.

Panpsychism is a family of theories within philosophy of mind, which seek to explain the existence of consciousness in the human person by positing mentality ('psyche') as fundamental throughout the natural world ('pan'). To claim that mentality is fundamental is to say that the mind can neither be explained in terms of, nor reduced to, anything non-mental. This is in contrast to physicalists, who claim that the mind can be reduced to physicality, and to emergentists, who claim that minds can be explained by the behaviour and structure of non-mental materials and forces. Note that panpsychism does not entail that the only things that exist are mental or immaterial, although it is certainly compatible with this idealist extension. Strictly speaking, panpsychism comments only on the nature and place of mentality within the cosmos and is not a total or complete ontological theory. While a traditional substance dualist will also describe the mind as fundamental, most substance dualists envision minds as given to a particular organism upon conception or embryonic development by God. Substance dualists do not typically describe mentality as fundamental *throughout* the natural world. One could, however, construe panpsychism as a kind of dualism all the way down.

When one compares panpsychism to neighbouring positions within philosophy of mind, its closest relative seems to be hylomorphism. Hylomorphism is a position deriving from Aristotelian philosophy, which sees all actual being as a combination of matter (*hyle*) and form (*morphe*). Matter without form exists only in potentiality and is known as *prime matter*, whereas actual matter, which has form, is a *corporeal substance*. The form of a thing, which makes it the kind of substance that it is, is also referred to by Aristotle as a *soul* (*psyche*); the form of human beings is a rational soul, the form of animals is an animal (irrational) soul, the form of plants is a vegetative soul, and so on. Moreover, like the indwelling powers of psyche in panpsychism, the form in hylomorphism determines the passive and active powers and dispositions of any given thing, such that causation arises from the inherent capacities within formed matter. In both panpsychism and hylomorphism this provides the basis for retaining teleology or final causes within the natural world.

In order to differentiate their position from panpsychism, a hylomorphist will most likely stress that psyche/form does not entail the capacity or even the proto-capacity for experience. However, in this case the capacity of experience will have to be sourced externally from the corporeal substance rather than be an inherent power, but this is something hylomorphists do not typically wish to do.[1] Instead, the demarcation between hylomorphism and panpsychism, I suggest, is that on hylomorphism each substance is fundamental such that 'there are metaphysically fundamental entities at multiple levels of scale'.[2] This is in contrast to panpsychism, where fundamentality is found at one level of reality, of which all other entities are aggregates, combinations or individuations.[3]

In this sense, hylomorphism and panpsychism both uncomfortably straddle the categories of monism and dualism, and both extend the duality of nature

---

1. This is because of the inherent powers view of properties, capacities and dispositions which hylomorphism entails. If hylomorphism is taken to mean that matter contains the potentiality for consciousness, such that when the matter has the correct form it manifests as a conscious corporeal substance, then this, as far as I can tell, is a type of panpsychism.

2. Robert C. Koons, 'Knowing Nature: Aristotle, God, and the Quantum', in *Knowing Creation: Perspectives from Theology, Philosophy, and Science*, ed. Andrew B. Torrance and Thomas H. McCall (Grand Rapids, MI: Zondervan, 2018), 216. Later, Koon clarifies this further in writing, 'In the Aristotelian image of nature, *substances* (metaphysically fundamental things) exist at many levels of scale and composition.' Koons, 'Knowing Nature', 220.

3. If fundamentality is found at every level of reality, then it seems that hylomorphism restricts the extent to which corporeal substances can combine or individuate at different levels. However, depending upon a hylomorphist's account of mereology and the possibility of different corporeal substances combining into a new, single unified corporeal substance such that the form of a thing changes, this difference may quickly disappear. I suspect that, in truth, the majority of variants of hylomorphism and panpsychism cannot be meaningfully distinguished.

to include all of reality, animate and inanimate alike. It may well turn out that the categories of monism, dualism and idealism are rather unhelpful. For while denying the reality of neither the mental nor the material, panpsychism often eschews traditional typologies by underlining that what we call 'material' and 'mental' always come together and cannot be separated. In the theological panpsychism proposed in the final three chapters of this book, it is argued that all divisions within the created world pale in comparison to this first act of creation *ex nihilo* and the utter distinction established between Creator and created.

In recent decades, emergence theory has become a popular via media between eliminative physicalism, which denies the reality of consciousness, and substance dualism, which separates mind and matter into separate ontological categories. Put simply, emergence theory argues that when physical processes become complicated in exactly the right way, such as in the human brain, the mind emerges. In lieu of the inability (or refusal) of emergence theorists to provide an account of how unconscious matter gives rise to the mind, a small but significant group of contemporary analytic philosophers are returning to the historical concept of panpsychism as a more satisfactory alternative. In contrast to emergence theory, panpsychists argue that in order for human beings to be conscious, the basic ingredients of mentality have to exist throughout the universe as a fundamental feature of reality. Only if this panpsychist thesis is granted, it is argued, can the complex minds of organisms, animals and humans develop or, perhaps, emerge.[4] Should this revival of panpsychism continue, what will the implications be for Christian theologians engaged in constructive and interdisciplinary articulations of the doctrine of creation? This is the driving question that this book sets out to answer.

Emergence theory has been enthusiastically embraced by some contemporary theologians, particularly those who work at the intersection of science and theology. The first chapter argues that this enthusiasm for emergence theory within Christian theology is misplaced. In addition to significant scientific and philosophical ambiguities, theologies built upon the theory of emergence contain unrecognized tensions. This is because emergence theory exhibits a tendency towards becoming a global theory of everything, rather than merely an explanation for the origin of consciousness. If this tendency for emergence theory to become emergent*ism*, then the transcendence of God as Creator, incarnate Saviour and indwelling Spirit is in danger of becoming problematically compromised. Before embracing emergence theory too quickly then, theologians should investigate alternative ontologies, which may serve Christianity better.

Chapter 2 examines the resurgence of interest in panpsychism from prominent analytic philosophers of mind. Thomas Nagel, David J. Chalmers and Galen Strawson are the knights of this tale, although they do not stand alone. Their

---

4. A panpsychist is then in a position to reintroduce weaker forms of emergence back into their account of the human consciousness and biological evolution. This emergent panpsychism is discussed in Chapter 2.

'campaign', although it was never planned as such, is the culminative effect of a growing dissatisfaction with both physicalism and emergentism within secular philosophy of mind, and the refusal to return too quickly to a substance dualism reliant on theism for coherence. After the central arguments for panpsychism have been narrated, this chapter turns to evaluate how well panpsychism fares in philosophic combat. The largest section of this chapter considers the objections levelled against panpsychism, the response offered by panpsychists and the shape of panpsychism when the dust has cleared from the battlefield. When all have counted their wounded, philosophy of mind is left in a stalemate, but it is a stalemate where panpsychism has earnt her seat at the table. The remaining question is, whom will panpsychism choose as an ally? The final section of this chapter brokers an accord between theism and panpsychism and argues that if the logic within contemporary panpsychism is consistently held then it leads to theism. In short, there is a natural alliance between panpsychism and theism.

The alliance between panpsychism and Christian theology is not as new and surprising as it might seem from the present literature; instead there is a very old friendship here that can be built upon. Chapter 3 provides a historical retrieval by arguing that the panpsychism of Gottfried Wilhelm von Leibniz arose out of theological concerns and was employed to serve theological argumentation. The theological arguments focused upon are: (1) the doctrine of creation *ex nihilo*, (2) a view of creation as a single, comprehensive order and (3) a sacramental ontology. These arguments are the seeds for the more constructive proposals found within Chapters 4 and 5. By highlighting how Leibniz employed panpsychism, not only in conjunction but also in defence of the doctrine of creation *ex nihilo*, this interlude disentangles panpsychism from the rejections of this doctrine put forth by process theology and feminist theologies (which often contain panpsychist tendencies). Panpsychism does not entail or commit one to any specific doctrine of God.[5]

In Chapters 1 and 2, the argument for the adoption of panpsychism within the Christian doctrine of creation has been rather cautious and defensive. It has only been argued that panpsychism is a more philosophically robust and theologically flexible theory of mind than emergentism for Christian theologians to adopt. Can panpsychism offer more than this by constructively interacting and integrating with other theological commitments central to the doctrine of creation? What theological benefits might panpsychism offer to Christian theologians? Chapters 4 and 5 assess the fecundity of panpsychism, one might say the potential growth of the three seeds gathered from Leibniz's theology, in two contentious areas of theological debate today: models of divine action and Christian responses to the ecological crisis.

Chapter 4 evaluates the scientific, ethical and theological challenges summarized by the epithet 'interventionism', and the responses by Robert J. Russell, David Ray

---

5. This chapter, therefore, is a response to dismissals of panpsychism on the grounds that it entails some form of process theism (see below) or pantheism. See John Macquarrie, *In Search of Deity* (London: SCM Press, 1984), 53.

Griffin and Kathryn Tanner. These are significantly different theological projects, and not directly compatible with one another. Yet, the flexibility of panpsychism as an ontology is shown in that a panpsychist ontology would strengthen each of these models of divine action. Although panpsychism does not commit theology to any one doctrine of God, it does make a distinctive contribution to the area of divine action. What panpsychism uniquely provides is an ontological 'space' for the personal and interactive presence of the Holy Spirit indwelling the depths of creaturely subjectivity and calling all creatures towards flourishing.

While Chapter 5 draws attention to panpsychism's importance within secular eco-philosophy, it is argued that an account of transcendence is also required such that nature is not an end in itself, but a sacrament pointing towards the Creator. It is then argued that central theological metaphors, depicting the relationship between humanity and creation, are distorted when human beings alone have the necessary ontology for reciprocal, dialogical relationship with God. Panpsychism enables theologians to realistically interpret neglected aspects of the biblical witness and church's liturgy, such that creation is a responsive community made to praise the Triune God.

The challenge of articulating a robust model of divine action and providing an adequate response to the ecological crisis are two of the most pressing concerns for the contemporary articulation of creation. These two chapters use panpsychism to build a call-and-response structure to a panpsychist doctrine of creation. The God, who spoke creation into being and whose active indwelling presence calls all creatures into union, receives the praises and the groanings of created beings. Moreover, these chapters reveal the possibility that panpsychism may not only be resourced from without but may also arise from within the Christian community's scriptural and liturgical reflection. Panpsychism facilitates a robust and realistic account of God's active presence within creation and the response of all created beings in praise. If nothing more, the revival of panpsychism within analytic philosophy of mind should be welcomed and may be partnered with by theologians in the coming years.

At this point, we might pay heed to Austin Farrer's advice for 'a proper distinction of saving faith from pious philosophy', whereby ontological theories are held lightly, in order to ensure that a theologian's 'vitals are not being torn away when their philosophy is jettisoned'.[6] Arguments, such as those discussed in this book, look at different ways of viewing the finite creation in light of theological claims, but the core claims regarding who God is and what God has done are not scrutinized here in the same philosophical method. It is often said that primary theology lies in the worship of the church, and the work of theologians is always secondary reflection. If so, then the consideration of this book might be considered tertiary reflection by examining the philosophical frameworks that best facilitate the secondary articulations of doctrinal theology and allow for greater synthesis

---

6. Austin Farrer, *Faith and Speculation: An Essay in Philosophical Theology* (London: A&C Black, 1967), 14.

between primary and secondary theological discourse. While such tertiary reflection is a necessary and helpful aid to theology, the conclusions reached are not matters of saving faith.

To confuse these forms of discourse would be to divinize philosophy or naturalize theology. It is one of the central critiques, found repeatedly in these chapters, that theology must resist the urge – most often arising in interdisciplinary discourse – to naturalize its claims and thereby speak of God as existing in metaphysical continuity, or within the larger category of 'nature' that humans investigate. As a result of this methodological conviction, it might be noted that in my argumentation panpsychism alone does not generate new theological insights. Instead, panpsychism is tested as an ontological framework, and judged as to its ability to allow theologians to speak more clearly and robustly of the distinction between God and creation, while simultaneously affirming the presence of God and the value of creation.

One example of naturalizing theology by subsuming theological claims under a particular ontology is process theology. Alfred North Whitehead (1861–1947), Charles Hartshorne (1897–2000) and the process theology movement that they ignited and championed is probably the most well-known integration of panpsychism within Christian thought. In many ways, this book is designed to refute the assumption that process theology is the only way to incorporate panpsychism into Christianity. As such, a brief exposition of process thought is offered here, such that it may be referenced in contrast to all that follows.

A brief exposition of process theology

During the metaphysical stage of his career, Whitehead saw that the dualism that Western thought had inherited from Descartes had led to the contradictions of scientific materialism.[7] In order to undo this 'world-knot', Western cosmology needed to be radically rethought.[8] Whitehead argued that such a solution would entail 'no arbitrary breaks' between mentality and nature, such that the mind was at the heart of 'the constitution of nature'.[9] While Whitehead's system is shot through with panpsychism, it is also highly idiosyncratic; process scholarship is neither a norm in panpsychist philosophy nor the best paradigm for panpsychist theology.

---

7. See, Alfred North Whitehead, *Science and the Modern World* (New York: Free Press, [1925] 1967).

8. Arthur Schopenhauer is credited with referring to the mind–body problem as the world-knot, which inspired the title of David Ray Griffin's book on a panexperientialist solution: *Unsnarling the World-Knot: Consciousness, Freedom, and the Mind-Body Problem* (Eugene, OR: Wipf and Stock, 1998).

9. Whitehead, *Science and the Modern World*, 73; Alfred North Whitehead, *Modes of Thought* (New York: Capricorn Books, 1938), 156. Whitehead's panpsychism was, then, initially motivated by the Argument from Continuity.

In preparation for the alternative that is argued for throughout this book, the remainder of this introduction will, first, show in what sense process philosophy is panpsychist and, second, argue that theologians interested in panpsychism can, and should, reject process theology's doctrine of God.[10]

Inspired by William James, Whitehead constructed a new theory of reality upon the foundation of experiential events; he called these 'occasions of experience' or 'actual occasions'.[11] These actual occasions are 'drops of experience, complex and independent', forming an 'ocean of feeling'.[12] These occasions are 'the final real things of which the world is made up'.[13] Whitehead's ontology has been labelled 'panexperientialist' (a subtype of panpsychism) since all reality is constituted by experiential events.[14] In contrast to the panpsychism discussed in this book, process philosophy contains no enduring substances or subjects beneath these experiences, but only a succession of experiences that form the 'becoming' (but never the 'being') of all the apparent substances and subjects in the universe. All of the subjects and objects that we encounter in the world are said to be collections of these actual occasions, which have achieved some level of unity to form a 'nexus' or interdependent 'society'.[15] It is due to this ever becoming, never restful, stream of experiential events that Whitehead's philosophy has birthed the movement known as *process* philosophy.

Actual occasions are fleeting moments of experience, which momentarily enjoy 'subjective immediacy' before being replaced by a successor.[16] The predecessor forms part of the experience (i.e. the reality) of the subsequent occasion, and

10. Due to the limitations of space, I simply refer readers less accustomed to the complexity and terminology of process philosophy to John B. Cobb and David Ray Griffin, *Process Theology: An Introductory Exposition* (Louisville, KY: Westminster John Knox Press, 1976).

11. Alfred North Whitehead refers to 'actual occasions' in *Adventures of Ideas* (New York: Free Press, [1933] 1967) and 'occasions of experience' in *Process and Reality*, corrected edition, ed. David Ray Griffin and Donald W. Sherburne (New York: Free Press, [1928] 1978); Whitehead credits William James for giving Whitehead the idea that human experience comes in drops; Whitehead, *Process and Reality*, 105–6.

12. Whitehead, *Process and Reality*, 18, 166.

13. Whitehead, *Process and Reality*, 18.

14. The term 'panexperientialist' was first used by John B. Cobb and David Ray Griffin in *Mind in Nature: Essays on the Interface of Science and Philosophy* (Washington, DC: University of America Press, 1977). Whitehead never used any such terminology, and Charles Hartshorne employed the term 'panpsychism' and later replaced it with 'psychicalism'. See, David Ray Griffin, *Reenchantment without Supernaturalism: A Process Philosophy of Religion* (Ithaca, NY: Cornell University Press, 2001), 97.

15. Whitehead, *Adventures of Ideas*, 258–61.

16. Whitehead, *Process and Reality*, 38, 336–8.

thus obtains what Whitehead calls 'objective immortality'.[17] It is because the relationship between occasions constitutes their very essence that occasions are 'internally related' (past to present, and simultaneous adjacent occasions) and process philosophy claims to be a 'relational ontology'. Herein lies Whitehead's account of efficient causality; an actual occasion carries within it the whole history of its predecessors, and this has 'causal efficacy' that the occasion 'prehends' or feels.[18] This process of the past being experienced by the present is the 'physical pole' of existence and gives the impression at the macro level of temporal duration of objects.[19] It is worth noting that even this 'physical pole' is entirely experiential.

Whitehead supplements this with the 'mental pole' of existence, which introduces novelty into how these physical feelings are integrated ('transmuted') into the next occasion in the sequence.[20] This is how change may occur in the universe. Novelty is introduced through the prehension, not of other actual occasions as at the physical pole, but by the 'conceptual prehension' of 'eternal objects'.[21] These eternal objects are *possibilities*, such as abstract relations or qualities, which are only actualized through the mental pole. All the past (physical) and abstract (mental) aspects of experience are together synthesized into a single present experience, a momentary actual occasion. All this occurs in a fraction of a second and it is a moment Whitehead refers to as 'satisfaction'.[22] The completion of this process is referred to as satisfaction because each aspect of experience carries with it, according to Whitehead, an emotional tone, called a 'subjective form' which is the 'sheer it-ness' of every experience.[23] What level of novelty is introduced into each occasion is governed by the 'subjective aim' of each occasion, which is its purposeful aspect, striving for 'enjoyment' in its 'satisfaction'; this is meant to account for teleological causation in the world.[24]

Where is God within this metaphysical maze? Whitehead famously wrote, 'God is not to be treated as an exception to all metaphysical principles, invoked to save their collapse. He is their chief exemplification.'[25] From this statement alone, it is clear that any notion of *creatio ex nihilo* or claims to radical discontinuity

---

17. Whitehead, *Process and Reality*, 89, 94. The subject-object distinction in Whitehead is therefore purely temporal; the subject is present, and the object is past. See, *Adventures of Ideas*, 227.

18. Whitehead, *Process and Reality*, 28–9.

19. Whitehead, *Process and Reality*, 35, 51–2, 66.

20. Whitehead, *Process and Reality*, 165.

21. Eternal objects are defined as 'any entity whose conceptual recognition does not involve a necessary reference to any definite actual entities of the temporal world'. Whitehead, *Process and Reality*, 69–70.

22. Whitehead, *Process and Reality*, 37, 130.

23. Whitehead, *Process and Reality*, 394, 398; Whitehead, *Adventures of Ideas*, 336–8.

24. Whitehead, *Science and the Modern World*, 250.

25. Whitehead, *Process and Reality*, 521. This is most clearly seen in Whitehead's famous list of antitheses on page 528.

between God and creation are ruled out.[26] The rejection of any separation between a transcendent Being and the world of endless becoming results in a doctrine of God whereby the divine is a part of – bound within – the metaphysical system of creation. It is in this sense that process theologians endorse 'naturalism', since the process God is not 'supernatural' and cannot interrupt or rewrite the processes of the world.[27] When Whitehead does introduce God-talk into his philosophy he identifies 'God' with an aspect of his metaphysics – first with the principle of limitation and later as an actual entity.[28]

The actual entity of limitation, or God for Whitehead, has three primary functions. First, God accounts for the reality and determination of the eternal objects, thereby actualizing what would otherwise be a boundless indeterminate reality. Thus, it is possible for Whitehead to say that without God there could be no concrete world and since the eternal objects enable novelty, God's envisioning and ordering of eternal objects is how God can attempt to act in the world.[29] Second, God's determining of eternal objects gives the all-important initial aim to each new occasion as it comes into existence, which is its location or initial standpoint on the world.[30] This is the primary creative task of God, since the standpoint of a new occasion influences what past or co-adjacent present occasions it is affected by, and thus impacts what it means for each occasion to be ideally satisfied. Third, God accounts for and orders relative values, since God is the principle of limitation and 'restriction is the price of value'.[31] God's purpose is to bring ideal values into

26. See David Ray Griffin, 'Creation Out of Nothing, Creation Out of Chaos, and the Problem of Evil', in *Encountering Evil: Live Options in Theodicy*, ed. Stephen T. Davis (Louisville, KY: Westminster John Knox Press, 2001).

27. See, Griffin, *Reenchantment*, 129–68.

28. Whitehead, *Science and the Modern World*, 257; cf. *Process and Reality*, 47. Whitehead switches from claiming that as the principle of limitation, 'God is not concrete' (*Science and the Modern World*, 137) to referring to God as a concrete 'actual entity'. See, Alfred North Whitehead, *Religion in the Making: Lowell Lectures, 1926* (Cambridge: Cambridge University Press, 1926), 90, 94, 99, 152. Cobb argues that this move is motivated by the concern that for the principle of limitation to function it must be concrete, rather than abstract – not due to any theological changes *per se*. See, John B. Cobb, *A Christian Natural Theology: Based on the Thought of Alfred North Whitehead* (London: Lutterworth Press, 1966), 147, 157–8.

29. Whitehead, *Religion in the Making*, 158–9; *Process and Reality*, 50. In this sense process theologians can claim that there would be 'no-*thing*' apart from God, but not absolute nothingness. See, Cobb and Griffin, *Process theology*, 66.

30. Whitehead, *Process and Reality*, 104–5.

31. Whitehead, *Science and the Modern World*, 256; Whitehead, *Religion in the Making*, 153–7. In identifying God with the principle of limitation which determines values, Whitehead chose to characterize God more decisively with goodness than with metaphysical ultimacy. This is because he thought the latter would, unacceptably, entail seeing God as the source of goodness and evil in equal measure. Whitehead, *Science and the Modern World*, 258. See, Cobb, *Christian Natural Theology*, 143.

the world, and this is known in process thought as the non-coercive 'lure' of God.[32] All of the above, the timeless envisioning of eternal objects, ideal possibilities and values are referred to in process thought as God's primordial nature.[33]

A more minor theme in Whitehead, but which has become more prominent through the influence of Charles Hartshorne, is the idea that God also has a consequent nature – the effect that the world has upon God.[34] This is God's *becoming*, which like all other entities in the world is what makes God concrete rather than abstract. An actual occasion is under no compulsion to accept the eternal objects and values that God orders and offers, as is explored in Chapter 4: 'Process theism … cannot provide the assurance that God's will is always done.'[35] This acceptance or rejection of God's lure by each actual occasion limits, or makes concrete, what God can offer to the next actual occasion in the sequence. In this way all the actual occasions in the universe internally (i.e. constitutively) affect who God is; and God prehends (feels) them, suffers with them all, just as one actual occasion prehends another. The consequent nature of God is often emphasized by process theologians as a way to articulate the intimate, vulnerable and mutually loving relationship between God and the world, over and against what is characterized as the tyrannical and indifferent God of classical theism. While seeking to overcome the problems implied by an Aristotelian account of God as an Unmoved mover, the consequent nature of God in process thought has been criticized for depicting God as a 'moved Unmover'; God is 'moved' because the divine nature is partly determined by the choices of creatures, and God is an 'Unmover' because he cannot guarantee any possible future.[36] This neat, if rather over simplistic, polemic reversal of Aristotle points towards the radicality and potential cost of the process doctrine of God.

As a Christian doctrine of God and creation, process theology falls foul of the same critique levelled against emergence theologies in Chapter 1 – the subsumption of God within a metaphysical framework of the world such that any dissimilarity between God and the natural world is already conditioned and relativized by a more fundamental similarity. What process theologians celebrate

---

32. A process account of divine action is discussed further in Chapter 4.

33. In his later writing, most notably *Adventures of Ideas*, Whitehead replaces the term 'God' with 'Eros' as the power urging the realization of ideals, but the content of his thought remains largely unchanged.

34. This is in large part due to Charles Hartshorne who wrote, 'My sharpest objection to classical theism is its making God the giver of everything and recipient of nothing … A "first" cause is not enough … There is equally need of a last effect, or rather an everlasting effect.' Charles Hartshorne, 'A Reply to My Critics'. in *The Philosophy of Charles Hartshorne*, ed. Lewis Edwin Hahn, Library of Living Philosophers, vol. 20 (LaSalle, IL: Open Court, 1991), 672.

35. Cobb and Griffin, *Process Theology*, 118.

36. Colin E. Gunton, *Being and Becoming: The Doctrine of God in Charles Hartshorne and Karl Barth* (London: SCM Press, 2001), 41.

as the naturalizing of God, Colin E. Gunton has argued, is equally the divinizing of the world.[37] The fundamental problem is not, as Gunton implies, that 'the primary category of the philosophy is found to be something less than personal', such as experience or relations, but that 'the attenuation is carried upwards into the concept of God'.[38] It is this equivocation of Divine and created categories (personal or impersonal, it matters not at this point) that lies at the heart of the process theologian's error – not the adoption of panpsychism *per se*. A certain humility is then required as to the scope of one's claims. Panpsychism will not solve all the problems of theology and philosophy, even if it may aid in answering recalcitrant philosophical problems and provide new insights for theologians with regard to the doctrine of creation, *but not to the nature of God*. The clearest way to ensure this humility and resist the temptation of naturalism is to affirm the importance of *creatio ex nihilo*.[39]

One might echo Keith Ward's use of process thought as not a final system, but 'a spur to thinking in new ways about our complex universe'.[40] In advocating his own dual-aspect idealism, Ward writes,

> Consciousness cannot just arise out of nowhere and be joined onto a brain in a completely accidental and unpredictable way. For many scientists it makes more sense to see consciousness as a natural development out of simpler elements, as an unfolding of potentialities inherent in matter from the first ... We do not have to be committed to the rather elaborate edifice of process philosophy to be attracted to this way of seeing consciousness as a natural development of simpler properties inherent in all material things.[41]

It is perfectly possible to be a panpsychist, without committing oneself to the idiosyncrasies of process thought.

Panpsychism is an ancient theory of consciousness with a cumbersome name, a central claim that sounds counterintuitive to modern ears, and its fair share of historical baggage.[42] It is perhaps for these reasons that, despite the recent resurgence of interest in panpsychism within analytic philosophy of mind and

37. Gunton, *Being and Becoming*, 223.

38. Gunton, *Being and Becoming*, 221.

39. See Chapters 3 and 4 for this affirmation of creation *ex nihilo* in conjunction with panpsychism in discussions of initial creation and ongoing divine action, respectively.

40. Keith Ward, *More than Matter? Is There More to Life than Molecules?* (Grand Rapids, MI: Eerdmans, 2010), 61.

41. Ward, *More than Matter?*, 82.

42. For an exposition for the long historical pedigree of panpsychism with Western philosophy, see David Skrbina, *Panpsychism in the West* (Cambridge, MA: MIT Press, 2005). It is widely understood that Eastern philosophy is almost universally panpsychist, although I know of no English-language analysis or argument for this claim. Another lacuna in the scholarship on panpsychism within the history of ideas is the recurrent strains of panpsychist thinking within Christian theology. Unfortunately, only Francis of Assisi

eco-philosophy, this ontology has been largely overlooked as a potential partner for theological reflection on creation. The gambit of this book is that panpsychism is worth reconsidering, not least because its recent increase in popularity and long historical pedigree enjoin theologians to this task.

Panpsychism has sufficient congruence with current theories within the natural sciences and enough philosophical plausibility to be adopted as a serious ontological option. So long as panpsychism is disentangled from the naturalistic frame that has come to burden it in secular philosophy and process metaphysics, then panpsychism offers some significant advantages to Christian theology over competing ontologies. Neither panpsychism nor any other ontology can generate or even arbitrate between the central claims of the Christian faith. Instead, the role of this tertiary reflection, this dialogue between philosophy and theology, is to find a suitable framework upon which doctrinal claims and biblical exegesis can rest and be most clearly articulated. As such a scaffolding, panpsychism provides powerful resources for seeing creation as a cathedral of praise for the glory of the Creator.

and Peirre Teilhard de Chardin feature as explicit theological figures within Skrbina's informative narrative.

Chapter 1

TAKING LEAVE OF EMERGENCE THEORY

Emergence theory is a philosophical framework that has been enthusiastically embraced by many Christian theologians, particularly those working at the intersection of science and religion. Although the general language of emergence is almost universal, what I refer to as 'emergence theology' (or the 'emergence theologians' who construct this theology) is the thorough and intentional employment of the theory of emergence from the natural sciences and from philosophy of mind to explicate core tenets of Christian theology.[1] Emergence theologians hail from a variety of denominations and countries, and include figures such as Philip Clayton, Arthur Peacocke, Niels Henrik Gregersen, Nancey Murphy, Denis Edwards, Elizabeth Johnson and Amos Yong. The current popularity of emergence theory among theologians means that before panpsychism can be properly explored in subsequent chapters, reasons for rejecting emergence theory need to be given.

The appeal of emergence theory for theologians is the promise of a scientifically aware view of God and creation, which on the one hand denies supernatural interventionism and anthropological dualism and on the other hand avoids physicalism and reductionism.[2] In contrast to reductionism, where reality is *nothing but* the determination of microphysical parts, emergence theory argues that reality includes '*something more* from *nothing but*'.[3] For theologians seeking to articulate their faith in dialogue with natural science, the appeal of emergence theory is clear and compelling: Emergence theory offers a framework for articulating an anti-reductionist evolutionary theism that places humanity, divine action and even the incarnation of Jesus Christ in congruity with the evolutionary

---

1. Emergence theology is when 'the new emergent picture of the world is used as the organizing principle for systematic theology'. Philip Clayton, *Adventures in the Spirit: God, World, Divine Action* (Minneapolis, MN: Fortress Press, 2008), 88.

2. Philip Clayton describes emergent properties as a *via media* allowing theologians to avoid either 'radical dualism of mind/soul and body *or* the physicalism that is widespread among scientists and philosophers today'. Philip Clayton, *God and Contemporary Science* (Edinburgh: Edinburgh University Press, 1997), 247.

3. Terrence Deacon and Ursula Goodenough, 'From Biology to Consciousness to Morality', *Zygon: Journal of Religion and Science* 36, no. 1 (2003): 802.

story. Emergent accounts of divine action are seen to be profitable because they depict a God who works with nature and does not suspend natural processes or violate the law of energy conservation in bestowing humanity with mental and spiritual capacities.[4] Thus, for many contemporary theologians the philosophical framework of emergence theory is seen as the essential link or the bridge for increased dialogue between the natural and theological sciences.

Despite its current popularity across academia, emergence theory is widely acknowledged to nevertheless contain several philosophical conundrums and scientific ambiguities. What has not been so widely recognized is that emergence theologies also contain a unique set of troublesome tendencies. After exploring the central claims and limitations of emergence theory within the natural sciences and philosophy of mind, this chapter argues that when emergence is accepted as the conceptual scaffolding for Christian theology, then there is a significant and undesirable theological slant given to, in particular, the doctrine of God. It is argued that emergence theologies struggle to resist the logical consequence of *emergent theism*, which makes God in some way emergent from the complexity of the natural world. If divinity is defined within the framework of emergence, then God cannot be the transcendent Creator of this natural process.

But can emergence theory be employed by Christian theologians in a more constrained way, limited, for instance, to theological anthropology? A constrained employment of emergence theory as an articulation of the origin of the animal soul inherits some of the philosophical conundrums of emergence theory, but largely avoids the theological problems discussed in the latter part of this chapter. A dualistic and restricted employment of emergence thus remains one possible option within theological anthropology, and there are notable examples of this approach.[5] Yet, these restricted uses of emergence theory cut against the global and interdisciplinary logic of emergent*ism*. In order to provide maximum interdisciplinary revenue emergence theory is often taken as an overarching framework that not only redefines articulations of creation (including humanity) but also articulations of God. Moreover, as a theory that presents the immaterial

---

4. Paul Davies, 'Introduction: Toward an Emergentist Worldview', in *From Complexity to Life: On Emergence of Life and Meaning*, ed. Niels Henrik Gregersen (Oxford: Oxford University Press, 2003), 14. See also Niels Henrik Gregersen, 'From Anthropic Design to Self-Organized Complexity', in *From Complexity to Life*, ed. Gregersen (Oxford: Oxford University Press, 2003), 206–31.

5. For example, Joshua R. Farris, who employs William Hasker's emergent dualism in conjunction with a creationist story of the soul in order to construct a new version of supernatural interventionism and anthropological dualism. See Joshua R. Farris, *The Soul of Theological Anthropology: A Cartesian Exploration* (New York: Routledge, 2016); William Hasker, *The Emergent Self* (Ithaca, NY: Cornell University Press, 1999). Keith Ward also employs a notion of weak emergence within the framework of 'dual-aspect idealism', rather than reductive or non-reductive physicalism. See Keith Ward, *More than Matter? Is There More to Life than Molecules?* (Grand Rapids, MI: Eerdmans, 2010).

as secondary to and dependent upon the material, even limited employments of emergence present some, hitherto unrecognized, challenges to traditional Christian theology. This conclusion should leave theologians wondering if there is not perhaps a better metaphysical theory available, a more suitable theory of consciousness with which Christian theology might partner.

This chapter will proceed by examining more closely what the claims of emergence theory are within different academic disciplines, including various fields within the natural sciences, within philosophy of mind and finally within theology. First, I provide a brief and general introduction to emergence theory. Second, I argue that theologians should be aware of the wide variety of emergence theories employed within the natural sciences, many of which are compatible with reductionism. Third, this is seen to be different again from emergence theory within philosophy of mind. The strong type of emergence that theologians most frequently employ is a highly critiqued concept within philosophy of mind. Emergence theory does not, at present, appear a secure foundation for Christian theology to build upon. Thereafter, this chapter examines the problematic hue with which emergence theory colours Christian theology through a Trinitarian structure by analysing the impact of emergence theory on the doctrine of God (the Father), the incarnation (the Son) and divine action (the Holy Spirit). The conclusion of this chapter is that the cost that emergence theory exacts must be carefully counted before one chooses emergence theory as the philosophical framework for articulating one's theology. In light of the concerns presented in this chapter, it seems prudent to consider what alternative philosophies might serve contemporary Christian theology better. Taking its cue from notable philosophers dissatisfied with emergence theory, Chapter 2 evaluates the recent revival of panpsychism within analytic philosophy of mind.

What is emergence theory?

John Stuart Mill (1806–1873), when examining the composite nature of table salt from two toxic substances, reaffirmed the Aristotelian principle that 'the whole is greater than the sum of its parts'.[6] Influenced by Mill, George Henry Lewes (1817–1878) distinguished between *resultants*, as additions of things, and *emergents*, which he described as 'a new qualitative class of phenomena' which 'cannot be

---

6. John Stuart Mill, *System of Logic* (London: Longmans, Green, Reader, and Dyer, 1843), Book III, chapter 6, §1. This oft-cited phrase comes from Aristotle's *The Metaphysics*, Book VIII, part 6, where he wrote, 'The whole is something over and above its parts and not just the sum of them.' Aristotle, *The Metaphysics*, in *The Complete Works of Aristotle*, ed. Jonathan Barnes (Princeton, NJ: Princeton University Press, 1998). This should not be taken, however, as Aristotle's explanation of the mind which is altogether more cosmic and widespread than contemporary emergence theorists. See John Rist, *The Mind of Aristotle* (Toronto: University of Toronto Press, 1989).

reduced to the sum of their difference'.[7] This idea was developed further by the British emergentists in the 1920s, most notably Samuel Alexander, C. Lloyd Morgan and C. D. Broad. They articulated emergence as *a naturalistic meta-theory*, which applied across disciplines on a cosmic scale and affected physical, mental and cultural spheres. The interdisciplinary aim of emergence theory is clear from the foundation of this movement; all levels of reality and all the academic disciplines that concern these different levels are drawn together under the one meta-theory of emergence. One might call this emergent*ism*. The naturalistic component of emergence theory, although parsed out in different ways by Alexander, Morgan and Broad, is important. All three of the British emergentists employed emergence theory to remove the need to invoke any mystical or supernatural agencies, which only some academic disciplines can claim to have knowledge of (most notably, theology), since this presents a barrier to interdisciplinary dialogue and thus cuts against the central purpose of emergentism.

Emergence theory states that reality is fundamentally layered into 'hierarchical divisions of stuff … organized by part-whole relations, in which wholes at one level function as parts at the next (and at all higher) levels'.[8] These wholes are often metaphorically referred to as 'higher levels' and their constituent parts, or base substrates, are 'lower levels'. Higher levels are not only conglomerates of lower levels, but as a result of the increase in complexity of the physical parts, new properties are said to *emerge*. This emergence of genuinely novel properties, from which emergence theory derives its name, means that higher-level phenomena are not merely quantitatively different to their lower-level substrates, but that there are qualitative differences between levels as well. The qualitative difference and novelty between levels is defended by the claim that emergent properties are *unpredictable* and *irreducible* from the parts at the lower levels.

The claim that the emergence of higher-level properties cannot be predicted is an epistemological claim regarding the limits of human knowledge. Since it remains possible that the ontological reality is in fact reducible, this epistemological form of emergence is known as 'weak emergence'. Contrarily, it may be that unpredictability points towards the reality of ontological irreducibility in the natural world. The criterion for this inference from epistemological unpredictability (weak emergence) to ontological irreducibility (strong emergence) is the existence of downward or whole-part causation, whereby the higher emergent level starts to exhibit power in some way over the parts. This strong emergentist thesis is, typically, what emergence theologies claim. Philip Clayton, the leading proponent

7. Niels Henrik Gregersen, 'Emergence and Complexity', in *The Oxford Handbook of Religion and Science*, ed. Philip Clayton and Zachary Simpson (Oxford: Oxford University Press, 2008), 768–83, 770; George Henry Lewes, *Problems in Life and Mind*, 1874–9, 5 vols. (New York: Houghton, Osgood, 1875), vol. II, 412.

8. William C. Wimsatt, 'The Ontology of Complex Systems: Levels of Organization, Perspectives, and Causal Thickets', *Canadian Journal of Philosophy* supplementary 20 (1994): 222.

of emergence theology, even argues, 'For theists who maintain that God as a spiritual being exercises some causal influence in the natural world, defending strong emergence may be a *sine qua non* for their position.'[9] The hope in emergence theologies is that downward causation provides the basis for human freedom and spirituality and an analogy for the God–world relationship.

From this brief description we can see that emergence theory is a way of viewing the whole of reality defined by three central criteria:

1. All reality is composed of a *hierarchy of levels* within a physicalist or monist framework.
2. The existence of some form of *novelty* so that each level is marked by something new (properties, entities, causalities, laws or substances) emerging out of organizational complexity.
3. As one moves up the levels either epistemological *unpredictability* (weak emergence) or ontological *irreducibility* through downward causation (strong emergence) can be discerned.[10]

Clayton writes, 'I would say that emergence is *the theory that cosmic evolution repeatedly includes unpredictable, irreducible, and novel appearances*.'[11] Put most simply, emergence is the thesis that more can come from less, captured in the well-known slogan that the whole is greater than the sum of its parts.

Varieties of emergence within the natural sciences

Beyond this general outline, one encounters a real difficulty in accurately describing emergence theory as it has become an umbrella term for a whole range of different processes and phenomena. As Mark A. Bedau and Paul Humphreys write in their anthology *Emergence*, 'The topic of emergence is fascinating and controversial in part because emergence seems to be widespread and yet the very image of emergence seems opaque, and perhaps even incoherent.'[12] As such, the

---

9. Philip Clayton, 'Conceptual Foundations of Emergence Theory', in *The Re-Emergence of Emergence: The Emergentist Hypothesis from Science to Religion*, ed. Philip Clayton and Paul Davies (Oxford: Oxford University Press, 2006), 27.

10. See Charbel Nino el-Hani and Antonio Marcos Pereira, 'Higher-Level Descriptions: Why Should We Preserve Them?' in *Downward Causation: Minds, Bodies and Matter*, ed. Peter Bøgh Andersen, Claus Emmeche, Niels Ole Finnemann and Peder Voetmann Christiansen (Aarhus: Aarhus University Press, 2000), 133. Philip Clayton, *Mind and Emergence: From Quantum to Consciousness* (Oxford: Oxford University Press, 2004), 60–2.

11. Clayton, *Mind and Emergence*, 39.

12. Mark A. Bedau and Paul Humphreys, 'Introduction', in *Emergence: Contemporary Readings in Philosophy and Science*, ed. Mark A. Bedau and Paul Humphreys (Cambridge, MA: MIT Press, 2008), 1.

ingredients of *hierarchy, novelty, unpredictability* and *irreducibility*, which I take as the working definition of emergence in this chapter, might be best described as indicators of possible examples of emergence rather than strict criteria. The result is an ongoing chicken-and-egg problem between citing possible examples of emergence within different areas of the natural sciences and the continual search for a definition of emergence by philosophers of science and philosophers of mind.

We can see a wide variety of potential examples of emergence from within different scientific fields, and indeed from the relationship between scientific disciplines. John Holland writes, 'Despite its ubiquity and importance, emergence is an enigmatic, recondite topic, more wondered at than analyzed. What understanding we do [have] is mostly through a catalog of instances.'[13] Since emergence theory is a 'philosophical elaboration of a series of scientific results', and emergence theologies are built upon these philosophies, understanding something of the catalogue of instances cited in the natural sciences is important for theologians interested in emergence.[14] However, what becomes apparent from the description below is that the concept of emergence can function very differently within (and between) different scientific disciplines; computational science, physics, chemistry, and biology are each examined in turn. Clayton raises the concern that too precise a scientific account of emergence may undermine its interdisciplinary potential as a meta-theory. As such, Clayton elects to speak of emergence as a general recurring pattern or a 'family resemblance' across scientific fields.[15] Whether the examples offered by scientists are true instances of emergence is, thus, entirely debatable. As a result, emergence, as a scientific hypothesis, does not currently provide a stable base for analogies of emergence in other areas, such as philosophy of mind and theology.

One of the reasons that there has been such a rise in interest in complex systems, which form the basis of emergence, is because of the advances in computer technology and information processors that enable us to model and virtually examine the organizational structures of the physical world with increasing precision. The concept of emergence in reference to computational complexity proposes that we think of the world as a whole as a computational device that contains, transmits and processes information.[16] Computational irreducibility

---

13. John Holland, *Emergence: From Chaos to Order* (Reading, MA: Addison-Wesley, 1998), 3.

14. Clayton, *Mind and Emergence*, 1–2.

15. Clayton, *Mind and Emergence*, 61.

16. Mark A. Bedau and Paul Humphreys, 'Introduction to Background and Polemics', in *Emergence*, 342. Perhaps the most famous example of this is John Conway's program 'Life' which simulates cellular automata. The programme's algorithm determines if a particular square on a grid lights up based on the lit or unlit state of neighbouring squares. Complex structures or patterns of lit and unlit squares appear in unpredictable ways. This has been compared to neural networks for visualization by John Holland and the behaviour of ant colonies by Deborah Gordon. See, Clayton, *Mind and Emergence*, 69–72.

often represents an example of diachronic emergence occurring over time as a result of increasing complexity.[17] The emergence of computational irreducibility amounts to unpredictability; the information we gather does not increase our ability to predict further into the future.[18] It is debatable if this unpredictability warrants computational complexity to be counted as an instance of genuine emergence; certainly it is at most a very weak form of emergence. Regardless, these are the larger questions: Is it justified to extrapolate emergence in the real world based on the apparent and clear cases of emergence that computational models exemplify? Is there a true analogy between the information processes of a computer and the transmission of information in the physical world? On this issue, scientists remain divided.[19]

More importantly, this weak form of emergence is, according to Carl Hempel and Paul Oppenheimer, 'not an ontological trait inherent in some phenomena: rather it is indicative of the scope of our knowledge at a given time ... what is emergent with respect to the theories of today may lose its emergent status tomorrow.'[20] The claim of computational emergence is one of epistemic limitations, and not ontological or causal novelty. Computational models are mathematic and, in that sense, already ontologically reduced.[21] The behaviour of the system can be derived from the boundary conditions and rules set up within the system, hence it is also already causally reduced. As a result, computational sciences provide examples of the closest relationship between emergence and reductionism (albeit a '*dynamic reduction in principle*'), which other versions of emergence in other disciplines, including emergence theologies, actively seek to distance themselves from.[22]

The physical and chemical sciences also cite a variety of potential instances of emergence. Some describe electromagnetism as an emergent phenomenon only occurring when a magnet is positioned in the direction of other metallic substances. Similarly, the formation of ordered structures (such as fluid convention resulting from increased temperatures, or the cone structure of a pile of sand, or the formation of ice crystals) is often cited as instances of emergence. The most

17. Bedau and Humphreys, 'Introduction to Background and Polemics', 341.

18. Paul Humphreys, 'Computation and Conceptual Emergence', *Philosophy of Science* 75, no. 5 (December 2008): 588.

19. Mark A. Bedau and Paul Humphreys, 'Introduction to Scientific Perspectives on Emergence', in *Emergence*, ed. Bedau and Humphreys, 212.

20. C. G. Hempel and P. Oppenheimer, 'Studies in the Logic of Explanation', *Philosophy of Science* 15 (1948): 567–79; quoted in Niels Henrik Gregersen, 'Emergence: What Is at Stake for Religious Reflection?' in *The Re-Emergence of Emergence: The Emergence Hypothesis from Science to Religion*, ed. Philip Clayton and Paul Davies (Oxford: Oxford University Press, 2006), 283.

21. Bedau and Humphreys, 'Introduction to Scientific Perspectives on Emergence', 211–12.

22. Bedau and Humphreys, 'Introduction to Scientific Perspectives on Emergence', 213, 342.

famous and oft-cited example of an emergent phenomenon is the liquidity that is found neither in single molecules nor in their parts but emerges from the more complex structure of multiple H_2O molecules. These instances have been labelled either *first-order emergence* in Terrence W. Deacon's typology, where the physical emergent property is entirely dependent on and caused by the physical parts, or *second-order emergence*, where physical (and reducible) environmental factors (such as temperature) also play a causal role in giving rise to the emergent phenomena. First-order and second-order emergence are both weak forms of emergence and, although they provide valuable insights for the natural sciences, they remain uncontroversial and unprofound from a theological point of view. In these cases, the emergent phenomena are fully reducible (ontologically, causally, explanatorily) to the physical. After all, I know of no reductionist who finds the appearance of water deeply troubling to their world view.

It is due to such instances of first- and second-order emergence that some, such as leading emergence theorist and biophysicist Harold J. Morowitz, see 'emergence and reduction, not as antagonistic approaches, but as complementary aspects of understanding'.[23] Similarly, William C. Wimsatt argues that 'most scientists in the complex sciences have compatible views of reduction and emergence'.[24] Philosophers and theologians have to be careful when appealing to the fluidity of water or the formation of ice crystals as analogies for the emergence of irreducible properties within human beings or models for divine action, since these physical instances of emergent phenomena remain reducible to their material substructures.[25] As Mark Bedau and Paul Humphreys write, 'Scientific examples of emergent phenomena are sometimes epiphenomenal; that is, they are effects that do not themselves cause anything else. This raises the question of whether such examples of scientific emergence are objective scientific facts or merely exist in the eye of the beholder.'[26] If emergent properties are, or even could be, merely epiphenomenal then it would appear a great risk to Christian theology to articulate divine action or the divinity of Christ through this form of emergence theory.

23. Harold J. Morowitz, 'Emergence of Transcendence', in *From Complexity to Life: On the Emergence of Life and Meaning*, ed. Niels Henrik Gregersen (Oxford: Oxford University 2003), 177.

24. William C. Wimsatt, 'Aggregativity: Reductive Heuristics for Finding Emergence', in *Emergence: Contemporary Readings in Philosophy and Science*, ed. Mark A. Bedau and Paul Humphreys (Cambridge, MA: MIT Press, 2008), 99.

25. Another way in which emergence and reductionism are combined is seen in the speculation that space-time itself is an emergent property of quantum interactions, or that Newtonian laws of classical physics are emergent from quantum mechanics. This would mean that the very laws of reductionism are emergent. This example also shows again that emergence theory is a *philosophy*, non-verifiable by the natural sciences, upon which much scientific reasoning is based. See Clayton, *Mind and Emergence*, 67–8.

26. Bedau and Humphreys, 'Introduction to Scientific Perspectives on Emergence', 216.

Deacon's category of *third-order emergence* moves us beyond the threat of epiphenomenalism by introducing concepts of causal constraint of the whole upon the parts. *Third-order emergence* is based upon the 'memory' of systems as wholes so as to develop autocatalytic reactions that function in a non-linear fashion to produce self-ordering structures.[27] The capacity of cell membranes, for example, to 'remember' and share information with their offspring is a central mechanism of evolutionary natural selection. That is, the mechanisms within evolution, 'genetic variation, fitness and genetic transmission are each emergent phenomena'.[28] Thus, emergence should not be a process independent of or in addition to evolution but is 'emergence *in* evolution'.[29] Emergence theory, then, becomes the philosophical framework *underpinning* evolution and tying physical, chemical and biological narratives of cosmic evolutionary development together.

The interweaving of emergence within evolution, or even the subsumption of evolution under the grand meta-theory of emergence, is an important part of the attraction to emergence for some theologians. In the cultural war of creationist versus neo-Darwinian evolutionist explanations of why there is such order, beauty and variety in the natural world, many theologians working at the intersection between science and theology seek to carve out a position known as *theistic evolution*. Theistic evolution states that God is ultimately responsible for the wonders of the universe, but that having set up the original conditions of creation, thereafter God *only* acts through and congruently with evolution to bring out the order and variety that we perceive. The role of emergence theory within this debate is to highlight the creativity latent within naturalistic evolution as a possible place for God to act without 'intervening'.[30] Since the emergence of new phenomena within evolution remains unpredictable and beyond human understanding, we cannot rule out divine action at this point. Moreover, since strong emergence posits the creation of causally irreducible phenomena, God's action within the process of emergence or within strongly emergent entities need not violate any natural laws (such as energy conservation). It is hard not to be caught up in the exciting possibility that emergence theory may provide a genuine way forward in the inflammatory cultural wars between creationism and neo-Darwinian evolution.

---

27. Third-order emergence is normally referred to in the context of biology, but it is worth noting that this type of emergence is sometimes posited in quantum physics when two quantum events interact so as to become permanently entangled. In such instances, it seems that they can no longer be measured or examined as individual phenomena but form a genuine whole, which acts as a whole to determine the behaviour (spin/velocity, etc.) of the parts. See Humphreys 'Computation and Conceptual Emergence', 586.

28. Mark Graves, *Mind, Brain and the Elusive Soul: Human Systems of Cognitive Science and Religion* (London: Routledge, 2008), 99.

29. Clayton, *Mind and Emergence*, 85.

30. See Chapter 4 for a more thorough discussion of 'intervention' and why it is perceived as a problem for theologies of divine action.

The emergence of life is a significant point of interdisciplinary contact between biology and theology. Since the gift of life is often attributed to the Holy Spirit ('The Lord the Giver of Life') in Christian theology, it is in such debates that emergence theologies are in full stride. However, the emergence of life also provides an apt example of the tension between emergentist and theistic explanations. The emergence of life is based on autocells that transmit information through semiotic processes to create a sustainable system.[31] Life, as an emergent phenomenon, is defined as when a system (or an emergent whole) exhibits *teleological behaviour*, which denotes purposeful survival (self-maintains through time) and interaction with its environment.[32]

It is worth highlighting that (in contrast to panpsychism) this is *apparent* teleological behaviour without experience of any kind; it is understood to be '*proto-purposiveness*' or '*purposiveness without purpose*'.[33] The most significant literature on this topic comes from Alicia Juarrero, who shows how wholes constrain their constituent parts without any new causal powers or new level of ontology.[34] As Deacon explains, 'Such concepts as information, function, purpose, meaning, intention, significance, consciousness, and value are intrinsically defined by their fundamental incompleteness. They exist only in relation to something that they are not.'[35] By setting boundaries for the activity of the parts, organisms can act in what merely appears to be, but is not (so it is argued), a self-interested and purposeful way.

The idea of emergent teleology has been taken up by, among others, Paul Davies, who writes that emergence provides a naturalistic understanding of purpose *without* evoking God as '*a force* pushing and pulling matter alongside

31. See Stuart Kauffman, *Investigations* (New York: Oxford University Press, 2000); Stuart Kauffman, *At Home in the Universe: The Search for Laws of Self-Organization and Complexity* (New York: Oxford University Press, 1996); Brian Goodwin, *How the Leopard Changed its Spots: The Evolution of Complexity* (Princeton, NJ: Princeton University Press, 2001); Christian de Duve, *Vital Dust* (New York: Basic Books, 1995); Simon Conway Morris, *Life's Solution: Inevitable Humans in a Lonely Universe* (Cambridge: Cambridge University Press, 2003).

32. Terrence Deacon, 'The Hierarchic Logic of Emergence: Untangling the Interdependence of Evolution and Self-Organization', in *Evolution and Learning: The Baldwin Effect Reconsidered*, ed. B. Weber and D. Depew (Cambridge, MA: MIT Press, 2003), 273–308. See also George F. R. Ellis, 'True Complexity and Its Associated Ontology', in *Science and Ultimate Reality: Quantum Theory, Cosmology, and Complexity*, ed. John D. Barrow, Paul C. W. Davies and Charles L. Harper, Jr (Cambridge: Cambridge University Press, 2004).

33. Clayton, *Mind and Emergence*, 97.

34. Alicia Juarrero, *Dynamics in Action: Intentional Behaviour as a Complex System* (Cambridge, MA: MIT Press, 1999).

35. Terrence Deacon, *Incomplete Nature: How Mind Emerged from Matter* (New York: Norton, 2012), 23.

other forces of nature'.[36] The emergence of purpose, and with it the emergence of life, is possible in a 'continually creative universe', which may be sustained by God but which requires no 'supernatural tinkering' within natural processes.[37]

The main use of emergence theory, in debates surrounding the origin of animation, life or purpose in the universe, is to remove any need to evoke mysterious or extra-physical forces, such as Aristotle's *entelecy* or Bergson's *élan vital*, or the Holy Spirit breathing into the nostrils of Adam.[38] These narratives 'believe in a non-physical drive which brings the emergent form [of life] into existence'; they are classified as vitalism.[39] Vitalism, which is largely (and perhaps prematurely) considered an obsolete philosophy in lieu of emergence, is defined as any theory that posits 'the existence of a life force that somehow bestowed order on the material contents of living systems'.[40] Therefore, to introduce God, or the Holy Spirit, or any form of divine action as part of the explanatory framework within the emergence of life would be to contradict the basic purpose and principle of employing emergence theory. This is the naturalistic component of emergence theory, taken by many to be necessary for interdisciplinary dialogue, since appeals to special revelation or non-verifiable (non-physical) forces are seen to stand in opposition to scientific progress.[41] Despite this, Clayton also writes that 'there must be a principle of development, something that drives the whole process, if there is to be an ongoing process of emergence', citing Samuel Alexander's 'nisus

36. Paul Davies, 'Teleology without Teleology: Purpose through Emergent Complexity', in *In Whom We Live and Move and Have Our Being: Panentheistic Reflections on God's Presence in a Scientific World*, ed. Philip Clayton and Arthur Peacocke (Grand Rapids, MI: Eerdmans, 2004), 97.

37. Davies, 'Teleology without Teleology', 108. However, given that emergence is an unpredictable and unexplainable process, the origins of life appear no closer to a scientific explanation in the emergentist framework than in the interventionist-theist belief.

38. There is a tension then, when Christian theologians, such as Amos Yong, seek to evoke emergence theory in conjunction with divine action in explaining the origin of life. Yong writes, '*ha'adam* is formed out of and thereby emergent from the dust of the ground,' but that *ha'adam* 'becomes a living being only with the breath of the Lord.' Amos Yong, *The Cosmic Breath: Spirit and Nature in the Christianity-Buddhism-Science Trialogue* (Leiden: Brill, 2012), 82.

39. David R. Copestake, 'Emergent Evolution and the Incarnation of Jesus Christ', *Modern Believing* 36 (1995): 28.

40. Paul Davies, 'Complexity and the Arrow of Time', in *From Complexity to Life: On the Emergence of Life and Meaning*, ed. Niels Henrik Gregersen (Oxford: Oxford University Press, 2003), 75; Monica Greco, 'On the Vitality of Vitalism', *Theory, Culture & Society* 22, no. 2 (2005): 15. Franz M. Wuketits concludes that all types of vitalism are 'untenable in the light of modern biological research'. Franz M. Wuketits, 'Organisms, Vital Forces, and Machines', in *Reductionism and Systems Theory in Life Sciences: Some Problems and Perspectives*, ed. Paul Hoyningen-Huene and Franz M. Wuketits (Dordrecht, NL: Kluwer Academic Press, 1989), 10.

41. As Philip Clayton writes,

in Space-Time' and Alfred North Whitehead's principle of Creativity as more acceptable notions of such a principle.[42] It is a thin line, perhaps a distinction without any real difference, between a force which gives form to systems (which is excluded by emergentists as vitalism) and positing a principle that drives the process as a whole (which is embraced as theistic emergence).[43]

In addition to the use of emergence theory as a scientific hypothesis regarding particular phenomena, emergence has become a popular way of articulating the relationship between scientific disciplines. This is perhaps the clearest example of how emergence is an expansive framework for understanding reality, 'an overarching rubric', rather than a verifiable or falsifiable scientific theory within any single discipline.[44] As mentioned above, the vision of reality as constructed into a smooth hierarchy of levels is perceived as having great interdisciplinary advantages as the various methods of enquiry exist on a continuum. As George Ellis writes, 'They [the various academic disciplines] are hierarchical, in that layers of emergent order and complexity build up on each other, with physics underlying chemistry, chemistry underlying biochemistry, and so on.'[45] Robert B. Laughlin and David Pines write, 'Rather than a Theory of Everything,' which refers to the reductionist dream of explaining all of reality at the level of physics and mathematics, 'we appear to face a hierarchy of Theories of Things, each emerging from its parent and evolving into its children as the energy scale is lowered.'[46] It is the idea of continuous levels of ontological dependency (bottom to top) with

> Emergentist panentheism begins with the assumption that language about God and divine action stand in some tension, at least initially, with the mindset of the conclusion of scientific research … this tension [is described] using the concept of *methodological naturalism*. This concept entails, to put it bluntly, that the last thing a scientist would or should appeal to in explaining some state of affairs in the world is the hand of God.

Clayton affirms that emergence theologies should make 'the assumption of naturalism at the outset'. Philip Clayton, 'Towards a Theory of Divine Action That Has Traction', in *Scientific Perspectives on Divine Action: Twenty Years of Challenge and Progress*, ed. Robert J. Russell, Nancey Murphy and William R. Stoeger SJ (Vatican State/Notre Dame, IN: Vatican State Observatory/Centre for Theology and the Natural Sciences, 2008), 106–7.

42. Clayton, *Mind and Emergence*, 27.

43. Interestingly, A. S. Pringle-Pattison describes what has come to be known as emergence theory as a 'neo-vitalism' at the beginning of the twentieth century. See A. S. Pringle-Pattison, *The Idea of God in the Light of Recent Philosophy: The Gifford Lectures, University of Aberdeen, 1912–1913* (New York: Oxford University Press, 1920), 71–2.

44. Clayton, *Adventures in the Spirit*, 67.

45. George F. R. Ellis, 'Physics, Complexity, and the Science-Religion Dialogue', in *The Oxford Handbook of Religion and Science*, ed. Philip Clayton and Zachary Simpson (Oxford: Oxford University Press, 2008), 752.

46. Robert B. Laughlin and David Pines, 'The Theory of Everything', in *Emergence*, ed. Bedau and Humphreys, 265.

epistemic or causal distinctiveness that forms the core thesis and the central premise for interdisciplinary cohesion.

However, it is this same idea that presents a uniquely difficult challenge for Christian theology. Emergence is no less expansive, no less cosmic or totalizing a philosophy than reductionism; but it is much less prescriptive in its thesis, such that each discipline maintains a level of explanatory power and integrity. Despite this flexibility, almost to the point of ambiguity as seen above, emergence does have *criteria* and as we enter the realm of philosophy of mind and beyond this into theology, these criteria become stretched beyond recognition. Antje Jackelén argues,

> Emergence seems to be yet another example of concepts that absorb meaning from different contexts of inquiry, transfer such meaning from one context to another, and thus develop the capacity of building ideology. Emergence theorists may wish to pay attention to such dynamics. They may as well be concerned about the effects of their concepts far from their origin.[47]

This warning about the effect of translating emergence theory across disciplines is sage advice for both philosophers of mind and Christian theologians seeking to build upon the emergentist ideology.

The mystery of emergence theory in philosophy of mind

The use of emergence across the natural sciences prompts theologians engaged in science and religion dialogue to readily employ emergence. However, the type of emergence most often employed within theology comes, in fact, from philosophy of mind. In recent decades, emergence theory has proven a popular way to approach the mind–body problem and this particular discourse of emergence now constitutes the main pillar of emergence theory more widely. Terrence Deacon testifies to the centrality of the emergence of mind within emergentist thinking when he writes,

> Human consciousness is not merely an emergent phenomenon; it epitomizes the logic of emergence in its very form … Consciousness emerges as an incessant creation of something from nothing, a process continually transcending itself. To be human is to know what it feels like to be evolution happening.[48]

This suggests that the mind is the next level up on a smooth continuum of nature's hierarchy. The emergence of mind is special because it (supposedly) provides the

---

47. Antje Jackelén, 'Emergence Everywhere?! Reflections on Philip Clayton's *Mind and Emergence*', *Zygon: Journal of Religion and Science* 41, no. 3 (September 2006): 624.

48. Deacon, 'The Hierarchic Logic of Emergence', 306.

paradigmatic instance of emergence, not because it is a *sui generis* instance of emergence. However, it is argued below that the phenomenon of mind, if taken in a realist fashion, stretches the model of emergence beyond any form of explanatory theory and takes it into the realm of mystery. To say that the emergence of mind epitomizes the theory of emergence more widely is bad news for the future prospects of emergence as an explanatory framework.

Tim Crane names only two basic requirements for an emergentist philosophy of mind: (1) the supervenience thesis, which describes a state of ontological *dependency* such that 'mental properties are properties of physical objects'; and (2) the emergence thesis, a sufficient *distinctness*, so that 'mental properties are distinct from physical properties' such that we can affirm the reality of phenomenal experience (*qualia*), intentionality and free will and escape the threat of epiphenomenalism. Whether it is possible to hold these two tenets of an emergentist philosophy of mind together is widely debated.[49] In light of this tension, some emergentists end up conceding to their critics (who liken emergentism to 'magic')[50] that emergence 'qualifies as a narrative, but scarcely an explanation. We are left none the wiser as to how biological systems actually achieve any sort of mental state, let alone are in a position to make claims that it is comprehensible, let alone rational.'[51] Similarly, emergence theorist Jerry Fodor admits, 'Nobody has the slightest idea how anything material could be conscious.'[52] Emergence theory restates the mind–body problem in emergentist language, and in the end this may prove useful, but it is not the kind of philosophical explanation originally intended.

The range of theories pertaining to the emergence of consciousness can be seen to roughly parallel the types of emergence within the natural sciences. On the reductionist end of the spectrum, drawing upon computational emergence, is the philosophy of Daniel Dennett. Dennett is strongly committed to functional materialism, so that if we talk about a mind we have to do so in a way that does not introduce any new ontology into the world. As a result, he seems happy to admit that much of what we perceive about the mind, for example the unity of experience arising from billions of individual neurons or the perception of free will, is mere appearance or illusion and so not worth defending.[53] In reference to David Chalmers's famous thought experiment of whether it is possible for a

49. Tim Crane, 'The Significance of Emergence', in *Physicalism and its Discontents*, ed. Carl Gillett and Barry Loewer (Cambridge: Cambridge University Press, 2001), 208.

50. Sewall Wright, 'Panpsychism in Science', in *Mind in Nature: The Interface of Science and Philosophy*, ed. John B. Cobb, Jr and David R. Griffin (Lanham, MD: University Press of America, 1977), 82; Thomas Nagel, *Mind and Cosmos: Why the Materialist Neo-Darwinian Conception of Nature Is Almost Certainly False* (Oxford: Oxford University Press, 2012), 56.

51. Simon Conway Morris, *The Runes of Evolution: How the Universe Became Self-Aware* (West Conshohocken, PA: Templeton Press, 2015), 295.

52. Jerry A. Fodor, 'The Big Idea: Can There Be a Science of the Mind', *Times Literary Supplement* (3 July 1992): 5.

53. Daniel Dennett, *Consciousness Explained* (Boston, MA: Little, Brown, 1991), 23, 458.

physically identical version of a human being to not be conscious (like a zombie), Dennett writes, 'Are zombies possible? They're not just possible, they're actual. We're all zombies. Nobody is conscious – not in the systematically mysterious way that supports such doctrines as epiphenomenalism!'[54] Thus, Dennett concludes that *qualia* do not exist (they are 'complex dispositional states of the brain'), and that the brain functions like a computer with 'Multiple Drafts' emerging, forming the appearance of consciousness.[55] Dennett denies epistemic predictability but he affirms ontological and causal reducibility of brain events, which is the thesis of very weak epistemic emergence seen in the theories of computational complexity.

John Searle's 'biological naturalism' draws upon analogies from the chemical form of emergence. Searle writes,

> Consciousness is a higher-level or emergent property of the brain in the utterly harmless sense of 'higher-level' or 'emergent' in which solidity is a higher-level emergent property of H_2O molecules when they are in a lattice structure (ice), and liquidity is similarly a higher-level emergent property of H_2O molecules when they are, roughly speaking, rolling around on each other (water). Consciousness is a mental, and therefore physical, property of the brain in the sense in which liquidity is a property of systems of molecules.[56]

In this description, 'mind' seems to be a purely semantic term used to describe the physical whole or the organized activity of the brain. Searle writes that like any other 'emergent property', minds 'have to be explained in terms of the causal interactions among the elements'.[57] As such, Searle uses emergence theory to encourage 'materialists [to] cheerfully embrace consciousness as just another material property among others'.[58] Unlike Dennett, Searle also wants to maintain a realistic view of subjectivity and consciousness. However, Searle himself admits that there is no current answer to the mechanics of emergence: 'How do unconscious bits of matter produce consciousness?'[59] The emergentist, as of yet, offers no explanation for this process. The problem, as Thomas Nagel rightly argues, is that 'however great the variety of physical phenomena may be, ontological objectivity is one of their central defining characteristics; and as we have seen Searle insists that consciousness is ontologically subjective'.[60] There is a fundamental clash between Searle's commitment to realist subjectivity and his commitment to naturalism. This is a clash that his employment of emergence theory serves to mask but does

---

54. Dennett, *Consciousness Explained*, 406.

55. Dennett, *Consciousness Explained*, 403–4, 431.

56. John R. Searle, *The Rediscovery of the Mind* (Cambridge, MA: MIT Press, 1992), 14.

57. Searle, *Rediscovery of the Mind*, 111.

58. Searle, *Rediscovery of the Mind*, 55.

59. Searle, *Rediscovery of the Mind*, 55.

60. Thomas Nagel, 'The Mind Wins!' *New York Review* (4 March 1993): 40; See Searle, *Rediscovery of Mind*, 16, 19.

not alleviate. Instead, Searle stretches the term 'physical' in such a way that it is emptied of any of its constraining definitions (such as ontological objectivity).[61] Searle acknowledges that his view entails the denial of free will, but admits that this is an unsatisfactory outcome. He concludes, as a result, 'that in our entire philosophical tradition we are making some fundamental mistake' and that the whole approach to the problem of the mind may have to be rethought.[62]

Neuroscientist Roger Sperry defended an emergentist picture of the mind–brain relationship on the basis of biological instances of emergence. His view is called 'emergent interactionism' because, although he maintains physicalism, his work on mapping neuro-correlation led him to posit genuine two-way interaction between the mind and the brain. Sperry writes,

> Mental phenomena are described as primarily supervening rather than intervening, in the physiological process … Mind is conceived to move matter in the brain and to govern, rule, and direct neural and chemical events without interacting with the components at the component level, just as an organism may move and govern the time-space course of its atoms and tissues without interacting with them.[63]

Based on an analogy with the emergence of organismic behaviour, the mind is viewed by Sperry as being in a whole-part relation to the brain. The mind is seen to have some top-down causal powers over the brain as a whole but cannot influence individual parts by interacting with them directly. Supervenience is the thesis of ontological dependence, such that the mind cannot exist or act without bottom-up causality in the brain. This is described in contrast to a pre-existent soul or independent mental substance that intervenes with the material firing of neurons. Unfortunately, this account of whole-part causation does not escape the threat of epiphenomenalism since without direct interaction there is no way to discern between discussions of the mind as a *description* of bottom-up causation taken as a single whole and discussions of the mind as exerting top-down *causal influence* over the whole. Indeed, Sperry emphasizes,

> The expectation that downward macrodetermination should thus effect reconfigurations … in the neuron-to-neuron activity of subjective mental states … indicates a misunderstanding of what emergent interaction is. From the

---

61. Interestingly, this is a similar semantic elasticity that Galen Strawson employs in his famous defence of panpsychism; Galen Strawson, 'Realistic Monism: Why Physicalism Entails Panpsychism', *Journal of Consciousness Studies* 13, nos. 10–11 (2006): 3–31.

62. John R. Searle, 'The Mind-Body Problem', in *John Searle and His Critics*, ed. Ernest Lepore and Robert van Gulick (Cambridge, MA: Basil Blackwell, 1991), 145.

63. Roger W. Sperry, 'Consciousness and Causality', in *The Oxford Companion to the Mind*, ed. Richard L. Gregory (Oxford: Oxford University Press, 1987), 164–6; cited in Clayton, *Mind and Emergence*, 23–4.

start I have stressed consistently that the higher-level phenomena in exerting downward control do *not disrupt* or *intervene* in the causal relations of the lower-level component activity. Instead, they *supervene* in a way that leaves the micro interactions, per se, unaltered.[64]

If downward causation does not, in any way, alter the physical behaviour of the parts, in what sense can the mind be said to have a causal effect on the brain? Sperry's description of downward causation without interaction remains utterly mysterious, if not epiphenomenal. This problem is important for emergence theologies which, as shall be explored below, describe the God–world relation or divine action in the same language of supervening upon but not intervening in the world.

Christian theologian Nancey Murphy uses Searle's 'biological naturalism' and Sperry's 'emergent interactionism' to argue for what she calls 'non-reductive physicalism', although it is 'no different from some forms of emergent monism'.[65] Murphy describes non-reductive physicalism as 'the acceptance of ontological reductionism, but the rejection of causal reductionism and reductive materialism'.[66] To accept ontological reduction means that, according to Murphy, 'humans are not hybrids of matter and something else, they are purely physical organisms'.[67] But Murphy argues that this does not lead to causal reductionism. Murphy emphasizes her denial of causal reductionism when she writes,

If free will is an illusion and the highest of human intellectual and cultural achievements can (*per impossibile*) be counted as the mere outworking of the laws of physics, this is utterly devastating to our ordinary understanding of ourselves, and of course to theological accounts, as well, which depend not only on a concept of responsibility before God, but also on the justification (not merely the causation) of our theories about God and God's will.[68]

Murphy is completely correct in outlining the devastating consequences of causal reductionism; if all events in the universe – including human actions and thought – could be exhaustively explained by physical laws such that there is no

---

64. Roger W. Sperry, 'In Defense of Mentalism and Emergent Interaction', *Journal of Mind and Behaviour* 12, no. 2 (1991): 230.

65. Nancey Murphy, 'Nonreductive Physicalism', in *In Search of the Soul: Perspectives on the Mind-Body Problem*, ed. Joel B. Green (Eugene, OR: Wipf and Stock, 2005), 115–16.

66. Nancey Murphy, 'Nonreductive Physicalism: Philosophical Issues', in *Whatever Happened to the Soul? Scientific and Theological Portraits of Human Nature*, ed. Warren S. Brown, Nancey Murphy and H. Newton Malony (Minneapolis, MN: Fortress Press, 1998), 130.

67. Nancey Murphy, *Bodies and Souls, or Spirited Bodies?* (Cambridge: Cambridge University Press, 2006), 69.

68. Murphy, 'Nonreductive Physicalism: Philosophical Issues', 129.

free will or rational thought, then all academic discussion, religious belief and human endeavour are a futile illusion. What remains to be seen is if Murphy's rejection of causal reductionism can be supported and maintained, given her acceptance of ontological reductionism.

If human beings (and all other complex organisms) are entirely composed of only the particles of microphysics, it would seem that the behaviour of those complex organisms will be entirely explicable in terms of the behaviour of these microparticles.[69] A higher level, when one accepts ontological reductionism, is only a way of describing complex organization; it does not refer to any newly existing concrete entity. The mind is not a *thing* for emergent monists; instead it can only be the absence of material possibility: 'Mind didn't exactly emerge from matter, but from constraints on matter.'[70] But, Murphy argues, to avoid causal reductionism 'what the emergentist needs to show is that as we go up the hierarchy of complex systems we find entities that exhibit new causal powers (or, perhaps better, participate in new causal processes or fulfill new causal roles) that cannot be reduced to the combined effects of the lower-level causal processes.'[71] Murphy makes analogies to the flight of a paper plane or the re-adjustment of a satellite watch to argue that the environment (the hand that throws the plane and air current or the information received from the satellite to the watch) provides causal input from outside the system. Unfortunately, interaction within a larger environment does not provide Murphy with the means to resist causal reductionism in the way that she hopes.[72] All the causal factors remain physical and reducible to micro-determination, and no new causal powers can be attributed to the systems themselves (in this case, the paper plane and the watch). Murphy uses these examples to suggest that 'mental events are not reducible to brain events, because mental events are largely constituted by relations to actions in the environment.'[73] However, if the environment remains entirely physical (and micro-determined), then the reductionist's way of explaining events may get more difficult, but it is not made impossible by the appearance of environmental causes and constraints.[74]

---

69. The now classic articulation of this argument is given by Jaewgon Kim's presidential address to the American Philosophical Association, 'The Myth of Nonreductive Materialism', in *Supervenience and the Mind: Selected Philosophical Essays* (Cambridge: Cambridge University Press, 1993).

70. Deacon, *Incomplete Nature*, 538.

71. Nancey Murphy and Warren Brown, *Did My Neurons Make Me Do It? Philosophical and Neurobiological Perspectives on Moral Responsibility and Free Will* (New York: Oxford University Press, 2007), 79–80.

72. See Mikael Leidenhag, 'From Emergence Theory to Panpsychism – A Philosophical Evaluation of Nancey Murphy's Non-Reductive Physicalism', *Sophia: International Journal of Philosophy and Traditions* 55 (2016): 381–94.

73. Murphy and Brown, *Did My Neurons Make Me Do It?*, 209.

74. J. P. Moreland, 'A Critique of and Alternative to Nancey Murphy's Christian Physicalism', *European Journal for Philosophy of Religion* 8, no. 2 (2016): 107–28. Murphy acknowledges that emergent downward causation cannot be employed as a model for

Beyond non-reductive physicalism, at the far end of the spectrum of emergence philosophies, is William Hasker's *emergent dualism*. In light of the continual threat of epiphenomenalism facing the physicalist and monist view of emergence, Hasker concludes that in the case of the emergence of the human mind,

> it is not enough to say that there are emergent properties here; what is needed is an *emergent individual*, a new individual entity which comes into existence as a result of a certain functional configuration of the material constituents of the brain and nervous system.[75]

On Hasker's view, the mind that emerges from and out of the complexity of the brain is a separate 'substance', an 'ontologically distinct entity from the physical brain' (hence, emergent *dualism*).[76] This is 'very strong' or 'hyper-strong' emergence, and very weak supervenience. Brian Leftow concludes that Hasker's emergent individual is no different to the Thomist soul with God left out of the picture.[77]

Despite its ability to articulate a more robust role for mental properties such as experience and free will, which are necessary for discussion of morality and the endurance of personal identity over time, most theologians who have adopted emergence theory in order to talk about the mind or the soul do not explicitly discuss Hasker's emergent dualism. Instead, most theologians and scholars in the science-religion dialogue draw upon Clayton's emergent *monism*, where there is no 'soul-substance', but only 'vital dust: the one stuff of the world whose history we work to reconstruct, taking on surprising forms'.[78] This is because emergent dualism, as a form of dualism, posits an ontological jump from the material to the mental. While Hasker's proposal is able, arguably unlike emergent monism, to sufficiently defend itself against the threat of reductionism and epiphenomenalism, it does so at the cost of emergence theory's interdisciplinary appeal. The mind, on Hasker's account, should no longer be taken to exemplify the general philosophy of emergence across reality, but constitutes a *sui generis* instance of emergence.

divine action, as is proposed by Arthur Peacocke because 'downward causation in the world is always mediated by ordinary physical forces'. Since downward causation embraces ontological reductionism, she fears that such a model of divine action could not escape falling into pantheism. As such, she prefers the quantum-based models of divine action discussed in Chapter 4. Nancey Murphy, 'Emergence, Downward Causation and Divine Action', in *Scientific Perspectives on Divine Action: Twenty Years of Challenge and Progress*, ed. Robert J. Russell, Nancey Murphy and William R. Stoeger, SJ (Vatican State/Notre Dame, IN: Vatican Observatory/Centre for Theology and The Natural Sciences, 2008), 129.

75. Hasker, *Emergent Self*, 90.

76. William Hasker, 'On Behalf of Emergent Dualism', in *In Search of the Soul: Perspectives on the Mind-Body Problem*, ed. Joel B. Green (Eugene, OR: Wipf and Stock, 2005), 77, 81.

77. Conference comment by Brian Leftow, quoted in Hasker, *The Emergent Self*, 195–6.

78. Clayton, *Mind and Emergence*, 198.

Hasker ponders the question, 'How far down the scale of biological complexity does consciousness go?'[79] He seems to remain agnostic on this point but does state that the potentiality for consciousness must go all the way down. Hasker acknowledges that some critics of emergence consider the jump from material complexity to mental properties to be ' "magical" because the emergent properties appear, as it were, out of the blue.'[80] Emergent dualism posits *anima ex nihilo*, repeatedly for every conscious organism. In response to this, Hasker posits the emergent power for mentality in the basic constituents, the elementary particles, of matter. He writes, 'It is an inherent power of ordinary matter that, when combined in the right ways, it produces an entity with the characteristics of the emergent mind.'[81] Indeed, he writes that as Christians, 'God has told us that he created us from the dust of the earth – so we have no choice, really, but to suppose that he endowed that dust with the powers required to enable the rich and various creation that he proposed to fashion from it.'[82] This is surprising terminology for a self-proclaimed emergentist philosopher since the concept of dust with inherent powers for consciousness has been a prominent way to describe panpsychism in contrast to strong emergence theory.[83]

Hasker goes on to say, 'It may be that in the end only belief in the power of such a creative God can make emergent dualism a viable and credible hypothesis.'[84] In the end, Hasker seems to concede that emergence is either 'magic', as its critics argue, or it requires additional theistic apparatus to support it. Indeed, philosopher Colin McGinn writes that when faced with the challenge of explaining how 'sentience sprang from the pulpy matter' of the brain, 'one is tempted, however reluctantly, to turn to divine assistance: for only a kind of miracle could produce *this* from *that*.'[85] If one is comfortable positing minds as a perpetual miracle or an intervention by God of new causal powers within the natural order, then Hasker's account of emergence is a viable model. However, many in the science-religion field would

79. Hasker, 'On Behalf of Emergent Dualism', 78.

80. Hasker, 'On Behalf of Emergent Dualism', 82.

81. Hasker, 'On Behalf of Emergent Dualism', 82.

82. Hasker, 'On Behalf of Emergent Dualism', 83. Denis Edwards makes a similar, but more pervasive move of interpreting all instances of emergence as supernaturally empowered, 'from the first nuclei of hydrogen and helium, to atoms, galaxies, the Sun, bacterial forms of life, complex cells, the wonderfully diverse life on Earth, and human beings' as the direct action of 'the Breath of God that empowers and enables the whole process from within'. Denis Edwards, *Breath of Life: A Theology of the Creator Spirit* (Maryknoll, NY: Orbis Books, 2004), 43–4.

83. For example, see J. van Cleve, 'Mind-Dust or Magic? Panpsychism versus Emergence', *Philosophical Perspectives* 4 (1990): 215–26.

84. Hasker, 'On Behalf of Emergent Dualism', 83.

85. Colin McGinn, *The Problem of Consciousness: Essays toward a Resolution* (Oxford: Basil Blackwell, 1991), 45.

find this an alarming conclusion, since it seems to undermine the sufficiency of the theory of natural selection within evolution. As Charles Darwin himself wrote,

> If I were convinced that I required such additions to the theory of natural selection, I reject it as rubbish ... I would give nothing for the theory of Natural selection, if it requires miraculous additions at any one stage of descent.[86]

If the evolutionary story is governed by purely physical forces, from which emerge mental properties, then despite all the advances in evolutionary biology over the last century that describe and explain the physical complexity, Darwin's account would still require a miraculous addition in the case of the appearance of the mind. This, as articulated by Darwin himself, is unacceptable for the theory of natural selection. As we shall see in the next chapter, this concern for the smoothness and sufficiency of evolutionary theory is part of the reason that some contemporary philosophers are taking leave of emergence theory and adopting panpsychism.

We have seen that emergentist philosophers often employ analogies to physical emergence to give credibility to their theory. Dennett likens the mind to a computational, purely epistemological, instance of emergence. Searle compares mental properties to the liquidity of water. Murphy compares the mind to a paper aeroplane and a satellite watch. William Hasker also uses a magnetic analogy: 'As a magnet generates its magnetic field, so an organism generates its consciousness,' although he admits that 'fields of physics [are not] emergent in the strong sense that applies to the conscious mind.'[87] These analogies (at best) reveal another chicken-and-egg problem for emergence theorists. The theory of emergence, as it exists in philosophy of mind, is often described as the exemplar instance of emergence providing clarity to other physical instances of emergence. And yet, philosophers of mind universally employ examples of physical emergence as analogies to help ground and explain the emergence of mind.

The problem is far worse than a mere chicken-and-egg problem. Appeals to physical emergence by philosophers of mind (and *vice versa*) are, in fact, a 'category mistake of the most egregious kind.'[88] The assumption that physical properties behave like mental properties, that there can be an analogy between the liquidity of water and the mentality of the brain, is the thesis that emergence needs to prove. As such, it is question-begging to assume that the analogy functions within the argument in this way. Unlike the liquidity of water, the supervenience of the mind upon the brain remains brute, merely correlative and

---

86. Charles Darwin, *The Life and Letters of Charles Darwin*, ed. Francis Darwin, 2 vols. (New York: D. Appleton, 1896), vol. II, 6–7.

87. Hasker, 'On Behalf of Emergent Dualism', 78.

88. David Ray Griffin, *Unsnarling the World-Knot: Consciousness, Freedom, and the Mind-Body Problem* (Eugene, OR: Wipf and Stock, 1998), 64; William E. Seager, *Metaphysics of Consciousness* (London: Routledge, 1991), 180.

not at all causal or explanatory as is the case for other physical examples of weak emergence. Nagel's warning that 'much obscurity has been shed on the [mind-body] problem by faulty analogies' rings especially true in current discussions of emergence.[89]

Jaegwon Kim points out that this mysterious correlation, which we call supervenience, between the mind and brain is 'a "phenomenological" claim, not a theoretical explanation. Mind–body supervenience, therefore, does not state a solution to the mind–body problem; rather it states the problem itself.'[90] As is often quoted, early emergentist Samuel Alexander conceded that emergence is 'something to be noted, as some would say, under the compulsion of brute empirical fact or, as I should prefer to say in less harsh terms, to be accepted with the "natural piety" of the investigator. It admits no explanation.'[91] The emergentist idea that something more arises from something less does not apply in the instance of consciousness; without panpsychism this is only something from nothing or emergence *ex nihilo*. Galen Strawson has called such 'brute emergence' a 'miracle ... every time it occurs'.[92] The mystery of emergence of mind is not due to a lack of current knowledge in practice but is 'one of principle'.[93] This is because no physical property (i.e. a property of spatial extension that is exhaustively known through perception) 'seems capable of rendering perspicuous how it is that damp grey tissue can be the crucible from which subjective consciousness emerges fully formed'.[94] It is largely due to the perceived failure of emergence theory that philosophers of mind have turned to re-examine the potential of panpsychism. Before evaluating this trend in Chapter 2, we need to consider more explicit theological reasons for being cautious of emergentism and taking leave of emergence theologies.

Problematic tendencies in emergence theology

This chapter has highlighted the wide variety of types of emergence, indicating that emergence is more easily understood to be an overarching world view, or ideology, rather than a testable scientific hypothesis or explanatory philosophy. Moreover, definitions of emergence have proven elusive and the logic of

---

89. Thomas Nagel, 'Panpsychism', in *Mortal Questions* (Cambridge: Cambridge University Press, 1979), 202.

90. Jaegwon Kim, *Supervenience and the Mind: Selected Philosophical Essays* (Cambridge: Cambridge University Press, 1993), 168.

91. Samuel Alexander, *Space, Time and Deity*, vol. 2 (London: Macmillan, 1920), 47.

92. Galen Strawson, 'Realistic Monism: Why Physicalism Entails Panpsychism', in *Consciousness and Its Place in Nature: Does Physicalism Entail Panpsychism?*, ed. Anthony Freeman (Exeter: Imprint Academic, 2006), 18.

93. McGinn, *Problem of Consciousness*, 213.

94. McGinn, *Problem of Consciousness*, 27.

emergence appears obscure. This was to show that emergence is a less secure foundation for theology, either scientifically or philosophically, than is often supposed by emergence theologians. An unstable foundation is troublesome on any construction site, and this chapter now explores the problematic slant that emergence theory gives to the building of Christian theology.

The promise of emergence theory for Christian theology has been described in the most optimistic and far-reaching terms. One emergence philosopher describes how 'theologians are hoping that emergence in one form or another will shed light on the nature and existence of God, divine action, the mind–body problem, and free will'.[95] Augustine Shuttle writes,

> The idea of evolution and the emergence of new forms of being – not simply in the biological sphere but in the cosmos as a whole and in human history itself – has in fact provided Christian theology with a new paradigm within which to conceptualize such basic elements of faith as the notion of creation, the doctrine of God's incarnation in Jesus, the indwelling in us of the Holy Spirit, and the function of the Church in the world.[96]

However, this new paradigm does not come without a significant cost to Christian theology. The leading proponent of emergence theology, Philip Clayton, admits that 'emergence is no silent ally, and it may require certain modifications to traditional versions of theism and to traditional theologies'.[97] The section below analyses the extent of the theological modifications that emergentism demands. It is argued that when the world view of emergence is employed within Christian theology, it pulls towards 'emergent theism', whereby God is a product of the emergent process. While it remains true that 'there is in fact a wide variety of ways in which a theology can be emergent', when emergence is applied as a general framework or global ontology then the same theologically problematic tendencies abound.[98] These tendencies might be characterized as a loss of radical transcendence and naturalization of the doctrine of God. The cost of emergence theory to Christian theology is far greater than previously realized, such that Christian theologians should consider viable alternatives before committing themselves to emergence theory too heavily.

95. Michael Silberstein, 'Emergence, Theology, and the Manifest Image', in *The Oxford Handbook of Religion and Science*, ed. Philip Clayton and Zachary Simpson (Oxford: Oxford University Press, 2008), 785.

96. Augustine Shuttle, 'Evolution and Emergence: A Paradigm Shift for Theology', *Philosophy & Theology* 22, nos. 1–2 (2010): 235.

97. Clayton, 'Conceptual Foundations of Emergence Theory', 28.

98. Clayton, *Adventures in the Spirit*, 103. Niels Henrik Gregersen provides an interesting fivefold typology of ways to combine emergence theory and theistic belief. Gregersen, 'Emergence: What Is at Stake for Religious Reflection?', 279–302.

The father: A dipolar doctrine of God and emergent theism

It was seen above that many emergence theorists see emergence as a totalizing or expansive framework for the whole of reality. Gillett writes, 'each of these emergentist views offers a plethora of new resources to apply in understanding not only the natural world but also ourselves as part of this world, and even our conceptions of the divine.'[99] Although this expansion from the realm of nature into conceptions of the divine is not an entailment of emergence theory, it is in continuity with the appeal of emergence theory as an interdisciplinary platform. Thus, while it remains possible for theologians to employ emergence as a narrative about the physical context in which God creates human souls *ex nihilo*, emergence theory was originally conceived and remains for many an overarching world view that structures our understanding of all of reality.

From the earliest days of emergence theory, in the first decades of the twentieth century, emergence theorists held differing positions on the relationship between religion and emergence. C. Lloyd Morgan seems to have been a theist with regard to the initial act of creation. However, like C. D. Broad and Roy Wood Sellars, Morgan saw emergence theory as thoroughly naturalistic so that the whole of reality can be framed according to the scientific method, without reference to God.[100] While not aiming to disprove the existence of God, these early British emergentists sought to remove the need to invoke supernatural causation or divine action of any sort within the universe after the initial God-given act of genesis. Morgan described emergence theory as

> a philosophy based on the procedure sanctioned by progress in scientific research, the advent of novelty of any kind is loyally to be accepted whenever it is found, without invoking any extra-natural Power (Force, Entelechy, Élan, or God) through the efficient Activity of which the observed facts may be explained.[101]

This should not be considered a theologically innocuous position since, as an expression of methodological naturalism, it places divine action in opposition, or explanatory competition, to emergence theory.[102] Ursula Goodenough and

99. Carl Gillett, 'The Hidden Battles over Emergence', in *The Oxford Handbook of Religion and Science*, ed. Philip Clayton and Zachary Simpson (Oxford: Oxford University Press, 2008), 803.

100. 'There is nothing, so far as I can see, mysterious or unscientific about a trans-ordinal [emergent] law or about the notion of ultimate characteristic of a given order … The only peculiarity of it is that we must wait till we meet with an actual instance of an object of the higher order before we can discover such a law.' C. D. Broad, *The Mind and Its Place in Nature* (New York: Routledge, [1925] 2013), 79.

101. C. Lloyd Morgan, *Emergent Evolution* (New York: Henry Holt, 1923), 2.

102. Morgan describes this as 'the naturalistic contention' of emergence. Morgan, *Emergent Evolution*, 2. As discussed in Chapter 2, 'naturalism' is a much-debated term. It seems to come in stronger and weaker forms, neither of which is neutral or easily

Terrence Deacon advocate this position today when they write, 'The emergence perspective offers us ways to think about creation, and creativity, that do not require a creator.'[103] However, because Morgan did not seek to use emergence to explicate the nature of God, the (problematic) impact of this form of emergence theory upon theology is, while hostile, fairly minimal.

By contrast, Samuel Alexander's Gifford Lectures, *Space, Time, and Deity*, posited God's deity to be an emergent phenomenon. Emergence theory, as an overarching metaphysic, was not used to remove the need for God-talk, but extended to become the framework of theology, in addition to natural science and philosophy of mind. Deity was defined as a property or ontological reality further up the hierarchy of emergent phenomena, beyond that of human minds. He wrote,

> God includes the whole universe, but his deity, though infinite, belongs to, or is lodged in, only a portion of the universe … As being the whole universe God is creative, but his distinctive character of deity is not creative but created.[104]

It seems that, for Alexander, God's deity is not an essential property of God's being. Instead, deity or God's transcendence emerges temporally from the increasing complexity of the physical universe, which, when taken as a unified whole, is referred to as 'the body of God' and accounts for the immanence of God.[105] As Niels Henrik Gregersen points out, Alexander's view 'places God in the position of the predicate, that is, as the secondary one, while the material universe would take the logical place of the subject'.[106] This follows the general logic of emergence theory as the immaterial property or entity emerges from and remains dependent upon the material substrate. Most clearly Alexander writes, 'God then, like all things in the universe … is in the strictest sense not a creator but a creature.'[107]

compatible with Christian theology. Stronger forms involve adherence to physicalism and determinism, whereas weaker forms 'only require expulsion of the supernatural, the theological, and the essentially normative-evaluative'. Kim, *Supervenience and Mind*, 297. See also David Ray Griffin, *Unsnarling the World-Knot*, 30–1.

103. Terrence Deacon and Ursula Goodenough, 'The Sacred Emergence of Nature', in *The Oxford Handbook of Religion and Science*, ed. Philip Clayton and Zachary Simpson (Oxford: Oxford University Press, 2008), 870.

104. Alexander, *Space, Time, and Deity*, vol. 2, 357, 397. Or again, 'As actual, God does not possess the quality of deity but is the universe as tending to that quality … Thus there is no actual infinite being with the quality of deity; but there is actual infinite, the whole universe, with a nisus to deity; and this is the God of the religious consciousness.' Alexander, *Space, Time, and Deity*, 361–2.

105. Alexander, *Space, Time, and Deity*, 357. See also Harold J. Morowitz, *The Emergence of Everything: How the World Became Complex* (Oxford: Oxford University Press, 2004), 195–9.

106. Niels Henrik Gregersen, 'Emergence in Theological Perspective: A Corollary to Professor Clayton's Boyle Lecture', *Theology & Science* 4, no. 3 (2006): 315.

107. Alexander, *Space, Time, and Deity*, vol. 2, 398.

Although widely recognized as undesirable by Christian theologians engaging with emergence theory, Alexander's view of God mixed with an emergent view of divine attributes (deity) continues to have a surprisingly strong impact on emergence theologies today.[108] Gregersen writes that, despite its undesirability for religion, 'the general outcome is inevitable if emergentist thinking is written large, metaphysically speaking.'[109] Philip Clayton rejects Alexander's 'radical emergent theism', but does admit that 'the success of the sciences of emergence does provide some impetus in the direction of the emergence of deity' and that Alexander's proposal is 'a logical extension' of emergence theory.[110] Emergence theory gives ontological priority to material existence by citing the organization of matter as the creative cause for all immaterial or higher-level properties. Emergence, in and of itself, has no way to conceive of an immaterial being or property existing independent of or prior to the material world. Therefore, Clayton concludes, 'To the extent that divine mind is held to be transcendent or to precede the existence of the cosmos, the framework of emergence has been left behind.'[111] Emergence must be left behind then, for God is neither partly transcendent nor pre-existent only to some extent, but wholly so in accordance with divine unity.

A similarly bipolar view of God is seen in process theologies' view of the Primordial (akin to the emergence process) and Consequent (akin to the emergent resultant) aspects of God.[112] Process thought endorses panexperientialism, and so has been more closely associated with panpsychist metaphysics than emergentist ontology. Despite emergence theorists' rejection of panexperientialism, the influence of process theology upon emergence theology is clear. Clayton, on this topic, writes,

> Arguably, metaphysics in the tradition of Whitehead should also be emergentist, since it is a philosophy of pervasive becoming, even including the thesis that at

---

108. Anthony Freeman is a contemporary scholar who explicitly embraces Alexander's approach. Anthony Freeman, 'God as an Emergent Property', *Journal of Consciousness Studies* 8, nos. 9–10 (2001): 147–59. Emily Thomas gives an intriguing defence of Alexander, in opposition to the panentheistic emergence theologies of Clayton, Peacocke and Morowitz in 'Samuel Alexander's Space-Time God: A Naturalist Rival to Current Emergentist Theologies', in *Alternative Concepts of God: Essays on the Metaphysics of the Divine*, ed. Yujin Nagasawa and Andrei A. Buckareff (Oxford: Oxford University Press, 2016), 255–73.

109. Gregersen, 'Emergence: What Is at Stake for Religious Reflection?', 290.

110. Clayton, *Adventures in the Spirit*, 87, 102. See also, Clayton, *Mind and Emergence*, 169, 180–7. Clayton also cites Samuel Alexander when expressing the following: 'And yet this core emergentist idea offers at least some support to the contention that the *telos* of the process of cosmic evolution is the emergence of God-like properties in the universe.' Clayton, 'Towards a Theory of Divine Action That Has Traction', 110.

111. Clayton, 'Towards a Theory of Divine Action That Has Traction', 179.

112. Alfred North Whitehead, *Process and Reality*, ed. David Ray Griffin and Donald W. Sherburne (New York: Free Press, [1928] 1978), 343–51.

least one 'pole' of the divine, the so-called consequent nature of God, emerges through the history of its interactions with finite occasions of experience.[113]

In both process and emergence theologies, the category of 'becoming' is emphasized over 'being'. In both theologies God is identified simultaneously with this process of emergence (immanence) and as emergent (relative transcendence). What emergence theology and process theology share is a grand and expansive metaphysic of becoming, under which the doctrine of God is redefined or subsumed. In Whitehead's words, 'God is not to be treated as an exception to the metaphysical principles, invoked to save their collapse. He is their chief exemplification.'[114] This suggests that theological concepts are not seen to be above our understanding of the natural world but are redefined in light of a meta-theory extrapolated from scientific paradigms and philosophical theories. The logical and ontological priority given to the universe by emergence and process theologians entails a redefinition of the concept of transcendence. This redefinition moves away from a pre-existent transcendence of all created entities and processes to a relative transcendence arising out of created entities and processes. This subsumption of the supernatural within the natural, which occurs through the adoption of naturalism, is a grave theological mistake. If one adopts emergent*ism* as a global ontology or expansive interdisciplinary framework, then this naturalizing subsumption becomes difficult to avoid.

The emergent Christ: Incarnation through emergent evolution

In so far as it is the perpetual charge of theologians 'to think out the meaning of the Christian conviction that God was incarnate in Jesus, that Jesus is God and Man', Christology is an unavoidable arena for theological metaphysics.[115] It is unsurprising then that the doctrine of the incarnation has undergone concentrated innovation within emergence theologies. Gregersen writes that a central theological question for Christian emergence theologians is, 'Is there a connection between the chemistry of emergence and the emergence of Jesus Christ?'[116] An example

---

113. Clayton, *Mind and Emergence*, 167. Further arguments for the compatibility between process thought and emergence theory come from Nancey Frankenberry, 'The Emergent Paradigm and Divine Causation', *Process Studies* 13 (1983): 202–17; and Ian Barbour, 'Neuroscience, Artificial Intelligence, and Human Nature: Theological and Philosophical Reflections', in *Neuroscience and the Person: Scientific Perspectives on Divine Action*, ed. Robert J. Russell, Nancey Murphy, Theo Meyering and Michael Arbib (Vatican City State/ Berkeley, CA: Vatican Observatory/Centre for Theology and the Natural Sciences, 1999), 249–80.

114. Whitehead, *Process and Reality*, 343.

115. Donald M. Baillie, *God Was in Christ: An Essay on Incarnation and Atonement* (London: Faber & Faber, 1961), 83.

116. Gregersen, 'Emergence in Theological Perspective', 310.

of an affirmative response comes from molecular biologist and Anglican priest, Arthur Peacocke.[117] As one of the leading and most prolific figures of emergence theology, Peacocke describes the incarnation as 'a new emergent, a new reality, had appeared within created humanity'.[118] Put another way, 'the significance and potentiality of all levels of creation may be said to have been unfolded in Jesus the Christ'.[119] Thinking through the meaning of Jesus Christ as God incarnate within the framework of emergence theory has two results. First, since emergence theory envisions reality as a hierarchy of ascending levels of complexity, it reconceives the incarnation as creaturely ascent rather than a divine descent into the world. Second, because emergence theory, for Peacocke, is the means of evolutionary adaptation then his incarnation-through-emergence is a process available to any biological creature, and not unique to the person of Jesus Christ. Peacocke embraces both these moves and envisions Jesus Christ as the summit of the ladder of emergent phenomena and defines 'incarnation' as a process in continuity with, and taking place through, the natural processes of evolution.

Jesus Christ, as a new emergent phenomenon, is placed on the scale of emergence theory more widely. In so far as what emerges in Jesus Christ is divinity or a divine nature, then this Christology tends towards emergent-theism – the emergence of a deity from the complexity of the world.[120] This logic of ascent, not gracious descent, can be seen in Peacocke's statement that 'incarnation'

> does not involve any 'descent' of a God, conceived of as 'above' man … but rather as being a unique manifestation of a possibility always inherently there for man by his potential nature, i.e. by virtue of what man was, or rather might be, in himself (which is, of course, as God evolved him). The 'incarnation' which occurred 'in' Jesus is an example of that emergence-from-continuity that we have seen characterized the creative process.[121]

117. Another very similar affirmation is articulated by Denis Edwards, who draws upon Karl Rahner, to argue, 'The incarnation is part of cosmic history … in fact the climax of, a massive movement of self-transcendence' within the universe. Denis Edwards, *Jesus and the Cosmos* (Eugene, OR: Wipf and Stock, 2004), 70.

118. Arthur Peacocke, *All That Is: A Naturalistic Faith for the Twenty-First Century* (Minneapolis: Fortress Press. 2009), 34–6.

119. Peacocke, *All That Is*, 40.

120. I previously argued more strongly that Peacocke's Christology of ascent in conjunction with emergence theory led to an emergent theism, like that of Samuel Alexander. I have since come to doubt whether the emergent properties exhibited by Christ are considered by Peacocke to be divine in any realist or ontological sense, rather than merely exemplary for humanity. Thus my analysis of Peacocke has changed markedly since, Joanna Leidenhag, 'Critique of Emergent Theologies', *Zygon: Journal of Religion and Science* 51, no. 4 (December 2016): 867–82.

121. Arthur R. Peacocke, *Creation and the World of Science* (Oxford: Clarendon Press, 1979), 241–2. Thus, Philip Clayton is wrong to claim that 'emergent thinking links most naturally with kenotic Christology'. Clayton, *Adventures in the Spirit*, 111. Kenoticism

Peacocke uses emergence theory to define 'incarnation' as the ascension of a single human being to reach a new evolutionary level, the potential for which was latent within all human beings.

The second result, where incarnation is a universal process, can be seen in Peacocke's claim that 'God has all along been instantiating, "incarnating" God's own "personalness" in that world'.[122] This constant 'incarnating' is identified with the process of evolutionary emergence throughout the natural world, but it is only in Jesus Christ that this process reached its perfect summit.[123] Peacocke's emergence-Christology here seems congruent with John Hick's *The Metaphor of God Incarnate* in that, for both Peacocke and Hick, 'the mythic story [of the incarnation] expresses the significance of a point in [evolutionary] history where we can see human life lived in faithful response to God and see God's nature reflected in that human response'.[124] For Peacocke, the incarnation is part of an ongoing process, indistinguishable from the natural processes of evolution, but which all humanity should strive to imitate.[125] As Oliver Crisp points out, this approach of low Christology puts 'the theological cart before the horse: Christian theology proclaims that Christ *as* God incarnate teaches us how we should live'.[126] It is not that as an emergent human Christ teaches us how to be God (which is what Peacocke suggests), but that as God Christ teaches us how to be truly human.

Peacocke is also self-consciously employing Geoffrey Lampe's (to whom Peacocke's own Bampton Lectures are dedicated) 'inspiration Christology'.[127] As such, Peacocke acknowledges that he has no desire to support views of a

refers, fundamentally, to a divine descent and stripping of divine attributes, and emergence refers to an ascent and a filling-up, as opposed to a self-emptying, of divine properties within a human being.

122. Arthur R. Peacocke, *Theology for a Scientific Age: Being and Becoming – Natural, Divine, and Human* (Minneapolis, MN: Fortress Press, 1993), 305–6. This view of emergent evolution as a kind of ongoing 'incarnation' of God is articulated by Franciscan and Teilhardian expert Ilia Delio. She writes, 'Incarnation does not take place in evolution; Christ does not intervene in creation and then become its goal. Rather, the whole evolutionary process is incarnational.' Ilia Delio, *The Emergent Christ: Exploring the Meaning of Catholic in an Evolutionary Universe* (Maryknoll, NY: Orbis Books, 2011), 53.

123. Peacocke, *Creation and the World of Science*, 212–13, 231.

124. John Hick, *The Metaphor of God Incarnate* (London: SCM Press, 1993), 105–6.

125. Although it is not made clear how we consciously convert to Jesus/to evolution and choose to imitate or participate more fully in our own evolution/incarnation. It seems that evolution is not something we can *choose* to participate in or not, especially given that the capacity for free will and choice is seen to be an emergent property produced by the evolutionary process.

126. Oliver Crisp, 'Incarnation', in *The Oxford Handbook of Systematic Theology*, ed. John Webster, Kathryn Tanner and Iain Torrance (Oxford: Oxford University Press, 2007), 165.

127. See, Geoffrey Lampe, *God the Spirit: The Bampton Lectures 1976* (Oxford: Clarendon Press, 1977).

pre-existent Logos, since as we saw above immaterial pre-existence contradicts the logic of emergence theory. This denial of Christ's pre-existence allows Peacocke to repeatedly affirm that any human being could become 'incarnate'.[128] However, this linking of an evolutionary emergence theology with a moral exemplar Christology is problematic. One might ask Peacocke, if emergence is an unpredictable event resulting from increased biological complexity, just how does one follow Christ's example and bring about the emergence of a new ontological level within oneself? Since mental properties (including those which reveal the nature of God in Jesus Christ) are conditioned by, and supervene upon, physical substrates according to emergence theory, it would seem that in emulating Christ, disciples would need a material (neurological) change before a spiritual change could occur; salvation as an emergent phenomenon becomes a product of evolutionary adaptation.

It is likely that a prior commitment to a low-Christology of exemplarism is reinforced by emergence theory, rather than Peacocke's commitment to emergence entailing a low-Christology; but, either way, the adoption of emergence theory and the expression of a low-Christology appear mutually reinforcing. Where emergence theory makes a distinctive contribution, over and above Hick's and Lampe's similarly low-Christologies, is in how it subsumes his concept of the incarnation specifically within the theory of evolution and the material processes of creation. Emergence theory provides a material-to-mental-to-spiritual narrative of linear development, a trajectory which Rowan Williams has described as 'the most fundamental mistake Christology can make' because it dissolves any 'unique and decisive contribution of Christological language' to the 'logic of creation'.[129]

Peacocke remains unclear on what the new emergent level or property that Jesus Christ instantiates in the world specifically refers to. It does not seem to be a new emergent self or mind, such as William Hasker's model of emergence (which would be one way to maintain a notion of dyothelitism with emergence theology). Instead, the perfect revelation of God that emerges in Jesus Christ seems to refer to a distinct set of mental properties. F. LeRon Shults follows Peacocke here and defines 'the doctrine of incarnation [as] an attempt to clarify this question about the coming-to-be of Homo sapiens', through the evolutionary process of emergence, which began the 'emergence of the symbolic capacity of our species'.[130] According to Shults, therefore, the new emergent level reached in Christ is a psychological and epistemological set of mental properties; the way-of-knowing and being-known that the persons of the Trinity share is repeated in Jesus of Nazareth.[131] Similarly, Philip Clayton describes the new emergent level reached in Jesus Christ as a set of dispositional properties such that Jesus's way of acting and being in the world is God's way of acting and being in the world.[132]

---

128. Peacocke, *Creation and the World of Science*, 233, 242. Arthur Peacocke, *God and the New Biology* (London: Dent, 1986), 132; Peacocke, *All That Is*, 38.

129. Rowan Williams, *Christ: The Heart of Creation* (London: Bloomsbury, 2018), 235.

130. F. LeRon Shults, *Christology and Science* (Aldershot: Ashgate, 2008), 23, 58, 60.

131. Shults, *Christology and Science*, 60.

132. Clayton, *Adventures in the Spirit*, 111.

Whichever set of properties are preferred, as the unique revelation of God within these emergence-Christologies, it is a set of properties that arises out of physical complexity and remains ontologically dependent upon the material substrate of biological evolution.

The crux of the problem for emergent Christologies is the limited definition of transcendence that emergence theory allows for. Emergence theory is often embraced by theologians for having any space for transcendence at all, namely the transcendence of higher properties from their bases such that (*contra* reductionism) we can speak of genuine novelty in the universe. It is often unclear in emergence theologies if the term 'transcendence' is meaningfully different from the terminology of 'irreducibility'. This is insufficient for any notion of divine transcendence, which is a transcendence that enters into, draws alongside and descends, rather than a transcendence that emerges out of or ascends. In so far as the uniqueness of Jesus of Nazareth, which legitimates this person alone to be the centre of the Church's worship as the Christ, is taken to be an emergent property, then Jesus Christ must *either* not be fully divine and pre-existent as the Creator of all things *or* divinity exists on a scale with physical and mental properties and as such remains supervenient and dependent upon the physical complexity of the world (emergent theism). Jesus Christ, on emergent Christologies, may transcend the psychological and ethical (and even ontological) capacities thus far actualized in evolutionary history, but he cannot be considered to manifest the *divine* transcendence that exceeds the universe; an emergent Christ cannot transcend the process of emergence itself.

The spirit of emergence: Divine action as an emergent phenomenon

For many emergence theologians there seems to be a natural coherence between the Holy Spirit, as the personal activity of God in creation, and emergence theory. Harold J. Morowitz notes this connection when he writes, 'The transition from mystery to complexity would be, in theological terms, the divine spirit.'[133] Or again, 'the rule of emergence associates more closely with what theologians call the Holy Spirit.'[134] Why does Morowitz observe this correspondence between the Holy Spirit and emergence, and what is the shape of pneumatology being proposed here?

Philip Clayton also articulates the importance of pneumatology for emergence theology when he writes, 'The understanding of the Spirit is central to emergent theology.'[135] However, it is clear that the shape of pneumatology within his emergence paradigm is, again, pulled towards emergent theism. Clayton writes,

---

133. Morowitz, 'Emergence of Transcendence', 185.

134. Harold J. Morowitz, 'The "Trinitarian" World of Neo-Pantheism: On Panentheism and Epistemology', in *In Whom We Live and Move and Have Our Being: Panentheistic Reflections on God's Presence in a Scientific World*, ed. Arthur Peacocke and Philip Clayton (Grand Rapids, MI: Eerdmans, 2004), 132.

135. Clayton, *Adventures in the Spirit*, 110.

The divine spirit … must also be temporal, the emergent result of a long-term process of intimate relationship with beings in the world. In this view, then, Spirit is not a fundamental ontological category but an emergent form of complexity that living things within the world begin to manifest at a certain stage in their development.[136]

Clayton explicitly refers to God's Spirit, not merely human minds or created spirits, as resulting from the physical complexity of the world in a parallel fashion to how Alexander described God's deity as an emergent result of the world. It would seem, at this point, that there is no pre-existent or transcendent Spirit of God on Clayton's schema. But this would not be entirely correct. Clayton goes on to say,

A theological corrective must be made to the 'straight emergence' view, however. The Spirit that emerges corresponds to the Spirit who was present from the beginning.[137]

In Clayton's pneumatology, we have the same duality that was described earlier in reference to God the Father. Clayton admits that emergence theory needs a 'theological corrective' to counterbalance the pull towards emergent theism. However, this corrective is not a minor adjustment, but forces Clayton to hold together two forms of logic that stand in tension, if not direct opposition, to one another. On the one hand, emergence theory holds that all immaterial, spiritual and higher-level entities must be ontologically, logically and temporally preceded by material substrates. On the other hand, theism holds that an immaterial, spiritual and transcendent Being is the Creator, the ontological and logical ground of all existence. This tension causes a confused duality within the doctrine of God for emergence theologies.

What motivates Clayton, who seems to perceive the tension and resists 'a fully emergentist theology' of Samuel Alexander, to positing the Holy Spirit as (partially) an emergent resultant?[138] The motivation seems to come out of the question of divine action. Divine action is addressed more fully in Chapter 4; it is sufficient at present to state that Clayton – like many in the science-religion dialogue in recent decades – argues that God cannot be seen to act in a way contrary to natural laws. This maxim, almost a rule in recent debates, is termed 'non-interventionism' and has been motivated by scientific, interdisciplinary, pastoral and theological concerns. Setting aside questions regarding the validity or need for non-interventionist divine action for the moment, we can see that what motivates Clayton's emergence theology is the hope that 'an emergentist theory of mind thus opens up the possibility of a divine influence at the mental or

---

136. Clayton, *Adventures in the Spirit*, 110.
137. Clayton, *Adventures in the Spirit*, 110.
138. Clayton, *Mind and Emergence*, 190.

spiritual level that does not require an exception to any natural laws.'[139] Speaking of the emergent level of personhood, the 'integrated self or psychophysical agent-in-community', Clayton writes, 'Here, and perhaps here alone, a divine agency could be operative that could exercise downward causal influence without being reduced to a manipulator of physical particles or psychotropic neurotransmitters.'[140] The hope of emergence theory, possibly the central motivation for Clayton's whole project, is the articulation of a non-interventionist account of divine action.

This emergence-based account for divine action, however, forces Clayton to construe the Holy Spirit (the personal agency of God) as the next level in the emergence hierarchy. Positively, Clayton celebrates: 'It is permissible to construe divine causality as one of these higher levels of causality' that has non-deterministic, top-down influence on the world.[141] However, Clayton notes the cost of his approach: 'The resources of emergence theory can help her [the theologian] introduce and defend divine action, but only if she construes the divine as the next emergent level in the cosmic evolutionary process.'[142] Thus, Clayton is compelled to divide his doctrine of God; as creator, God pre-exists and transcends the emergence process, as agent in the world – as the Holy Spirit in particular – God is an emergent resultant at the next level of a created hierarchy.

Conclusion

Emergence theory is often praised for offering an interdisciplinary framework that avoids the inadequacies of physicalist reductionism and the mysteries of Cartesian dualism; but such celebration appears premature. Emergence theologies seek to reconstruct the core tenets of Christianity upon the foundation of emergence theory as it exists within the natural sciences and philosophy of mind. This chapter argued, first, that the foundation provided by the natural sciences was less secure than emergence theologians often admit because no clear definition of emergence is forthcoming, and many scientists view emergence as entirely compatible with reductionism. The form of emergence theory employed within theology most often draws upon philosophy of mind. This chapter went on to argue that emergence within philosophy of mind is an ambiguous concept, in part because the idea that the mind is analogous to physical emergence appears to be either a

---

139. Philip Clayton and Steven Knapp, *The Predicament of Belief: Science, Philosophy and Faith* (Oxford: Oxford University Press, 2011), 58. Elsewhere, Clayton writes, '*Divine action is to be located not within specific scientific disciplines but in the interrelationships between them.*' Clayton, 'Towards a Theory of Divine Action That Has Traction', 108 (italics in original). This claim seems notably different from his idea elsewhere that divine action works primarily at the highest level of reality (the personal and spiritual).

140. Clayton, *Mind and Emergence*, 198.

141. Clayton, *Adventures in the Spirit*, 198.

142. Clayton, *Adventures in the Spirit*, 198.

false analogy or entirely mysterious. Emergence theory, as currently construed in either the natural sciences or in philosophy of mind, is an unstable foundation for constructive theology avoiding neither the inadequacies of reduction nor the mysteries of dualism.

These are serious challenges, certainly, but the problems that beset emergence theology are far more serious still. Emergence theory was originally conceived for two related purposes. First, emergence theory was intended to provide a naturalistic explanation for complex and mysterious phenomena (such as life and purpose in the natural world) and remove the need to evoke supernatural agencies. Second, this commitment to naturalism, at least in part, served an interdisciplinary purpose. As such, the adoption of emergence theory as an interdisciplinary framework is closely linked to its commitment to naturalism and the hope for a sufficient, expansive framework for understanding all of reality. A theologian, such as William Hasker, may adopt an emergentist understanding of the soul (and accept the various philosophical problems therein) without adopting the world view of emergence *in toto*. However, this is not what emergence theologies typically do because it is against the grain of the logic of emergence itself as an expansive framework for understanding all of reality.

Theologians who do accept the logic of emergence *in toto* accept a significant tension in their work. On the one hand, as emergentists they are committed to the idea that the material precedes (both temporally and logically) the immaterial. On the other hand, as theists they are committed to the idea that an immaterial (or other than material) Creator pre-exists the universe (either temporally or logically). The hope placed in strong emergence theory by emergence theologians is the expectation that it can provide a realistic account of irreducible immaterial properties or entities (souls, minds, freedom, angels, demons and even God or God's action), in accordance with the naturalistic and monistic framework of contemporary natural science. However, the nature and place of these emergent properties within the world is highly constrained by emergence theory, making it less promising for Christian theology than first appears. Even if emergence affirms irreducibility, the mental and spiritual aspects of life are still subordinated and secondary to the physical and material, thus the threat of disenchantment and devaluation looms.

Emergence theologians claim to remove any dualism within the human person and, instead, to place the great divide between God and the universe. Accordingly, God should remain outside of the framework of emergence. This intuition about the proper place of dualism within Christian theology seems entirely correct. However, the maximizing goals of emergence theory and the commitment to interdisciplinary naturalism make this almost impossible for emergence theologies to maintain. Instead, emergence theory exhibits a tendency to place the dualism *inside* the doctrine of God. In this duality, God's immanence is equated with the process of emergence and the transcendence of God is redefined to be akin to the self-transcendence that creatures can achieve through the process of emergence. In Christian theology, God is seen to be in continuous interaction with creatures for the sake of salvation through the incarnation of the Son and the indwelling of the Spirit. This makes the possibility of protecting the doctrine of God from the distortive effect of emergence theory extremely difficult. In their articulations of the incarnation and in discussions of divine action, emergence theologies inadvertently lower God the Son and God the Holy Spirit to the level of created realities. If Clayton is worried 'that too much theological discourse will wreck the theory of emergence', then I am concerned that too much emergence theory will wreck Christian theology.[143] Christian theologians searching for a metaphysical theory to employ within the doctrine of creation (and theological anthropology) need to look elsewhere for a less expansive or inherently naturalistic ontology. To that end, the remainder of this book evaluates the potential of panpsychism for the doctrine of creation.

143. These are Amos Yong's words, but they are a fair summary of Clayton's concern. Amos Yong, *The Spirit of Creation: Modern Science and Divine Action in the Pentecostal-Charismatic Imagination* (Grand Rapids, MI: Eerdmans, 2011), 169.

Chapter 2

WELCOMING CONTEMPORARY PANPSYCHISM

Panpsychism is an umbrella term for a variety of positions within philosophy of mind which all hold that psyche is fundamental throughout the universe. In contemporary philosophy, panpsychism is undergoing a significant resurgence of interest and seems to be gathering momentum.[1] This chapter seeks to introduce and critically evaluate the contemporary literature on panpsychism within analytic philosophy of mind. If panpsychism becomes widely accepted among philosophers in the coming decades, what might theology wish to critique or affirm in dialogue with this position? This important question, to my knowledge, has not yet been asked and explored by theologians.

This chapter has a narrative structure; it is a story of a campaign, a battle and the possibility of a new alliance. 'The campaign' is the story of panpsychism's resurgence within contemporary philosophy of mind, largely (but not always intentionally) through the efforts of three notable philosophers: Thomas Nagel, David J. Chalmers and Galen Strawson. 'The battle' section of this chapter explores the main objections against panpsychism. In outlining the various responses from panpsychists this section also surveys the variety of positions currently gathered beneath the panpsychist umbrella. The battle resolves into a stalemate; panpsychism is equally as attractive (or unattractive depending on one's disposition) as its main metaphysical rivals within philosophy of mind. This is not a total loss for the panpsychist, who is typically viewed as the underdog, barely worthy of consideration. Instead, it is concluded that panpsychism *is a serious option* within philosophy of mind that Christian theologians should seriously consider and could respectably adopt.

After times of war come times for making new alliances. The hope is that if two compatible theories offer their respective strengths to one another, they might

---

1. Since 2017, there have been several major publications such as Godehard Brüntrup and Ludwig Jaskolla, eds, *Panpsychism: Contemporary Perspectives* (Oxford: Oxford University Press, 2017); David Skrbina, *Panpsychism in the West*, 2nd edn (Cambridge, MA: MIT Press, 2017); Philip Goff, *Consciousness and Fundamental Reality* (Oxford: Oxford University Press, 2017); William Seager, ed., *Routledge Handbook of Panpsychism* (New York: Routledge, 2020).

combine to create an altogether more satisfactory position. The alliance, brokered in the 'A new alliance: Panpsychism and belief in God' section, is between panpsychism and theism. This chapter points towards an original argument that panpsychism is not merely compatible with belief in God, but that the structure of the arguments in favour of panpsychism invites or implies a theistic stance regarding the origin of the universe. That is, if a panpsychist philosopher follows through the logic of her own arguments consistently, she should abandon any lingering association with naturalism and instead adopt theism. In addition, it is argued that panpsychism should be an attractive option for the theist when she is choosing between different theories of the mind. As a result, the resurgence in panpsychism is a movement that Christian theologians should welcome and tentatively lend their support to.

The campaign: The revival of panpsychism within philosophy of mind

The revival of interest in panpsychism is a story punctuated by the work of Thomas Nagel (1979), David J. Chalmers (1996), Galen Strawson (2006) and Thomas Nagel (2012) again. Their arguments stand in continuity with one another, and the cumulative effect is an impressive transformation of a very old, fairly counter-intuitive theory of mind into a scientifically plausible and analytically precise model of consciousness.

Thomas Nagel: The 'true father of contemporary panpsychism'

Throughout most of the nineteenth and twentieth centuries panpsychism was a small component within elaborate metaphysical schemes such as Absolute Idealism (in the work of Gustav Fechner, Rudolf Lotze and more recently Timothy Sprigge) and process philosophy. It wasn't until Nagel published an essay simply entitled 'Panpsychism' in 1979 that panpsychism was disentangled from this history and presented as a stand-alone theory within philosophy of mind. In this 're-igniting' essay, Nagel defined panpsychism as 'the view that the basic physical constituents of the universe have mental properties'.[2] This still popular definition captures the fact that many panpsychists wish to talk of mental properties rather than immaterial substances, and that most seek to keep idealism and process metaphysics at arm's length. This disassociation of contemporary panpsychism from larger metaphysical frameworks should embolden contemporary theologians to seriously consider

---

2. Sam Coleman 'The Real Combination Problem: Panpsychism, Micro-Subjects, and Emergence', *Erkenntnis* 79 (2014): 22; Thomas Nagel, 'Panpsychism', in *Mortal Questions* (Cambridge: Cambridge University Press, 1979), 181. The epiphet 'true father of contemporary panpsychism' in the section heading is taken from Sam Coleman, 'The Evolution of Nagel's Panpsychism', *Klesis* 41 (2018): 180.

panpsychism without fearing they are inadvertently committing themselves to either of these larger frameworks.

Nagel's 1979 essay mounted an argument for the plausibility of panpsychism from four simple premises:

1. Ontological materialism or monism: Human beings are wholly composed out of matter, which in principle can be shared or replaced by any other matter in this great universe. This is a denial of substance dualism.
2. Mental realism: Consciousness is a real phenomenon, regardless of our current difficulty to explain it. Moreover, consciousness is a property of the human organism, and hence it is a property of material beings.
3. No psycho-physical reduction: Conscious experience cannot be explained by physical properties alone. Physical properties are the sort of properties that can be quantified by scientists, but all quantified explanations will leave out some qualitative element.[3]
4. Non-emergence: All properties of any complex physical body can be transparently traced to the properties of the constituent parts, including their arrangement and interaction.

Taking these four premises together, the argument commonly runs that if mental properties are a real property of material entities, which cannot be reduced to or emerge from the organizational complexity of material parts, *then the only remaining option* (aside from employing divine action to inject souls into human subjects) is to posit consciousness as fundamental (panpsychism). Put another way, if wholly material creatures have conscious states that cannot be explained by their material properties, but which must still be explained in terms of the creature's constituent parts, then the constituent parts (and matter in general) must have additional non-material properties that explain the appearance of consciousness. As Sam Coleman characterizes the argument, 'There must be some secret properties of matter with a direct connection to consciousness, such that when you put matter together in the right way, as a brain (and perhaps a body too), you get a conscious being.'[4] These are the initial bones of contemporary arguments for panpsychism. It is sometimes referred to as *The Genetic Argument* for panpsychism.

Despite giving clear expression to these arguments Nagel's essay 'Panpsychism' concluded that panpsychism 'appears to follow from a few simple premises, each of which is more plausible than its denial, though not perhaps more plausible than the denial of panpsychism.'[5] Nagel had shown, without invoking process

---

3. This would later become known as the 'explanatory gap' between scientific explanation and conscious experience. J. Levine, 'Materialism and Qualia: The Explanatory Gap', *Pacific Philosophical Quarterly* 64 (1983): 354–61.

4. Coleman, 'Nagel's Panpsychism', 185.

5. Nagel, 'Panpsychism', 181.

metaphysics, how one might defend panpsychism in a wholly rational and logical manner. At this point, Nagel judged panpsychism to be too counter-intuitive, and placed it among the 'hopelessly unacceptable solutions to the mind-body problem'.[6] Nevertheless, this essay successfully introduced the structure of a panpsychist solution to contemporary analytic philosophers of mind.

David J. Chalmers: The science of consciousness

Following Nagel's 1979 essay, panpsychism remained an intriguing but unattractive position for most philosophers of mind. Throughout the 1980s and early 1990s psychophysical reduction and/or emergence theory, the rejection of which form two of the core premises for Nagel's argument, remained foundational for most philosophers of mind. However, in 1994 Chalmers gave a conference paper entitled 'Towards a Scientific Basis for Consciousness', which, in addition to the subsequent volume *The Conscious Mind*, irrevocably altered the playing field and added considerable support to the panpsychist position.[7] Chalmers's primary contribution to philosophy of mind has been his distinction between so-called 'easy problems' and 'the hard problem' of consciousness.

The 'easy problems' are, according to Chalmers, explaining the mind's ability to discriminate between categories and react to environmental stimuli; the integration of information by a cognitive system; the reportability of mental states; the ability of a system to access its own internal states; the focus of attention; the deliberate control of behaviour; and the difference between wakefulness and sleep.[8] Chalmers acknowledges that explaining these phenomena is a very difficult *puzzle* facing neuroscientists and cognitive scientists and that it may take 'a century or two of difficult empirical work'.[9] However, these puzzles can, in principle, be solved by such empirical methods. This is because all of the 'easy problems' listed above are, according to Chalmers, *abilities* or *functions*. Chalmers refers to these problems as *psychological consciousness*, and he is content to leave neurological and cognitive scientists to struggle with them.

Chalmers's argument is that no matter how much progress is made in understanding psychological consciousness there will always remain the so-called 'hard problem of consciousness'. The hard problem is characterized by

6. Nagel, 'Panpsychism', 193.

7. This conference paper was later published as 'The Puzzle of Conscious Experience', *Scientific American* 273 (1995): 80–6. See also the reprint of this argument, 'Facing Up to the Hard Problem of Consciousness', with responses in *Explaining Consciousness: The Hard Problem*, ed. Jonathan Shear (Cambridge, MA: MIT Press, 1997), 9–33; David J. Chalmers, *The Conscious Mind: In Search of a Fundamental Theory* (Oxford: Oxford University Press, 1996).

8. This list is taken from, David J. Chalmers, *The Character of Consciousness* (Oxford: Oxford University Press, 2010), 4. See also, Chalmers, *Conscious Mind*, 26–7.

9. Chalmers, *Character of Consciousness*, 5.

the question: Why are any of these functions accompanied by experience? Why are 'the lights on' inside the human machine? Chalmers calls this *phenomenal consciousness* and it refers to the experience, the feeling of what it is like to be a subject that accompanies many of the cognitive functions of the human brain. Chalmers gives five compelling arguments, by way of thought experiments, that seek to show that phenomenal consciousness will never be explained by reduction to physical facts; no matter how much we know about the brain (and body), we will never have explained *phenomenal* consciousness.[10] These arguments have turned the tide in favour of Nagel's second premise, no psychophysical reduction, and lend support to mental realism and non-emergence as well.

Although Chalmers's legacy is the success of this negative argument against materialism (and other forms of psychophysical reduction), much of his effort has been spent more positively in trying to construct – or at least point the way towards the possible construction of – a fundamental theory of consciousness.[11] In addition to his desire to '*take consciousness seriously*' as a phenomenon that cannot be reduced to physical function, Chalmers strives to '*take science seriously*'.[12] In order to hold to both commitments, Chalmers argues that we must make consciousness fundamental to the natural world; we must adopt panpsychism. In this way, Chalmers presents panpsychism as a middle way between reductionist materialism and supernaturalist dualism.[13]

Chalmers's positive argument runs that if consciousness is 'a scientific subject matter', then, although it 'is not open to investigation by the usual methods', it can still be explained by the usual scientific structure, namely 'a few fundamental entities connected by fundamental laws'.[14] Consciousness may be irreducible to physical

---

10. These five arguments show that experience does not logically supervene upon the physical, such that no amount of empirical understanding can even start to explain it: The Zombie Thought Experiment, The Inverted Spectrum; From Epistemic Asymmetry; The Knowledge Argument (from Frank Jackson and Thomas Nagel), The Absence of Analysis; See Chalmers, *Conscious Mind*, 94–124; Frank Jackson, 'Epiphenomenal Qualia', *Philosophical Quarterly* 32 (1982): 127–36; Thomas Nagel, 'What Is It Like to Be a Bat?' in *Mortal Questions* (Cambridge: Cambridge University Press, 1979), 165–80.

11. Hence the subtitle of his major volume, *The Conscious Mind: In Search of a Fundamental Theory*.

12. Chalmers, *Conscious Mind*, xii–xiii.

13. David J. Chalmers, 'Panpsychism and Panprotopsychism', in *Panpsychism: Contemporary Perspectives*, ed. Godehard Brüntrup and Ludwig Jaskolla (Oxford: Oxford University Press, 2017), 19–47.

14. Chalmers, 'Facing Up', 20; Chalmers, *Conscious Mind*, xiv. Thomas Nagel makes a very similar case for the scientific status for panpsychism when he writes, 'Major scientific advances often require the creation of new concepts, postulating unobservable elements of reality that are needed to explain how natural regularities that initially appear accidental are in fact necessary.' Thomas Nagel, *Mind and Cosmos: Why the Materialist Neo-Darwinian Conception of Nature Is Almost Certainly False* (Oxford: Oxford University Press, 2012), 42.

entities and laws, but there need be 'nothing particularly spiritual or mystical' about fundamental *phenomenal* entities and *psychophysical* laws.[15] These fundamental entities and laws are required to keep the explanation of consciousness within the same overall shape as any other scientific explanation.[16] Chalmers makes the comparison to James Clerk Maxwell's idea that electromagnetic forces had to be taken as fundamental, as well as positing new laws governing these forces, in order to explain the apparently spooky effect of electric and magnetic phenomena.[17] In short, Chalmers argued that panpsychism is not merely a possible move in the logical space of metaphysics (as Nagel had demonstrated), but that panpsychism might be deemed credible within a scientific framework.[18]

As with Nagel, in 1996 Chalmers was still uncomfortable with the label of panpsychism and considered association with this historical position a threat. Instead, he preferred to call his position 'naturalistic dualism'.[19] This he defined as the view, simply, that 'there are both physical and nonphysical features of the world'.[20] Chalmers was aware that by advocating dualism, he would meet resistance from many of his fellow philosophers, whether agnostically secular or adamantly atheistic. As such, Chalmers remains vigilant against any spiritual connotations of his position. He writes, 'There is nothing especially transcendental about consciousness; it is just another natural phenomenon … to embrace dualism is not necessarily to embrace mystery.'[21]

From the perspective of Christian theology, what are we to make of Chalmers's stubbornly anti-religious treatment of consciousness? Should this threaten Christian theologians? Quite the opposite. I suggest that Chalmers's naturalization of panpsychism, as a kind of 'dualism all the way down', is an important aspect of contemporary panpsychism in dialogue with theology. This is because Chalmers's description of consciousness as a purely natural phenomenon provides an important buffer against false characterizations of Christian views of the human soul as 'divine', a little piece of God or autonomously immortal.[22] If consciousness

15. Chalmers, 'Facing Up', 20.

16. Chalmers, *Conscious Mind*, 126–9.

17. Chalmers, *Conscious Mind*, 127.

18. Godehard Brüntrup and Ludwig Jaskolla 'Introduction', in *Panpsychism: Contemporary Perspectives*, 4.

19. Chalmers, *Conscious Mind*, 128. He later acknowledges that 'it is probably fair to say that [this] view is a variety of panpsychism … we ought to take the possibility of some sort of panpsychism seriously: there seem to be no knockdown arguments against the view, and there are various positive reasons why one might embrace it.' Chalmers, *Conscious Mind*, 299.

20. Chalmers, *Conscious Mind*, 124; Chalmers, *Character of Consciousness*, 17.

21. Chalmers, *Conscious Mind*, 126, 128. The accusation that 'dualism wallows in mystery, accepting dualism is giving up' is a common one, but it is here paradigmatically expressed by Daniel Dennett, *Consciousness Explained* (Boston, MA: Little, Brown, 1991), 37.

22. David Skrbina, for example, writes that panpsychism is incompatible with monotheistic religion because, 'In all monotheistic Western religions, humans alone possess

were a divinely transcendent phenomenon or slice of uncreated light, then any realist philosophy of mind would slide towards emergent theism, pantheism, polytheism or paganism. Consciousness, in Christian theology, must remain a created phenomenon of creaturely minds that, in keeping with the principle of *creatio ex nihilo*, neither emanate from God nor collectively constitute a divine mind or world-soul. By arguing for fundamental consciousness as 'just another natural phenomenon', Chalmers points the way forward for a Christian panpsychism to posit creaturely or created finite minds throughout the universe as fundamental and possibly ubiquitous, without implying that these minds are identical to God or in any way constitutive of divinity; but more of that later.

Galen Strawson's gauntlet: The argument for entailment

The third major figure in the recent history of panpsychism is Galen Strawson. Strawson took panpsychism onto the offensive and argued in such a way that his physicalist and emergentist colleagues found themselves having to justify how their positions managed to avoid or deny panpsychism. Whereas Nagel's essay placed panpsychism back on the philosophical map, and Chalmers framed panpsychism as a scientific and naturalistic option, it was Strawson who threw down the gauntlet and made panpsychism impossible for contemporary philosophers of mind to ignore.

In 2006, Strawson published an article entitled 'Realistic Monism: Why Physicalism Entails Panpsychism'. Strawson argued that 'something akin to panpsychism is not merely one possible form of realistic physicalism, but the only possible form, and hence, the only possible form of physicalism *tout court*'.[23] Given Strawson's own standing within the philosophical community and the dominance of physicalist ontology in the latter half of the twentieth century, it is unsurprising that this article was 'something of a watershed event in recent analytic philosophy of mind',[24] which brought 'panpsychism to the attention, and critical scrutiny, of mainstream philosophers of mind, also making a new generation aware of its appeal'.[25]

Strawson's argument can be formulated in the following way:

1. Physicalists hold that every real, concrete[26] phenomenon is wholly physical.

a *divine and immortal soul*.' David Skrbina, 'Panpsychism in history: An Overview', in *Mind That Abides*, ed. David Skrbina (Amsterdam: John Benjamins, 2009), 1.

23. Galen Strawson, 'Realistic Monism: Why Physicalism Entails Panpsychism', in Galen Strawson et al., *Consciousness and Its Place in Nature*, ed. Anthony Freeman (Exeter: Imprint Academic, 2006), 9.

24. Leemon B. McHenry and George W. Shields, 'Analytic Critiques of Whitehead's metaphysics', *Journal of the American Philosophical Association* (2016): 492.

25. Coleman, 'Real Combination Problem', 22.

26. 'Concrete' means a spatiotemporally located, non-abstract, entity.

2. Nothing is more certain than that consciousness is a real, concrete phenomenon.

Therefore,

3. (Realistic) physicalists must hold that consciousness is wholly physical.

How can (3) possibly be the case? To our ordinary (neo-Cartesian) definitions of 'consciousness' and 'physical', this conclusion appears to be a direct contradiction in terms. The catch is that Strawson argues that the definition of 'physical', as used at the end of the first premise, is an utterly mysterious category in and of itself. Strawson points to John Locke, David Hume, Joseph Priestly, Arthur Eddington, Bertrand Russell and Noam Chomsky as each coming to this conclusion in their own time, namely that 'we have *no* good reason to think that we know anything about the physical that gives us any reason to find any problem in the idea that mental phenomena are physical phenomena.'[27] This is not because the mind can be reduced to the functional interaction of physical parts, but because even the physical – properly understood – cannot be exhaustively described by physics.[28] When Strawson agrees with other materialists that experience is 'really just neurons firing', he means that 'there is a lot more to neurons than physics and neurophysiology record (or can record).'[29] At its core, Strawson's argument for panpsychism is primarily a refutation of dualism. He describes 'Descartes' greatest mistake' to be the assumption that we really know enough about the nature of spatial-extension to place it in opposition to conscious experience.[30]

What about emergence theory? Given Strawson's argument so far, a materialist could respond that all microparts are wholly non-experiential, but consciousness

27. Galen Strawson, *Real Materialism and Other Essays* (Oxford: Oxford University Press, 2008), 20, 39.

28. This argument is distilled from Strawson, *Real Materialism*, 19–20, 46–7; Strawson, 'Realistic Monism', in *Consciousness and Its Place*, 3–31. Interestingly, therefore, Strawson is unimpressed with David J. Chalmers's hard problem of consciousness, zombie thought experiments or naturalistic dualism, because these imply that we know more about non-experiential reality than we really do.

29. Strawson, *Real Materialism*, 56. Strawson is aware of the accusation that he is playing fast and loose with accepted terminology here, and that his argument is little more than a language game. Arguments about terminology are common enough in philosophy and, in this case, it is intended to provoke his interlocutors to see the 'silliness' of their own version of physicalism/materialism. Strawson, *Real Materialism*, 48–9.

30. Strawson, *Real Materialism*, 46. The idea that dualism went wrong over its characterization of matter, rather than of mind, is becoming common among panpsychists. Gregg Rosenberg writes, 'I argue that Descartes' most dangerous errors were the ones he made about matter, not mind.' Gregg Rosenberg, *A Place for Consciousness: Probing the Deep Structure of the Natural World* (Oxford: Oxford University Press, 2004), 7–8. David Ray Griffin writes, Descartes's 'view of the mind is indeed problematic, but even

certainly exists at some macro level by virtue of some strong emergence-based relation. At this point, Strawson added his voice to the growing number of philosophers who – inspired by Nagel's 1979 essay – argue,

> It is built into the heart of the notion of emergence that *emergence cannot be brute* in the sense of there being absolutely no reason in the nature of things why the emerging thing is as it is (so that it is unintelligible even to God).[31]

Strawson iterates that emergence is, by definition, an in-virtue-of relation whereby there must be something about the material base (the brain, for example) *in virtue of which*, it gives rise to the mind. For (super-)strong emergentists, who reject panpsychism and state that matter is wholly non-experiential, there can be nothing about the brain in virtue of which it gives rise to the mind.[32] In Strawson's words, 'You can make chalk from cheese, or water from wine, because if you go down to the subatomic level they are both the same stuff, but you can't make experience from something wholly non-experiential.'[33] For the emergence relation to work, mental properties must be built in at the bottom – found at the fundamental level.[34]

Strawson most often articulates his position as a form of Russellian monism.[35] Russellian monism states there is one type of stuff in the universe (monism), but that it has intrinsic and extrinsic qualities. The extrinsic quality of things is the behavioural structure, which is measured mathematically in how things relate. This is what we call the physical.[36] If physicality is merely the measurement of

---

more problematic is his view of matter'. David Ray Griffin, *Unsnarling the World-Knot: Consciousness, Freedom, and the Mind-Body Problem* (Eugene, OR: Wipf and Stock, 1998), 46–7.

31. See Strawson, *Real Materialism*, 65.

32. Interestingly, Alvin Plantinga affirms this argument against emergence and reduction when he writes, 'If electrons and quarks can't think, we won't find anything composed of them that can think by way of the physical interaction of its parts.' Alvin Plantinga and Michael Tooley, *Knowledge of God* (Oxford: Blackwell, 2008), 53.

33. Strawson, *Real Materialism*, 74.

34. In response to Strawson, Colin McGinn writes, 'It isn't *physicalism* that entails panpsychism: it's his commitment to emergence … if you agree that experiences are irreducible to non-E facts, and if you accept emergence, then you end up with panpsychism – which is not a very surprising outcome given the assumptions.' Although McGinn may be correct, many strong emergentists would find this very surprising, if not alarming. Colin McGinn, 'Hard Questions: Comments on Galen Strawson', in Strawson et al., *Consciousness and Its Place in Nature*, 92–3.

35. Chalmers now also sees Russellian monism as the most important version of panpsychism, since it is best suited for explaining mental causation. David J. Chalmers, 'Panpsychism and Panprotopsychism', *Amherst Lecture in Philosophy* 8 (2013): 1–35.

36. Strawson, *Real Materialism*, 27–38; Bertrand Russell, *An Outline of Philosophy* (London: Routledge, [1927] 1992), 125; Bertrand Russell, 'Mind and Matter', in *Portraits from Memory* (Nottingham: Spokesman, [1956] 1995), 153.

behaviour and relations, what is it that behaves or relates? What is the stuff of the world, in and of itself? Bertrand Russell argued that, since we only have access to the intrinsic nature of ourselves and not of anything else it is justifiable to imagine (although by no means certain) that all other things have the same intrinsic quality as human beings, namely the quality of experience.[37] This is the *Intrinsic Natures Argument* for panpsychism; the intrinsic nature of all things (that which is related in causal relations or that which is measured by scientists) is experiential.

Thomas Nagel again: The evolutionary argument for panpsychism

In 2012 Thomas Nagel published the slim volume *Mind and Cosmos*. Here, Nagel defended panpsychism as the most satisfactory explanation as to both 'why specific organisms have the conscious life they have' and 'why conscious organisms arose in the history of life on earth'.[38] Nagel's affirmation of panpsychism, of a neutral monist variety, was made partly on the basis of his previous 1979 argument and partly on the demystifying effect that the passing of years can have upon even the most unusual philosophies.[39] However, Nagel's primary motivation was due to a larger dissatisfaction with the whole neo-Darwinian interpretation of evolution, which he refers to as 'a heroic triumph of ideological theory over common sense'.[40] Hence, his book's controversial subtitle, *Why the Materialist Neo-Darwinian Conception of Nature Is Almost Certainly False*.

Nagel's evolutionary argument for panpsychism is neatly summarized in the following quote:

> But since conscious organisms are not composed of a special kind of stuff, but can be constructed, apparently, from any of the matter in the universe, suitably arranged, it follows that this monism will be universal. Everything, living or not, is constituted from elements having a nature that is both physical and non-physical – that is, capable of combining into mental wholes. So this reductive account can also be described as a form of panpsychism: all the elements of the physical world are also mental.[41]

This argument for panpsychism based on ontological continuity within the universe has been made not only by contemporary panpsychists but is also found in the work of early evolutionary biologists Ernst Haeckel, William Kingdon Clifford, Morton Price, Sir Charles Scott Sherrington, Sir Julian Huxley and Pierre

---

37. Bertrand Russell, *The Analysis of Matter* (London: Routledge, [1927] 1992).

38. Nagel, *Mind and Cosmos*, 50-1.

39. As Galen Strawson writes of his own position, 'This sounded crazy to me for a long time, but I am quite used to it, now that I know that there is no alternative short of "substance dualism"'. Strawson, *Real Materialism*, 71.

40. Nagel, *Mind and Cosmos*, 128.

41. Nagel, *Mind and Cosmos*, 57.

Teilhard de Chardin.[42] The most famous historical statement of the panpsychist argument from evolutionary continuity was penned by William James, and continues to influence panpsychist philosophers today. In *The Principles of Psychology*, James wrote,

> If evolution is to work smoothly, consciousness in some shape must have been present at the very origin of things. Accordingly, we find that the most clear-sighted evolutionary philosophers are beginning to posit it there. Each atom of the nebula, they suppose, must have had an aboriginal atom of consciousness linked with it; and, just as the material atoms have formed bodies and brains by massing themselves together, so the mental atoms, by an analogous process of aggregation, have fused into those larger consciousnesses which we know in ourselves and suppose to exist in our fellow-animal … Some such doctrine … is an indispensable part of a thorough-going philosophy of evolution.[43]

As James expressed, panpsychism is a '*philosophy* of evolution' found at the interface of metaphysics and evolutionary biology, and not a testable hypothesis. Yet, as a philosophy of nature, panpsychism does seem to find traction with the underlying principle of continuity within evolutionary theory.[44]

The mind–body problem, as the name implies, is commonly localized to humanity. However, since bodies arise from, interact with and return to the dust of the ground and stars, the mind–body problem is truly a cosmic problem. How can we locate the phenomenon of experience, not just in connection to the brain but in the universe at all? As Nagel posits, if we take the biological evolution of *Homo sapiens* seriously then we are confronted with the fact that the mind–body problem 'is not just a local problem … but that it invades our understanding of the entire cosmos and its history'.[45] Moreover, if evolution brought about consciousness then evolution cannot be 'just a physical process', but 'may have to be something more than physical all the way down'.[46] Nagel refers to the materialist neo-Darwinian claim to be able to answer everything through random efficient causation as a 'Darwinism of the gaps' approach; the sooner abandoned the better.[47]

---

42. Skrbina, *Panpsychism in the West*, 131–3, 141–4, 191–2.

43. William James, *The Principles of Psychology* (New York: Dover, [1890] 1950), 149. It can be noted that by the time of his Hibbert Lectures in 1907, published as *A Pluralistic Universe* in 1909, James had reconciled himself to panpsychism despite the combination problem. See Skrbina, *Panpsychism in the West*, 147–9.

44. Contemporary zoologist, Donald R. Griffin, describes the acceptance of panpsychism as 'the final crowning chapter of the Darwinian revolution' in 'From Cognition to Consciousness', in *A Communion of Subjects: Animals in Religion, Science, and Ethics*, ed. Paul Waldau and Kimberley Patton (New York: Columbia University Press, 2006), 498.

45. Nagel, *Mind and Cosmos*, 3.

46. Nagel, *Mind and Cosmos*, 46.

47. Nagel, *Mind and Cosmos*, 127. Nagel is adapting the pejorative label, 'god-of-the-gaps', first used by Charles Coulson to refer to the positing of divine action as the explanation for

Rounding up The Campaign

What I have referred to as 'The Campaign' was neither planned nor organized as such. It presents a slow, but steady, trend of dissatisfaction in recent philosophy of mind with both materialist reduction and emergentist mystery. In one sense, the most powerful argument for panpsychism is the *Last Man Standing Argument*; all other theories seem to fail, and (so far) panpsychism remains. The more positive version of this argument is *The Genetic Argument*, stating that consciousness at the human level needs a compelling, naturalistic, evolutionary, origin story; panpsychism alone provides such a story. The other main argument for panpsychism is *The Intrinsic Natures Argument*, outlined in reference to Strawson and Russell. This has been a secondary argument in comparison to *The Genetic Argument* in recent history, but it seems to be growing in importance due to its explanatory promise within philosophy of causation (but that's another story).[48] The arguments for panpsychism are radical, but persuasive. Are they enough to overcome the various objections that have been brought against panpsychism? It is to this question that this chapter now turns.

The battle: Contemporary objections to panpsychism

The resurgence of panpsychism has not been without resistance. To discern if panpsychism has the potential longevity within philosophy of mind, such that theologians will need to be in dialogue with panpsychism in the coming decades, the power of these objections needs to be assessed. The objections against panpsychism can be grouped into three main categories, presented in ascending order of severity. First, what I refer to as 'The Incredulous Stare' is the set of objections that panpsychism is too counter-intuitive to take seriously. Second, it has been argued that panpsychism is unscientific and, as such, cannot be accepted in the light of scientific progress. Third, and by far the most serious, is the challenge that even when accepted on its own terms panpsychism simply fails to deliver on its promise of an explanation for human consciousness.

The incredulous stare objections

The first type of objection that most theories of panpsychism encounter are made on the basis that it is simply incredible, implausible or beyond the scope of a reasonable explanation. Initially, this objection is often made through the tacit, but

any and every currently unexplained event in the universe. Charles A. Coulson, *Science and the Idea of God* (Cambridge: Cambridge University Press, 1958), 32.

48. Rosenberg, *Place for Consciousness*, 129–297; Galen Strawson, 'Realism and Causation', in *Real Materialism*, 387–408; Patrick Lewtas, 'Panpsychism, Emergentism and the Metaphysics of Causation', *Pacific Philosophical Quarterly* 99, no. 3 (2016): 392–416. doi: 10.1111/papq.12167.

powerful *Incredulous Stare Objection*. This is an a priori objection that panpsychism is too counter-intuitive to take seriously. Colin McGinn gives voice to this objection when he writes that the view that 'elementary particles enjoy an inner life' or that 'rocks actually have thoughts' is 'outrageous' and 'absurd'.[49] Despite its persuasive power for many, The Incredulous Stare Objection is easy to respond to since no concrete argument is being made here. That panpsychism is surprising, unusual or counter-intuitive does not entail its falsity. As Philip Goff writes, 'It is hard to see why the fact that most Westerners living today happen to be pre-theoretically inclined to think panpsychism false constitutes a reason to think that it is false.'[50] Panpsychists are quick to point out that most people today believe a whole series of highly counter-intuitive things on the basis of modern science: time slows down at high speeds, quantum particles have determinate positions only after they are measured, the Earth goes around the Sun and our ancestors were apes. However, the fact that our modern Western intuitions, modelled as they are by a mechanistic scientific picture, fail to account for consciousness is perhaps reason to doubt that these intuitions are reliable.

The *No Sign Objection* tries to give an account for the incredibility of panpsychism by arguing that there is no evident sign from our everyday experience or scientific experiments that the inanimate world contains mentality. However, not having signs or direct experience of a theory, especially a theory of consciousness, does not rule out its possibility. As Gregg Rosenberg writes, 'From my own perspective, any theory that attributes consciousness to people other than myself is going beyond my evidence for the existence of consciousness.'[51] Typically, we attribute consciousness to other creatures based on a preconceived notion of what constitutes consciousness. For example, if I believe language constitutes consciousness, I will exclude animals, whereas if I believe neurology constitutes consciousness, I will extend it to all animals with a sufficiently similar nervous system to my own. Therefore, it is hard to make an argument for or against consciousness on the basis of evidence without predetermining the outcome in some way.

The Incredulous Stare and No Signs Objections derive from The Analogical Argument for Other Minds. Since the primary way we think about the existence of other human minds is based on a perceived analogy between others and oneself, it is understandable that this is often the first objection to be levelled against panpsychism. The problem is that the panpsychist does not argue for fundamental minds based on an analogy to perceived behaviour or biology. This is because, to the panpsychist, all behavioural signs of consciousness are *inessential* features of experience, such as volitional movement and language, which the panpsychist denies exist at the fundamental level. As Gregg Rosenberg writes,

49. Colin McGinn, *The Character of Mind* (Oxford: Oxford University Press, 1982), 32.
50. Goff, *Consciousness and Fundamental Reality*, 174.
51. Rosenberg, *Place for Consciousness*, 93.

When we speak of the qualitative field of some other, noncognitive, system, we are obviously not attributing to it the qualities of our own experiences. We are not attributing little pangs of pain or experiences of tiny blue dots to noncognitive systems. Whatever we are attributing, it is not any kind of feeling with which we can empathize.[52]

If panpsychists claimed that objects such as rocks and telephones, which give no visible sign of being conscious, have a *unified* consciousness with functional abilities, then the No Sign Objection becomes more serious. However, no contemporary panpsychists I know of posit such a unified consciousness or psychological abilities in rocks (or most other inanimate objects).[53] Instead, they posit that rocks (and other such objects) contain mentality in a non-unified form, which we should *not expect to see signs of* at the level of the rock. In this way, contemporary panpsychism successfully sidesteps the No Sign Objection.

Panpsychists are untroubled by the No Sign Objection, not only because the level of consciousness at the fundamental level is minimal and barely recognizable if placed alongside human experience but also because raw experience gives no behavioural evidence for itself. It is because there is no work for consciousness to do that Chalmers's zombie argument *against* materialism is *successful*; phenomenal consciousness is something other than 'work' (material causation), it is experience.[54] When a panpsychist is asked by the sceptic, 'But what does it really mean for a fundamental wave/particle to be conscious?' one way to interpret the question is as an appeal for a description of fundamental consciousness that contains a sign or function analogous to consciousness at the human level. To any such appeal, the panpsychist cannot give satisfaction without overstepping her own claims, and so should resist the temptation to say too much.

Another way that these objections are expressed is through the *Uneconomic Objection* – the complaint that panpsychism is ontologically excessive and uneconomic because it posits unnecessary and superfluous phenomena. Philip Goff previously wrote that, when facing the hard problem of consciousness, there is always 'a parallel, non-panpsychist strategy which is more economical and more plausible'.[55] Similarly, J. P. Moreland describes panpsychism as 'a bizarre, incredible,

---

52. Rosenberg, *Place for Consciousness*, 95.

53. Historically, a (very) few panpsychists have argued that rocks are conscious; see Griffin, *Unsnarling the World-Knot*, 95–6.

54. A more dubious, but possible, response to this objection might be that there are 'signs' of fundamental consciousness in various interpretations of quantum physics. See Michael Lockwood, *Mind, Brain and the Quantum* (Oxford: Blackwell, 1989); and Michael Lockwood, 'The "Many Minds" Interpretation of Quantum Mechanics', *British Journal for the Philosophy of Science* 47, no. 3 (1996): 159–88.

55. Philip Goff, 'Why Panpsychism Doesn't Help Us Explain Consciousness', *Dialectica* 63, no. 3 (2009): 310.

and ontologically bloated . . . claim'.[56] McGinn employed this objection when he described panpsychism as 'extravagant'.[57] The implication is that panpsychism *unnecessarily* overloads our ontology of the universe with mentality. And yet, on the same page that McGinn calls panpsychism extravagant, he also admits that 'something pretty remarkable is needed if the mind-body relation is to be made sense of'.[58] Indeed, he writes that *if* we credit neurons with proto-consciousness then 'it seems easy enough to see how neurons could generate consciousness'.[59] Positing mentality as fundamental certainly appears lavish to our miserly mechanistic intuitions. However, until there is another satisfactory explanation for the awkward anomaly of consciousness, the claim that panpsychism is excessive or unnecessary does not reach beyond rhetorical polemics. Perhaps we live in a more extravagantly endowed universe than the austere ontology of the natural sciences is able to describe.

The unscientific objection and the question of naturalism

It was stated above that the natural sciences are particularly effective in convincing contemporary Western people to believe highly counter-intuitive ideas. The reign of the natural sciences also means that it is unsurprising that the second type of objection against panpsychism, that it is *incompatible with the natural sciences*, is perceived by many as a sufficient reason to dismiss panpsychism without recourse to any court of appeal. Achim Stephan jokes that panpsychism 'is what happens when philosophy throws a party and forgets to invite science'.[60] Philip Clayton rebukes panpsychism as a 'robustly metaphysical move' that 'cuts [itself] off from the evidential considerations that science could otherwise provide'.[61] Willem Drees accuses panpsychism for being 'substantially at odds with current science'.[62]

And yet it was shown above that panpsychism claims traction with the underpinning principles in evolutionary biology, and one can point to (minority) interpretations of quantum mechanics.[63] Moreover, Chalmers's defence of

56. J. P. Moreland, *Consciousness and the Existence of God* (New York: Routledge, 2008), 128.

57. Colin McGinn, *The Problem of Consciousness: Essays Toward a Resolution* (Oxford: Basil Blackwell, 1991), 2.

58. McGinn, *Problem of Consciousness*, 2.

59. McGinn, *Problem of Consciousness*, 28n.

60. Achim Stephan, 'Emergence and Panpsychism', in *Panpsychism: Contemporary Perspectives*, 347.

61. Philip Clayton, *Mind and Emergence: From Quantum to Consciousness* (Oxford: Oxford University Press, 2004), 130.

62. This is based on a misunderstanding that panpsychism denies the evolution of, and thus layered nature of, consciousness. Willem B. Drees, *Religion and Science in Context: A Guide to the Debates* (New York: Routledge, 2010), 92.

63. Examples of contemporary interpretations of quantum mechanics that place mentality at the fundamental level include: Henry Stapp's 'orthodox collapse' in *Mindful*

panpsychism is due to his commitment to finding a scientific explanation for consciousness. Whence the objection that panpsychism is unscientific? Answering this question reveals that panpsychism complicates philosophical assumptions about the natural sciences in truly intriguing ways. This question also takes us to the core of current debates regarding the relationship between religion and the natural sciences, and so forms a side entrance into this book's main task – evaluating the possibility of a forthcoming relationship between panpsychism and theology.

It is clear that panpsychism is not unscientific in the sense of being totally contrary to, or disproved by, the best scientific theories of our day; there are no quick dismissals here. What is less clear is the relationship that panpsychism has to the philosophical position of *naturalism*. This is a term that was encountered in Chapter 1's critical expositions of emergence theology, but now needs to be given more detailed analysis. In the following description, I distinguish between naturalism's positive truth claims, regarding what *does* exist, and naturalism's negative truth claims, regarding what *does not* exist. I argue that contemporary panpsychism entails a rejection of naturalism's positive truth claims. It is this rejection that lies at the heart of what can be described as a question-begging objection that panpsychism is unscientific. I also note that panpsychists typically choose to align themselves with naturalism's negative truth claims, and this creates problems for the possibility of a theistic panpsychism. Panpsychism's relationship to naturalism seems one of unrequited love; many naturalists want little to do with panpsychism, but panpsychists still want to associate themselves with naturalists, vainly hoping that their beloved naturalism will turn from the error

Universe. Quantum Mechanics and the Participating Observer (Berlin: Springer, 2007). Stuart Hameroff's and Roger Penrose's 'objective reduction' and the experiential collapse of the wave function in 'Conscious Events as Orchestrated Space-Time Selections', *Journal of Consciousness Studies* 3, no. 1 (1996): 36–53; and 'Consciousness in the Universe: A Review of the "Orch OR" Theory', *Physics of Life Review* 11, no. 1 (2014): 39–78. Michael Epperson's 'decoherence' theory in *Quantum Mechanics and the Philosophy of Alfred North Whitehead* (New York: Fordham University Press, 2012). In addition to prominent historical figures in evolutionary thinking, a few contemporary evolutionary biologists suggest that common bacterium and unicellular *Paramecium caudatum* are sensing, experiencing and goal-directed: Sam P. Brown and Rufus A. Johnstone, 'Cooperation in the Dark: Signalling and Collective Action in Quorum-Sensing Bacteria', *Proceedings of the Royal Society of Biological Sciences* 268, no. 1470 (2001): 961–5; Cornforth et al., 'Combinatorial Quroum Sensing Allows Bacteria to Resolve Their Social and Physical Environment', *Proceedings of the National Academy of Science of the United States of America* 111, no. 11 (2014): 4280–4; Jonathan T. Delafield-Butt et al., 'Prospective Guidance in a Free-Swimming Cell', *Biological Cybernetics* 106 (2012): 283–93. For more on panpsychism in the history of quantum theory and its relevance for science and religion, see Joanna Leidenhag, 'The Revival of Panpsychism and Its Relevance for the Science-Religion Dialogue', *Theology & Science* 17, no. 1 (2019): 90–106.

of her positive truth claims. Fortunately, this chapter has no interest in arbitrating between panpsychism and naturalism, and instead advises panpsychists to realign themselves with theism.

Naturalism is a controversial concept and notoriously difficult to define.[64] It seems wisest to gather definitions given by leading naturalists themselves in order to see why deviation from naturalism is heralded as unscientific. Michael Devitt describes naturalism as the view that 'there is only one way of knowing: the empirical way that is the basis of science (whatever that way may be)'.[65] Brendan Larvor articulates naturalism as the belief that 'the sciences of nature are the best (and in some versions, the only) guides to what there is, what it is like, and why'.[66] Therefore, all 'methodological naturalism is the view that philosophy – and indeed any other intellectual discipline – must pursue knowledge via empirical methods exemplified by the sciences, and not by *a priori* non-empirical methods'.[67] Most bluntly, naturalism states that 'science is the measure of all things, of what is that it is and of what is not that it is not'.[68] Wilfred Sellars, in this quote, points the way to showing how the epistemological and methodological definitions of naturalism quickly become ontological and metaphysical. Since the empirical method of the sciences can only provide knowledge of physical phenomena and law-like events, it might seem that reality really is a closed system of material and efficient causation in a giant mechanical universe. Perhaps unsurprisingly, when the physical sciences are taken as all-sufficient, this leads to physicalism. Thus, David Armstrong characterizes naturalism as an ontological commitment to the view that reality is nothing but a closed spatio-temporal system.[69] It is this web of interconnected commitments that inspires Jaegwon Kim to characterize naturalism as 'imperialistic; it demands "full coverage" … and exacts a terribly high ontological price'.[70]

64. This is exemplified by the fact that some naturalists, such as David Papineau, find it simpler to refuse to offer a definition for their position. David Papineau, *Philosophical Naturalism* (Oxford: Basil Blackwell, 1993). Perhaps the most succinct presentation of how many incompatible definitions of naturalism currently exist is found in Owen Flanagan, 'Varieties of Naturalism', in *The Oxford Handbook of Religion and Science*, ed. Philip Clayton and Zachary Simpson (Oxford: Oxford University Press, 2008), 430–51.

65. Michael Devitt, 'Naturalism and the A Priori', *Philosophical Studies* 92 (1998): 45.

66. Brendan Larvor, 'Naturalism', in *The Wiley Blackwell Handbook of Humanism*, ed. Andrew Copson and A. C. Grayling (Oxford: Wiley-Blackwell, 2015), 37.

67. Jean Hampton, *The Authority of Reason* (Cambridge: Cambridge University Press, 1998), 20.

68. Wilfrid Sellars, 'Empiricism and the Philosophy of Mind', in *Science, Perception and Reality* (London: Routledge & Kegan Paul, 1963), 173.

69. David Armstrong, 'Naturalism, Materialism, and First Philosophy', in *Contemporary Materialism*, ed. Paul Moser and J. D. Trout (New York: Routledge, 1995), 35.

70. Jaegwon Kim, 'Mental Causation and Two Concepts of Mental Properties', presented at the American Philosophical Association Eastern Division Meeting (December 1993): 2–23.

This is an ontological price panpsychism is unwilling to pay. Panpsychism cannot be naturalistic in any of the senses outlined above. In fact, panpsychism stands in direct and deliberate opposition to these anti-rationalist presuppositions and reductive or physicalist conclusions.[71] Although psyche at the fundamental level might (for some) be a reasonable conjecture taken from the strange results produced by quantum mechanics and the principles of evolutionary biology, there can be no direct empirical test for phenomenal consciousness. Instead, the panpsychists' commitment to the realism of consciousness is taken as a priori and self-evident (for, at least, the very good reason that any empirical tests presuppose the experience of the scientists conducting them). Therefore, the a priori nature of the panpsychist argument is not because the physical sciences have *not yet* designed a test for consciousness, but because phenomenal or experiential consciousness is defined as that which is left over *even if we had a complete and perfect scientific understanding of the world*. If consciousness could be established on the basis of empirical tests, then it could be functionally reduced and measured in terms of behaviour. The panpsychists' commitment to the reality of experiential consciousness is precisely the rejection of any such psychophysical reduction.

The panpsychist looks for the best way to explain and locate consciousness in the world that the natural sciences describe, but the existence of consciousness is accepted a priori. If panpsychists' opposition to restrictive naturalism is what is implied by the charge that panpsychism is 'unscientific', then panpsychism stands guilty as charged. However, most panpsychists would shrug their shoulders and go about their business. It is simply part of the argumentative appeal of panpsychism, an appeal that includes the claim that natural science cannot proceed without conscious agents, that it rejects naturalism in this sense.

Increasingly, naturalists are seeking to soften their position in various ways such that a rejection of physicalism and empiricism does not warrant the objection that any given theory is unscientific.[72] A softer or more liberal naturalism affirms that the

---

71. Roy Wood Sellars describes panpsychism as historically the main alternative to materialism through philosophical history in 'Panpsychism or Evolutionary Materialism', *Philosophy of Science* 27, no. 4 (October 1960): 329–50.

72. There are numerous titles for naturalisms that expand the ontological toolbox beyond that of mindless, valueless, matter. Fiona Ellis uses 'expansive naturalism', in *God, Value and Nature* (Oxford: Oxford University Press, 2014). Jeffry King refers to 'linguistic naturalism' in 'Can Propositions Be Naturalistically Acceptable?', *Midwest Studies in Philosophy* 19 (1994): 53–75. Mikael Leidenhag has critically evaluated a group of philosophers who all defend 'religious naturalism' as well as other such liberal approaches to naturalism. See Mikael Leidenhag, *Naturalizing God? A Critical Evaluation of Religious Naturalism* (New York: SUNY Press, forthcoming). Sean Carroll argues for 'poetic naturalism', in *The Big Picture: On the Origins of Life, Meaning, and the Universe Itself* (New York: Dutton, 2016). Perhaps most problematically, some theologians claim the position, 'theistic naturalism', which is often parsed out in terms of divine action but ultimately entails fitting God into the metaphysical framework of the natural world. See Arthur Peacocke, *Paths from Science towards God: The End of All Our Exploring* (Oxford: OneWorld, 2001), 138–44; Christopher

natural sciences are an important route to knowledge, but that other phenomena (such as values and minds) exist and other paths to truth can also be taken. That is, a liberal naturalist might claim that all knowledge must be 'continuous with' scientific knowledge or that we must go 'beyond the natural sciences as little as possible'.[73] This idea is typically affirmed by panpsychists (indeed, who denies it?). Strawson describes 'good philosophy' as that which 'stays close to the science of its day and is continuous with it in certain respects'.[74] Chalmers writes that his ideas are '*compatible* with contemporary science' but that he has 'not restricted [his] ideas to what contemporary scientists find fashionable'.[75] In endorsing panpsychism Chalmers argues that 'our picture of the natural world is broadened, not overturned'.[76] Clearly panpsychists do not abandon all commitment to the natural sciences, but I find it implausible that they (or any so-called liberal naturalism) can be regarded as naturalists in so far as the term connotes any positive propositions that distinguish it from other positions. How, or to what degree, philosophy should be continuous with the natural sciences is rarely specified. The question immediately arises, how far is too far and on what grounds could such a judgement be made?[77] As a positive truth claim (that the empirical methods of the natural sciences are one source of knowledge among others and that we should seek mutual compatibility between various truth-seeking practices) these softer forms of naturalism are fairly uninteresting; that is, they cannot be distinguished from almost any other epistemological or methodological position.

The claim that panpsychism adheres to naturalism is not entirely fraudulent if taken to refer to the negative, rather than the positive, part of the naturalist's credo – anti-supernaturalism. Barry Stroud writes, 'Naturalism on any reading is opposed to supernaturalism' and supernaturalism means 'the invocation of an agent or force which somehow stands outside the natural world and so whose doings cannot be understood as part of it'.[78] Soft or liberal naturalists (such as

Knight, 'Theistic Naturalism and "Special" Divine Providence', *Zygon: Journal of Religion and Science* 44, no. 3 (2009): 533–42.

73. Jack Ritchie, *Understanding Naturalism: Supervenience* (New York: Routledge, 2014), 1, 195–201; Brian Leiter, 'Naturalism and Naturalized Jurisprudence', in *Analyzing Natural Law: New Essays in Legal Theory*, ed. Brian Bix (Oxford: Clarendon Press, 1998), 81; Arthur Danto, 'Naturalism', in *The Encyclopaedia of Philosophy*, ed. Paul Edwards, vol. 5 (New York: Macmillan and Free Press, 1967), 44; Peter Forrest, *God without the Supernatural: A Defence of Scientific Theism* (Ithaca, NY: Cornell University Press, 1996), 89.

74. Strawson, *Real Materialism*, 1.

75. Chalmers, *Conscious Mind*, xiii.

76. Chalmers, *Conscious Mind*, xiv.

77. Thomas Nagel, for example, claims to be a naturalist, but also admits that his argument for moral realism is 'relying on a philosophical claim to refute a scientific theory supported by empirical evidence'. Nagel, *Mind and Cosmos*, 106, see also 4, 18 and 69.

78. Barry Stroud, 'The Charm of Naturalism', *Proceedings and Addresses of the American Philosophical Association* 70, no. 2 (1996): 44.

panpsychists) often give definitions for their position along the lines that 'the natural world is the whole world' or 'everything is natural'.[79] If understood as a positive statement about the character of the cosmos this is an almost vacuous definition. Instead, it should be taken as a negative truth claim asserting that there is no transcendent reality, or nothing exists 'outside of' this universe. More importantly this means that no entities, property or event within this universe can be explained by reference to any transcendent or divine reality. In its negative form, naturalism is a commitment to atheism (with negotiating room left for pantheism).

In a subversive move, Kathryn Sonderegger argues that this 'methodological atheism, or "naturalism"' is also to be interpreted as testifying and witnessing to the Invisibility of God's Omnipresence.[80] For the reasons argued throughout this book, I do not think theologians should accept naturalism or construct naturalistic theologies. However, we can affirm the idea that 'God cannot be an element in the explanatory models used to take account of the data or event under study', as a way to avoid inadvertently creating idols or reducing God into a finite object.[81] As explored in later chapters, panpsychism may help articulate the omnipresence of God, whereby we need not look for gaps within the natural world for God's presence to fill locally but as a way to affirm God's intimacy with the whole comprehensive created order. When panpsychists claim that their model of consciousness is the last hope for naturalism, they allude to the ever-looming possibility that the only explanation for the existence of consciousness is that souls are created *ex nihilo* by God (or some other immaterial agent) and attached to embryos. As J. P. Moreland argues, if this is the best or only explanation for consciousness, it adds substantial evidence to arguments for the existence of God.[82]

Moreland has given panpsychism one of the few evaluative examinations from the perspective of Christian theism. He argues that panpsychism is 'a rival to and not an appropriate specification of naturalism'.[83] Given this antagonism

79. Jaegwon Kim, 'From Naturalism to Physicalism: Supervenience Redux', *Proceedings and Addresses of the American Philosophical Association* 85, no. 2 (2011): 109.

80. Kathryn Sonderegger, *Systematic Theology: The Doctrine of God* (Minneapolis, MN: Augsburg Fortress, 2015), 53–4.

81. Sonderegger, *Systematic Theology*, 54.

82. Moreland's *Consciousness and the Existence of God* is a monograph-length example. Alvin Plantinga claims that the naturalists' often visceral rejection of substance dualism is not because of any commitment to science or best explanations but because 'immaterial selves would be too much like God, who, after all, is himself an immaterial self'. Alvin Plantinga, *Where the Conflict Really Lies: Science, Religion, and Naturalism* (Oxford: Oxford University Press, 2012), 319. Nagel seems to say much the same thing when he speculates that 'this cosmic authority problem', which prevents him from becoming a theist, 'is not a rare condition and that it is responsible for much of the scientism and reductionism of our time'. Thomas Nagel, *The Last Word* (New York: Oxford University Press, 1997), 131.

83. Moreland, *Consciousness and the Existence of God*, 115, 133.

between naturalism and panpsychism, it is surprising that Moreland states that 'panpsychism follows only if classical theism is ruled out', thereby placing panpsychism in competition to, rather than in support of, his argument for the existence of God from consciousness.[84] Contrary to Moreland, this chapter will conclude by suggesting that panpsychism and theism function best in partnership, not in competition. In the choice between theological panpsychism and J. P. Moreland's event/property dualism is not the *existence* of God, but the perceived relationship between God and creation.

This section has unpicked the origin of why panpsychism is sometimes critiqued as unscientific by examining its strenuous relationship to philosophical naturalism. The accusation that panpsychism is unscientific has little to do with the current conclusions and theories of the natural sciences. Instead, it arises from naturalistic philosophers who 'wrap themselves in the mantle of science like a politician in the flag' such that to question strong naturalism is to appear 'unscientific'.[85] I am under no illusion that the description above would satisfy all who take upon themselves the auspicious mantle of naturalism. After all, there are almost as many types of naturalism as there are philosophers advocating the position. I argued that all of the positive claims made by naturalism, which can be taken as a genuinely distinctive position, must be rejected by panpsychists. In their negative commitments, naturalists present a more united front against supernaturalism, which a panpsychist can choose to adopt or reject at will. I will argue in my final section that it makes more sense for panpsychists to also reject the negative, anti-supernaturalist, claims of naturalism and instead align themselves with theism.

The objection from explanatory failure and questions of combination

The final type of objection is not concerned whether panpsychism is a *scientific* explanation, but whether it is an *explanation* at all. Most positions within philosophy of mind claim superiority over competing frameworks on the basis of increased explanatory power.[86] The further the position lies from present-day intuitions, the more explanatory power is needed. Since panpsychism is widely accepted to be more counter-intuitive than most of its rivals, any deficit in explanatory power hits the panpsychist particularly hard. I consider two forms of the *Explanatory Failure Objection*: *The Brute Objection* and *The Combination Problem*.

There is a brute feature within every theory within philosophy of mind. For something to be 'brute' is to say, 'it just is that way, and there is no explanation for why it is so'. The brute element is the terminus of explanation. All theories have such a terminus; it is just a question of where. Every small child knows that

---

84. Moreland, *Consciousness and the Existence of God*, 118.

85. Plantinga, *Where the Conflict Really Lies*, 307.

86. This is not the case with Colin McGinn's *mysterianism*, nor with all defences of substance dualism.

the question 'Why?' can be asked *ad infinitum*, and the inevitable answer 'Just because!' is more satisfactory at some points than at others. If all theories contain an element of bruteness, then *The Brute Objection* is only such when the location of bruteness lies at the heart of the explanation itself, thereby landing a fatal blow to the theory's explanatory power.

Since that which is fundamental can neither be derived from nor explained in terms of anything else, the location of fundamental features of the world is often identical to the locations of bruteness within a theory. Thus, D. S. Clarke writes, 'Mentality, like matter, simply is a fundamental feature of what is, and all questions about its origins must therefore be dismissed as meaningless.'[87] Geoffrey Madell voices this fundamental bruteness as an objection when he complains that

> the sense that the mental and the physical are just inexplicably and gratuitously slapped together is hardly allayed by adopting … a pan-psychists…view of the mind, for [it does not] have an explanation to offer as to why or how mental properties cohere with [the] physical.[88]

Coleman calls this 'brute accompaniment' and wonders that 'if brute accompaniment is acceptable at the lowest level, it is hard to see why it should be objectionable at the macro-level'.[89] Since substance dualists also posit minds as fundamental, but only in conjunction with the human (or animal) organism, brute accompaniment is often seen as one of the main explanatory weaknesses of substance dualism. Substance dualism states that human minds and bodies just happen to go together and causally interact. Since human minds are fundamental in a way that is radically discontinuous with the rest of the (non-panpsychist) natural order, substance dualists can offer little explanation from within the natural order as to why this might be the case. As a result, contemporary defenders of substance dualism tend to be theists and draw on the additional explanatory power of theism from outside of the natural order to support their substance dualism. The question is, does the brute accompaniment of mind and matter at the fundamental level of reality (as in the panpsychist's thesis) lead to the same explanatory weakness in panpsychism as it does in substance dualism? If so, then it would seem sensible – especially for a theologian – to defer to the more intuitive and economic position, substance dualism.

The main reason that the panpsychist can claim explanatory power over the substance dualist, despite its own instance of brute accompaniment, is that the panpsychist gives an account of the human person that is not radically different

---

87. D. S. Clarke, *Panpsychism and the Religious Attitude* (New York: SUNY Press, 2003), 120.

88. Geoffrey Madell, *Mind and Materialism* (Edinburgh: Edinburgh University Press, 1988), 3.

89. Sam Coleman, 'Being Realistic: Why Physicalism May Entail Panexperientialism', in Strawson et al., *Consciousness and Its Place in Nature*, 43.

from the rest of the universe. That is, the panpsychists' brute accompaniment is ubiquitous and integrated, whereas (arguably) the substance dualists' brute accompaniment has the additional disadvantage of being patchy. Not only does the substance dualist leave unanswered the question of *why* mind and matter are slapped together, but also the question '*why here* (in the case of human beings) and not elsewhere' cries out for some kind of explanation.

Contrarily, the panpsychist offers an answer to the question 'why *here*?' by giving an account of the ontology of the universe more widely and taking into consideration the evolutionary history of humans as organisms (whether one thinks the panpsychists' explanation is adequate is a separate matter at this point). The panpsychist cannot account for why the universe contains material and mental properties in the first place, but she does offer a more substantial answer to the question of why, within this dualistic universe, human beings have mental and material properties. It seems, then, that *The Brute Objection* (on the grounds of brute accompaniment) does not force the panpsychist to defer to substance dualism.

By far the most serious challenge facing contemporary panpsychism is *The Combination Problem*: How do the experiences at the fundamental physical level combine to yield the experiences humans typically enjoy? It is important to note that the combination problem is not, in and of itself, an objection; it is a challenge. The combination problem is important because it is a weakness that the various objections examined above can exploit to significantly bolster their claims. In the words of Sam Coleman, the combination problem 'plausibly represents the major theoretical "I owe you" of the panexperientialist/panpsychist. But that there is work to be done does not imply the falsity of a view, and there are avenues to be explored.'[90] In the metaphorical narrative of this chapter, it is the lack of an understanding of 'mental chemistry' – that is the lack of a solution to the combination problem – that stalls the panpsychists' campaign for philosophical dominance, and as such leaves contemporary philosophy of mind more widely in a stalemate.

The combination problem is so-called because it was originally presented as the problem of articulating how minds at the fundamental level *combine*, rather than merely aggregate, to bring about the experience of a complex human mind with a unified first-person perspective. However, the combination problem now refers to a large network of problems regarding how to relate the explanans (fundamental mentality) to the explanandum (the human mind).[91] Panpsychism's explanatory promise rests upon the idea that human minds can be explained by fundamental mental entities. If panpsychism fails in providing a satisfactory account of the relationship between fundamental mentality and human minds, then fundamental mentality adds nothing to the explanatory power of panpsychism. As such, critics who decry panpsychism for being uneconomic (see the objection above) can

---

90. Coleman, 'Being Realistic', 51.
91. Chalmers, 'Combination Problem', 179–214.

justifiably call upon Ockham to use his infamous razor and cut away all 'bloated' notions of fundamental mentality from our ontology.[92] Fundamental properties have to earn their 'explanatory keep' so to speak.[93]

The 'combination problem' was a phrase coined by contemporary philosopher William Seager, but the problem itself was famously articulated a century earlier by William James. It is worth quoting at length:

> Take a hundred [feelings], shuffle them and pack them as close together as you can (whatever that may mean) till each remains the same feeling it always was, shut in its own skin, windowless, ignorant of what the other feelings are and mean. There would be a hundred-and-first feeling there, if, when a group or series of such feelings were set up, a consciousness *belonging to the group as such* should emerge. And this 101st feeling would be a totally new fact; the 100 feelings might, by a curious physical law, be a signal for its *creation*, when they came together; but they would have no substantial identity with it, nor it with them, and one could never deduce the one from the others, or (in any intelligible sense) say that they *evolved* it.[94]

The upshot of this monadic view of fundamental consciousness is that 'private minds do not agglomerate into a higher compound mind'.[95] The idea that minds are just not the sort of things that can combine boils down to an intuition, but it is one that many philosophers find highly compelling.

Much ink has been spilt on the combination problem in the contemporary literature surrounding panpsychism. This is not only because it represents the greatest gap in the panpsychists' account of human consciousness, but it is also the anvil upon which different versions of panpsychism are formed. The panpsychist needs to tell a story of combination to alleviate this intuitive objection against mental combination. There are three main types of such a story. First, a panpsychist might reformulate their position, and adopt either *cosmopsychism* or *panprotopsychism*. Both these reformulations of panpsychism claim to not need a theory of combination at all. Second, *constitutive panpsychism*, claims that

---

92. Goff, 'Why Panpsychism Doesn't Help'.

93. Sam Coleman, 'Panpsychism and Neutral Monism: How to Make Up One's Mind', in *Panpsychism: Contemporary Perspectives*, ed. Godehard Brüntrup and Ludwig Jaskolla (Oxford: Oxford University Press, 2017), 255–6.

94. James, *Principles of Psychology*, 160. Importantly, James based this denial of mental combination on his prior denial of material combination, such that water 'exists only for the bystander' (158–9). James writes, 'Atoms of feeling cannot compose higher feelings, any more than atoms of matter can compose physical things!' (161). Thus, James does not argue that mental combination is uniquely problematic, but that *all combination* is impossible and no higher-level wholes of any kind exist anywhere in the universe, other than in the mind of the beholder, or in the human soul (181).

95. James, *Principles of Psychology*, 160.

macro-experience is grounded in, realized by or constituted by micro-experience in the same way macrophysical facts are constituted by microphysical facts. Constitutive panpsychism seeks to tell a story that leaves the overall framework of physicalism intact; it retains causal closure and reductive explanations and merely adds unobservable intrinsic natures to the scientific image. Third, *non-constitutive panpsychism* reintroduces emergence theory in order to account for mental combination; macro-experience is a non-additive emergent from micro-experience. Non-constitutive panpsychism opts for downward causation and free will over causal closure.

In order to provide an adequate introduction to contemporary panpsychism, the various positions given below need to be surveyed. However, it would be an overindulgent use of space to explore each position in detail. This section concludes that, although no one solution has achieved a general consensus among panpsychist philosophers, there are a number of ways to approach this challenge. From this it can be concluded that *The Combination Problem*, although a serious challenge, is not yet a defeater against panpsychism; it does not make panpsychism an unrespectable position for theologians to seriously consider.

First, instead of taking on the task of solving the combination problem some scholars seek to find ways to avoid or deflate the need for such an account. The most common forms of this tactic are *Cosmopsychism* and *Panprotopsychism*. Panpsychism, as it has been explicated thus far, might be specified as *atomistic panpsychism*, which assumes *smallism* as the structure of explanation. *Smallism* is the view that all facts are determined by the facts about the smallest things, or those entities existing at the lowest level of ontology (which may not, in fact, be small at all – such as super strings or black holes). It is the lowest level of reality that is seen as the fundamental level. Smallism is the explanatory structure of most of the natural sciences; complex entities are explained by referring to their various parts. However, not all panpsychists adopt smallism, and instead, they argue for *cosmopsychism*.

Different versions of cosmopsychism have been referred to as 'panexperiential holism', 'priority cosmopsychism' and 'cosmological panpsychism', but they all share the common thesis that the whole is more fundamental than the parts.[96] As panpsychist positions, they all must state that mentality is found *at the fundamental level of reality*, but they take the 'highest' or 'largest' level of reality

96. For defences of cosmopsychism under these different headings, see Ludwig Jaskolla and Alexander Buck, 'Does Panexperiential Holism Solve the Combination Problem?', *Journal of Consciousness Studies* 19, nos. 9–10 (2012): 190–9; Yujin Nagasawa and Khai Wager, 'Panpsychism and Priority Cosmopsychism', in *Panpsychism: Contemporary Perspectives*, ed. Godehard Brüntrup and Ludwig Jaskolla (Oxford: Oxford University Press, 2017), 113–30; Goff, *Consciousness and Fundamental Reality*, 220–6; Itay Shani, 'Cosmopsychism: A Holistic Approach to the Metaphysics of Experience', *Philosophical Papers* 44, no. 3 (2015): 389–437; Freya Mathews, *For Love of Matter: A Contemporary Panpsychism* (New York: SUNY Press, 2003).

as the fundamental level. The cosmos as a single whole is, then, fundamental as opposed to the 'building blocks' of reality.[97] For *cosmo*-psychism it is the cosmos as a single whole which instantiates consciousness. If the atomistic panpsychist felt threatened by the incredulous stare of modern Western intuitions, cosmopsychism is far worse off since, by abandoning reductive explanations, cosmopsychism seems a step further away from contemporary natural science.[98] What then is the appeal of cosmopsychism? The main reason why a panpsychist may opt for cosmopsychism, rather than atomistic panpsychism, is because, *prima facie*, cosmopsychism faces no combination problem.[99] If cosmopsychism has no combination problem and provides a more satisfactory account of human consciousness, then the problems of intuitive incredulity and empirical implausibility pale in comparison with the promise of explanatory success. However, cosmopsychism can currently claim no such victory.

Although cosmopsychism faces no problems of combination, it runs into the arms of the equally difficult problem of the boundedness of consciousness, merely from the other direction – the individuation of experience to be 'my' experience alone. Cosmopsychism must provide an account of the *individuation* of consciousness and although this problem is sometimes gestured towards, I know of no systematic treatments of it.[100] There are, to my mind, at least four individuation problems:

97. Ludwig Jaskolla and Alexander Buck do this through 'existence monism', which states that the universe as a whole is the only truly existing entity. This seems to have the unappealing result that human subjects cannot be truly said to exist. All of the other cosmopsychists listed above employ Jonathan Schaeffer's 'priority monism'. Schaeffer argues that we should consider the universe as a genuine whole and not an aggregate of parts, just as we intuitively consider a whole circle as prior to semi-circles. See Jonathan Schaeffer, 'Monism: The Priority of the Whole', *Philosophical Review* 119, no. 1 (2010): 31–76; Jonathan Schaeffer, 'The Internal Relatedness of All Things', *Mind* 119, no. 474 (2010): 341–76; Jonathan Schaeffer, 'The Action of the Whole', *The Aristotelian Society: Proceedings of the Aristotelian Society Supplementary Volume* 87 (2013): 67–87.

98. See Nagasawa and Wager, 'Panpsychism and Priority Cosmopsychism', 126–7.

99. Nagasawa and Wager also argue that cosmopsychism avoids the potential problem of infinite decomposition where physics reveals that there is no final fundamental level at the lowest level to which panpsychism can attribute mentality. See Nagasawa and Wager, 'Panpsychism and Priority Cosmopsychism', 118–20.

100. What I call 'the individuation problem' has also been referred to as the 'decombination problem' by Miri Albahari, 'Beyond Cosmopsychism and the Great I Am: How the World might be grounded in Universal "Advaitic" Consciousness', in *Routledge Handbook on Panpsychism*, ed. William Seager (London: Routledge, 2020). The 'decomposition problem' by Chalmers, 'Panpsychism and Panprotopsychism', 19–47. The 'derivation problem' by Nagasawa and Wager, 'Panpsychism and Priority Cosmopsychism'. It may well be that future panpsychism research will have to re-examine attempts by Absolute Idealists, such as F. H. Bradley, to answer precisely these questions.

1. How does one consciousness give rise to many distinct subjects, whose experience and perspective is neither identical to each other nor to the former single consciousness? (The Subject Individuation Problem)
2. How does one experiential or quality-laden field individuate into distinct qualities and experiences, which may be distinguished by individual subjects within their own total experience, and which may be had by one subject but not another? (The Quality Individuation Problem and The Experience Individuation Problem)
3. How does the sparsely structured, unbounded cosmic consciousness or field of experience structure itself in such a way as to hold within it distinct (compactly structured) subjects and qualities? (The Structural Individuation Problem)
4. What prevents the continuous individuation of consciousness so that every configuration of matter at every level of reality is a discrete subject? (The Over-Individuation Problem)

These problems appear at least as difficult as the various combination problems. This, then, removes any advantage that cosmopsychism might claim to have over the (relatively) more intuitive position of (atomistic) panpsychism, and so in the remaining discussion we shall return to assuming (atomistic) panpsychism.[101]

The second way that contemporary panpsychists sometimes seek to escape the combination problem is by adopting panprotopsychism. *Pan*-proto-*psychism* is the view that fundamental physical entities have protophenomenal properties. Protophenomenal properties are not phenomenal properties; there is nothing it is like to be a protophenomenal property, and there is nothing it is like to have a protophenomenal property. Panprotopsychism seems to be a form of neutral monism; the fundamental level consists of neither wholly physical nor wholly experiential properties, but something else that constitutes both the physical and the experiential. There are two popular options for what kind of properties protophenomenal properties might be: raw experiences or unexperienced qualities. These positions are called panexperientialism and panqualityism, respectively.

Panexperientialism, as adopted by process philosophers, states that experience and spontaneity are fundamental and ubiquitous. David Ray Griffin gives two reasons why he prefers to call his position panexperientialism, rather than panpsychism.[102] First, he is concerned that 'psyche' suggests subjects which, independent of the stream of experience, endure through time. As a process

---

101. For a more in-depth discussion of holistic panpsychism and possible solutions to the various individuation problems, see Joanna Leidenhag, 'Unity between God and Mind? A Study on the Relationship between Panpsychism and Pantheism', *Sophia: International Journal of Philosophy and Traditions* 58, no. 4 (2019): 543–561.

102. Griffin, *Unsnarling the World-Knot*, 78; David Ray Griffin, *Reenchantment without Supernaturalism: A Process Philosophy of Religion* (Ithaca, NY: Cornell University Press, 2001), 97.

theologian within a strictly event-based ontology, he rejects any temporal endurance of substances. Second, he is concerned that 'psyche' implies higher levels of cognition beyond experience and spontaneity. Panexperientialists emphasize the rejection of complex subjects with cognition, volition (although they accept basic spontaneity), self-consciousness and other such psychological properties.

It is unclear, however, that panexperientialism is as distinct from subject panpsychism as the former often claim. Most self-proclaimed panpsychists do *not* posit that complex psychologically functioning subjects are fundamental – only basic phenomenal subjects. Moreover, due to the flux and instability of the fundamental level of (physical) reality, many panpsychists do not posit fundamental subjects that endure for long periods of time. This is why Strawson argues that ' "panpsychism" doesn't have any implications that the word "panexperientialism" doesn't also have ... the word "panpsychism" doesn't in itself imply that there are subjects of experience in addition to experiential reality'.[103] If this is correct, then the panexperientialist will face the same puzzles regarding combination that the panpsychist faces.

An alternative version of panprotopsychism is *panqualityism*. Panqualityism is commonly associated with Herbert Feigl and is currently advocated by panpsychist philosopher, Sam Coleman.[104] As the name suggests, panqualityism posits qualities as fundamental and ubiquitous, not experiences. Qualities are not phenomenal but become phenomenal when perceived or experienced by a subject. For example, we might say that redness is a quality. This means there is nothing it is like to be redness, but there is something it is like to perceive redness. So far, panqualityism seems quite sensible.

In addition to abandoning the counter-intuitive idea of subjects and experience at the fundamental level, the main theoretical motivation behind panqualityism is that it needs no theory of subject combination. Instead qualities combine to yield a subject that perceives reality in an experiential way. On panqualityism, subjects remain self-contained, bounded and unified entities of a metaphysically primitive nature; they can neither combine nor individuate; instead they are simply created as they are and cease to exist as they are. Subjectivity is not a diffused sort of 'stuff' or generalized property but exists only in the form of particular subjects.[105] The main disadvantage of panqualityism is the need to account for how micro-qualities yield a macro-subject and there is no reason to think this will be an easier problem than the panpsychists' subject-summing problem. To the contrary, the

---

103. Galen Strawson 'Panpsychism? Reply to Commentators with a Celebration of Descartes', in Strawson et al., *Consciousness and Its Place in Nature*, 189.

104. Herbert Feigl, 'The "Mental" and the "Physical" ', *Minnesota Studies in the Philosophy of Science* 2 (1958): 370–497. See also Herbert Feigl, 'Some Crucial Issues of Mind-Body Monism', *Synthese* 3, no. 4 (1971): 295–312; Sam Coleman 'Mental Chemistry: Combination for Panpsychists', *Dialectica* 66 (2012): 137–66; Coleman, 'The Real Combination Problem'; Coleman, 'Panpsychism and Neutral Monism'.

105. Coleman 'Panpsychism and Neutral Monism', 259.

panpsychist's denial of radical, brute emergence means that a panpsychist will most likely be predisposed to see this as the greater mystery. The panqualityist needs to show why their position is not a return to brute emergence. It seems that neither cosmopsychism nor various forms of panprotopsychism truly avoid the need for a compelling account of combination.

The second type of response tackles the combination problem head-on by constructing possible models of how micro-subjects necessitate the appearance of a single unified macro-subject. Two representative positions of this second type are *Identity Panpsychism* and *Phenomenal Bonding*.

Identity Panpsychism is the theory that macro-experience is (or can be) identical to micro-experience. Historically, this was the theory put forward by Leibniz, who argues that a single dominant monad 'makes up the centre of a composite substance (an animal, for example) and is the principle of its unity, is surrounded by a *mass* composed of an infinity of other monads, which constitute the *body belonging* to this central monad'.[106] Leibniz left woefully unanswered questions of why some collections of monads obtain a dominant monad and subsequent unity, whereas other collections do not, and even which types of objects or systems are aggregates or unities.[107] The human subject is, for Leibniz, *identical* to one single monad.

This is not a model of combination strictly speaking, since Leibniz's 'windowless' monads are never seen to combine in any internal sense, but each remains entirely private and independent.[108] This response to *The Combination Problem* has never been popular; the instability of fundamental entities over time, the extremely limited causal role they play, the fact that all fundamental entities appear physically replaceable with one another (and so, presumably, are almost phenomenally identical) and the absurdity that a single electron has the same internal life as a human subject immediately make this an unattractive model for contemporary panpsychists.[109] One might even go so far as to say that if this were the *only* possible way to relate fundamental mentality and human subjects, it would be a reason to abandon panpsychism all together. Happily, this is not the case.

The second attempt to solve the combination problem is Philip Goff's notion of phenomenal bonding.[110] Goff argues that combination is primarily a problem

106. Goffried Wilhem Leibniz, *Principles of Nature and of Grace*, in *Philosophical Essays*, ed. R. Ariew and D. Garber (Indianapolis, IN: Hackett, [1714] 1989) [hereafter, Ariew and Garber], part 3, section 3.

107. Skrbina, *Panpsychism in the West*, 97–8.

108. Yet Leibniz remained dissatisfied with this aspect of his theory because of the need for a real unity in the person of Jesus Christ. See Maria Rosa Antognazza, 'Leibniz's Theory of Substance and His Metaphysics of the Incarnation', in *Locke and Leibniz on Substance*, ed. Paul Lodge and Tom Stoneham (London: Routledge, 2015), 231–53.

109. Chalmers, 'Combination Problem', 195.

110. Philip Goff, 'The Phenomenal Bonding Solution to the Combination Problem', in *Panpsychism: Contemporary Perspectives*, ed. Godehard Brüntrup and Ludwig Jaskolla (Oxford: Oxford University Press, 2017), 284–302.

when one imagines that the relations by which mental combination occurs are spatio-temporal or causal relations. This assumption arises from the fact that most physical combinations are related in this way; bricks form a tower only when certain spatio-temporal relations between the distinct bricks hold. Goff argues that it is unrealistic to suppose that mental entities, if they are irreducible to physical entities, will be combined through the same relations as physical unities; fitting phenomenal properties into physical relations is like fitting a round peg into a square hole.

Instead, Goff argues we need phenomenal bonding relations, 'which bond subjects of experience together to constitute other subjects of experience'.[111] He points out that it is hardly surprising that we are unable to perceive any such bonds, since we are unable to perceive only one subject through introspection and cannot directly perceive any other subjects at all. In order to perceive a relation between multiple subjects, it would first have to be possible to perceive multiple subjects. In this way, it seems perfectly possible that there are phenomenal bonding relations which we should not expect to have direct knowledge of.

The weakness with this solution is that it introduces a significant mystery into panpsychism. The less mystery introduced into any theory of mind, the more attractive the theory is to most philosophers.[112] Therefore, from a competitive perspective (in relation to emergence theory and substance dualism, for example) the introduction of unknowable phenomenal relations comes at a cost to the panpsychist. One proposal is that just as Russellian panpsychism posits that physical properties have intrinsic natures that are phenomenal, spatio-temporal relations might have phenomenal intrinsic natures that allow for co-consciousness or something similar. Rosenberg has argued that this proposal gives a robust account of causation.[113] However, since spatio-temporal relations are ubiquitous, this proposal needs additional work to avoid entailing that the universe as a spatio-temporal whole (and everything in it) is mentally related. The phenomenal bonding solution cannot be taken as a comfortable resting place for a theory of panpsychism, but it shows that mental combination is not a conceptual impossibility and it might point the direction for further investigation.

The third, and most promising, approach to the combination problem is exhibited by *Emergent Panpsychism* and *Panpsychist Infusion,* which offer non-constitutive accounts of combination by reintroducing a qualified form

---

111. Philip Goff, 'Can the Panpsychist Get around the Combination Problem?', *Mind That Abides*, ed. David Skrbina (Amsterdam: John Benjamins, 2009), 132.

112. Uwe Meixner characterizes this disposition in the following: 'Philosophers are rather uncomfortable with *miracles-* and *wonder* is felt to be more of a burden than a joy … Panpsychism comes to the rescue' of the uncomfortable philosopher in this regard. Uwe Meixner, 'Idealism and Panpsychism', in *Panpsychism: Contemporary Perspectives*, ed. Godehard Brüntrup and Ludwig Jaskolla (Oxford: Oxford University Press, 2017), 387.

113. Rosenberg, *Place for Consciousness*, 230–48.

of emergence into their position.[114] Given the panpsychists denunciation of traditional emergence as a form of 'magic' parading as an explanation, any employment of emergence within panpsychism has to be careful not to be self-refuting. That said, emergent panpsychism currently seems the most promising form of panpsychism for theologians wishing to maintain a robust notion of freewill via downward causation.

Emergence is a non-combinatorial relation between parts and wholes and so *Emergent Panpsychism* is a non-combinatorial and non-constitutive response to *The Combination Problem*. That is to say emergent panpsychism posits contingent laws of nature, which allows (but not necessitate in a strong sense) macro-experience to emerge from micro-experience and then downwardly act upon the micro-experiences from which it emerged. The downward causation thesis means that these wholes are only weakly supervenient and irreducible to their micro-experience parts, and so this is a *strong emergence* thesis (a weak emergent thesis between micro-experience and macro-experience would most likely, in effect, be a combinatorial solution similar to Goff's Phenomenal Bonding). Emergent panpsychism, like panprotopsychism, maintains the intuition that human subjects are irreducible, non-combining and non-divisible.

Emergent panpsychism appears, then, very similar to traditional strong emergence with the essential qualification that emergent panpsychism denies brute, or radical, emergence *from one categorical attribute to another*. Just as abstract entities cannot give rise to concrete entities (and *vice versa*), emergent panpsychism maintains that physical (non-mental) entities cannot emerge from mental entities (and *vice versa*). Godehard Brüntrup refers to this inter-attribute emergence as 'superstrong emergence' because it argues that whole new metaphysical categories are created, as in the case of emergent dualism or emergent theism.[115] Emergent panpsychism, like all contemporary panpsychists, rejects inter-attribute emergence from one category to another, but reintroduces intra-attribute emergence within categories – that is, from mental parts to mental wholes (or from physical parts to physical wholes).

---

114. Rosenberg, *Place for Consciousness*, 273–4; Gregg Rosenberg, 'Land Ho?': We Are Close to a Synoptic Understanding of Consciousness', in *Panpsychism: Contemporary Perspectives*, ed. Godehard Brüntrup and Ludwig Jaskolla (Oxford: Oxford University Press, 2017), 164–5; Liane Gabora, 'Amplifying Phenomenal Information: Toward a Fundamental Theory of Consciousness', *Journal of Consciousness Studies* 9, no. 8 (2002): 3–29; Giulio Tononi, 'Consciousness as Integrated Information: A Provisional Manifesto', *Biological Bulletin* 215, no. 3 (2008): 216–42; David Ray Griffin, *Religion and Scientific Naturalism: Overcoming the Conflicts* (Albany, NY: SUNY Press, 2000), 175–6; Strawson, *Real Materialism*, 72; Philip Goff, 'There Is No Combination Problem', in *The Mental as Fundamental*, ed. Michael Blamauer (Frankfurt: Ontos Verlag, 2011), 131–40.

115. Godehard Brüntrup, 'Emergent Panpsychism', in *Panpsychism: Contemporary Perspectives*, ed. Godehard Brüntrup and Ludwig Jaskolla (Oxford: Oxford University Press, 2017), 69.

One subtype of emergent panpsychism is panpsychist infusion.[116] This is a solution to the combination problem proposed by William Seager, whose article, 'Consciousness, Information and Panpsychism', was an early contribution to the campaign to give panpsychism renewed attention within analytic philosophy of mind.[117] Infusion is merging or blending of two entities, which then cease to exist in their own right, and are instead superseded by a new whole. Seager gives two examples of possible analogies from physical instances for fusion. The first is Paul Humphreys's interpretation of quantum entanglement as a type of fusion where the merged quantum particles can only be measured as a unity. The second is the formation of black holes, whereby the physical entities prior to the black hole no longer exist but are replaced by a single fundamental entity.[118] It is important to note that the fusion of consciousness is not reducible to physical theories regarding fusion, even spooky quantum theories or black hole theories. These physical examples only point to a possible analogy, not to evidence or even intelligibility of mental fusion. In either its typical or fusion subtype, the emergent panpsychist solution appears by far the most promising of all the solutions given here.

Emergent panpsychism has neither the philosophical nor the theological problems articulated in Chapter 1; since it does not posit ontological jumps, it cannot slip into emergentism or emergent theism. Emergent panpsychism also has the added advantage of being the strongest guarantor of downward causation/ free will and the closest position to dualism, whence most theologians come. If one approaches panpsychism, having become discontent with previous loyalties to substance dualism or traditional emergentism (or emergent dualism), then emergent panpsychism is likely to be an attractive option. However, if one has boxed a few rounds with materialism (or physicalism, etc.), then the constitutive combinatorial responses are more likely to appeal.

What is the outcome of all this duelling over objections and dancing around the combination problem? Panpsychists and their critics alike need to be careful not to overstate their claims; the outcome of this battle is best categorized as a stalemate. Most of the objections levelled against panpsychism (The Incredulous Stare Set and The Unscientific Objection) can be adequately responded to by panpsychists.

---

116. William Seager, 'Panpsychism, Aggregation and Combinatorial Infusion', *Mind and Matter* 8, no. 2 (2010): 167–84; William Seager, 'Panpsychist Infusion', in *Panpsychism: Contemporary Perspectives*, ed. Godehard Brüntrup and Ludwig Jaskolla (Oxford: Oxford University Press, 2017), 229–48. Another model of panpsychist infusion has recently been developed by Hedda Mørch and is attracting attention in the field. Hedda Hassel Mørch, *Panpsychism and Causation: A New Argument and a Solution to the Combination Problem*, (PhD thesis, University of Oslo, 2014).

117. William Seager, 'Consciousness, Information and Panpsychism', *Journal of Consciousness Studies* 2, no. 3 (1995): 272–88. Since then, Seager has authored the entry on 'Panpsychism' in *The Oxford Handbook to Philosophy of Mind* and authored the entry in *Stanford Encyclopaedia in Philosophy* (Summer 2001).

118. Seager, 'Panpsychist Infusion', 239.

However, in the absence of a satisfactory account of mental combination, these prior objections cannot be dismissed entirely; they remain waiting in the wings. The combination problem itself is 'significant but not insurmountable' and remains a weakness in the panpsychists' account of consciousness; but it is not a deep metaphysical mystery of the same kind that brute emergence seems to be and does not land a fatal blow.[119] This means that at present panpsychism 'offers only the form of an explanation without any content' and although this is perhaps only a small advance on competing theories, it points in a promising direction and may yet be able to fill out the content in the future.[120] Contemporary panpsychism is a robust and growing philosophical movement that has earned its place at the philosophical table and is worthy of further theological consideration.

A new alliance: Panpsychism and belief in God

This chapter first outlined how the arguments from three leading philosophers culminated in bringing about a resurgence of interest in panpsychism within contemporary philosophy of mind. Second, I examined the battlefield of debate by evaluating the main objections and responses to panpsychism. In particular, it was seen that the combination problem has scattered the troops and created a plurality of versions of panpsychism currently at play in analytic philosophy of mind. At several points in this chapter, the contemporary literature on panpsychism has been seen to bump up against issues of spirituality and raise the question of God's existence. It is now my intention to examine these issues more closely and broker an alliance between panpsychism and belief in God.

When responding to the objection that panpsychism is unscientific, it was acknowledged that many panpsychists affirm naturalism's negative truth claim against supernaturalism. This rejection of supernaturalism bears no logical relationship to panpsychism. In the remainder of this chapter, it is argued that although panpsychism does not entail belief in God, panpsychism is more logically consistent with theism than with atheistic naturalism. In other words, unbeknownst to most contemporary panpsychists, the arguments made in the recent turn to panpsychism invite or imply belief in a Creator. Thereafter, it is suggested that not only should panpsychists be open to theism, but conversely, theists should seriously consider panpsychism a suitable theory of consciousness to employ within their world view.

The argument that is most central in the recent resurgence of interest in panpsychism is the Genetic Argument. As seen above, this argument is the rejection of superstrong emergence from the physical to the mental based on the causal principle *ex nihilo nihil fit* – nothing can emerge out of nothing, or nothing can give something a property that it does not itself possess. Superstrong emergence

---

119. David Skrbina, 'Realistic Panpsychism: Commentary on Strawson', in Strawson et al., *Consciousness and Its Place in Nature*, 156.

120. Nagel, *Mind and Cosmos*, 62.

argues that the process of emergence can introduce ontological novelty, such as minds where there was only dead matter before, into the universe. This ontological jump, the panpsychist argues, violates this causal principle and so warrants the pejorative adjectives of being 'brute' or 'magic'. Panpsychists not only reject the emergentists' ontological thesis, they also reject the epistemological thesis of unpredictability as a violation of the Principle of Sufficient Reason. The Principle of Sufficient Reason states that 'no fact can be real or existent, no statement true, unless there be a sufficient reason why it is so and not otherwise'.[121] It is because the panpsychist cannot abide the abandonment of these two principles that, despite years of objections and dismissive stares of incredulity, an increasing number of contemporary philosophers have been motivated enough to posit mentality as fundamental and ubiquitous.[122] It is the commitment to the causal principle *ex nihilo nihil fit* and the Principle of Sufficient Reason that has motivated the recent revival of panpsychism within analytic philosophy of mind.

These two core principles, *ex nihilo nihil fit* and the Principle of Sufficient Reason, are similarly employed within various cosmological arguments for the existence of God. Cosmological arguments seek to demonstrate the existence of a *sufficient* reason or an ongoing *first* cause for the existence of the cosmos.[123] The Causal Principle is a central component in the Thomistic Cosmological Argument and the Principle of Sufficient Reason in the Leibnizian Cosmological Argument. Theists who employ either of these cosmological arguments affirm that it is impossible that something could contingently exist in an uncaused way, or that a contingent universe could pop into existence without some prior cause. The ontological division between not-existing and existing is too wide. Panpsychists employ this principle of causation with regards to the ontological divide between matter and mind when they reject (super)strong emergence. Indeed, Strawson

121. Gottfried Wilhelm von Leibniz, 'The Monadology', in *Leibniz Selections*, ed. P. Wiener (New York: Charles Scribner's, 1951), 527. Christian philosopher Alexander R. Pruss implies that theists may need to reconsider their embrace of emergence when he writes, 'The axiom that the perfects of the effect must be found in the cause is one that needs further exploration, both in connection with the cosmological argument, as well as in connection with emergentist theories of mind.' Alexander Pruss, 'The Leibnizian Cosmological Argument', in *The Blackwell Companion to Natural Theology*, ed. William Lane Craig and J. P. Moreland (Malden, MA: Blackwell, 2012), 98.

122. Nagel gives a colloquial articulation of the Principle of Sufficient Reason (or something close enough) in his argument for panpsychism, when he writes, 'Everything about the world can at some level be understood, and that if many things, even the most universal, initially seem arbitrary, that is because there are further things we do not know, which explain why they are not arbitrary after all.' Nagel, *Mind and Cosmos*, 17. Patrick Lewtas writes, 'Panpsychism issues from a steadfastly rationalist outlook rooted in a strongish principle of sufficient reason.' Patrick Lewtas, 'Russellian Panpsychism: Too Good to be True?', *American Philosophical Quarterly* 52, no. 1 (2015): 58.

123. William Lane Craig, 'The Cosmological Argument', in *The Rationality of Theism*, ed. Paul Copan and Paul K. Moser (London: Routledge, 2003), 112.

even makes the comparison to the creation of the universe when he writes that if emergence is intelligible then 'it will be intelligible to suppose that existence can emerge from (come out of, develop out of) non-existence'.[124] This too is something, by implication, Strawson cannot find intelligible; if consciousness needs an explanation so presumably does existence.

The Genetic Argument for panpsychism provides an account of the evolution and manifestation of minds *within* the universe, but does not aim to answer the why of existence itself; again, why is there mind (or anything) at all? It would seem then that brute contingencies are unsatisfactory to the panpsychist logic; and yet without a Creator or First Cause of some kind, this is exactly what the panpsychist is forced to claim with regards to the existence of the universe. In order to avoid such inconsistency, panpsychists need to posit some necessary being, or adopt the theory that the universe itself exists necessarily.[125] It should also be remembered that the idea that being cannot come from non-being, or that something cannot come into existence uncaused, is not a physical law but a metaphysical principle which therefore applies to all of reality, including the totality of the universe, and not merely to the things inside the universe. In Charles Taliaferro's words, 'Theism can thus provide an explanation for the existence of the panpsychistic cosmos as well as for the different levels of consciousness pervading it.'[126] Taliaferro goes on to say that, from the perspective of a theist and interactive dualist, 'panpsychism's willingness to recognize the mind or the mental … goes well beyond contemporary naturalism' and provides 'an eminently challenging position' in contemporary debate.[127] This gestures towards the conclusion that, although theism is not a strict entailment of panpsychism, if the central arguments for panpsychism were extended towards the universe as a whole then this would result in theism; one might say that panpsychism implies theism.[128]

The question as to why a theist might want to adopt panpsychism is less straightforward. Panpsychism and theism are clearly compatible, but would a theistic panpsychism be an overdetermined theory of consciousness? After all, a theistic substance dualism can state that God acts directly to infuse or inject embryos with souls and directly sustains the causal interaction between the mind and the body throughout a person's life (this is a traditional creationist account of

124. Strawson, *Real Materialism*, 66.

125. Clarke, *Panpsychism and the Religious Attitude*, 120.

126. Charles Taliaferro, 'Dualism and Panpsychism', *Panpsychism: Contemporary Perspectives* (Oxford: Oxford University Press, 2017), 369.

127. Taliaferro, 'Dualism and Panpsychism', 369.

128. It can be noted that this approach to correlating a position in philosophy of mind with philosophy of religion is very different to the approach taken by emergentists and process theists who maintain some level of commitment to naturalism, just that God is fitted into the metaphysic that the respective position in philosophy of mind describes. My approach is built on the opposite premise, that naturalism and the Christian doctrine of *creatio ex nihilo* are incompatible, and panpsychism is more consistently combined with the latter rather than the former.

the origin of the soul). This view remains a permissible account of consciousness and, as with panpsychism, there are no defeating objections to it. However, this account has weaknesses of its own to bear in mind. For example, it has given rise to a problematic ontological divide between humanity and other creatures, which sits uncomfortably with the theory of evolution. It also gives the soul and the body two radically different origin stories, which have been used to contribute to a perceived axiological difference between the soul and the body in Christian thought such that, despite the incarnation and resurrection accounts, materiality remains a second-class substance.

Furthermore, there remains a lingering dissatisfaction in employing divine action as an explanation for a widespread and systematic feature of the universe before all other possibilities have been exhausted.[129] This is the core of Nagel's critique against theistic explanations – that pushing 'the quest for intelligibility outside the world' into the intentionality of God cannot provide the explanation as to '*how* beings like us fit into the world'.[130] The objection against the creationist view of souls whereby God created each soul *ex nihilo* (with or without the guise of emergence) implies a denial of the comprehensiveness of the natural order. As stated above, these are not defeating objections against the traditional account of the soul (or consciousness) within Christian theology; God could have set things up to require continuous additions of souls. However, these issues are unsettling, and it is worthwhile for theologians to consider what other accounts of consciousness philosophy of mind suggests that are compatible with, perhaps even beneficial to, the wider concerns of Christian thought and practice.

This is not to say that special divine acts are impossible or should not be posited at all. To the contrary, in Chapter 4 I will argue that panpsychism provides a framework for a robust articulation of special divine action. However, appeals to special divine activity should not be taken as an alternative to scientific or philosophical explanations. This approach has been labelled 'god-of-the-gaps' theology. As an objection it is portrayed in what might be called a fable in contemporary science and religion dialogue, the story of Isaac Newton's hypothesis that God might need to regularly adjust the orbits of the planets to avoid disaster. This idea was ridiculed by Leibniz as equivalent to the idea that 'God Almighty wants to wind up his watch from time to time: otherwise it would cease to move. He had not, it seems, sufficient foresight to make it a perpetual motion.'[131] When Laplace's

---

129. This concern is famously articulated by Leibniz who, although never denying the possibility of miracles or sudden additions into the natural order, saw them as exceptions to be kept to a bare minimum since it is of more glory to God to have created a more complete system (apart from the disruptive influence of evil).

130. Nagel, *Mind and Cosmos*, 62, 26.

131. Gottfried Wilhelm von Leibniz, 'The Controversy between Leibniz and Clarke', in *Philosophical Papers and Letters*, ed. Leroy Loemker, 2 vols. (Chicago: University of Chicago Press, 1956), 1096.

equations of elliptical orbits replaced Newton's model, there was no longer any use for God within the theory; God was squeezed out of the explanation, so to speak. The moral of the story is that it is a risky strategy to employ special divine action within one's explanation of systematic aspects of creation. This goes for accounts of the origin of consciousness as it does for the movement of the celestial spheres. If the principle that systematic features of the world should not be explained via appeal to special divine action is accepted, then so long as panpsychism offers an otherwise compatible account of consciousness within God's creation alongside the evolution of matter, theologians have a responsibility to seriously consider, if not lend their support to, panpsychism.

Conclusion: Taking panpsychism forward

The story of contemporary panpsychism is a tale of how old problems die hard (or rarely die at all) and even the strangest solutions do not go out of fashion forever. It is a tale of how three eminent philosophers stubbornly argued that an account of consciousness could not be swept under the physicalist carpet and should not be rocketed into the heavenly sphere of transcendence if at all possible. Instead, Nagel, Chalmers and Strawson – now joined by many others – have dared to imagine that the physicalist, emergentist and even traditional substance dualist picture of the fundamental features of the world has been too barren; consciousness may go all the way down. The arguments for panpsychism, surveyed under the heading of 'the campaign', took reason and science together and have successfully brought about a revival of interest in this ancient and eccentric theory. This is not a negligible achievement, but neither is it a total victory. The various objections levelled against panpsychism, the philosophical 'battle' so to speak, were evaluated. Although panpsychism still stands, she is not unscathed for she has her own 'old problem' of the one mind and the many minds to contend with; there is still work to be done. However, it seems the panpsychist has found work worth doing, and what may turn out to be another blind alley has not been proven such yet.

But is there panpsychist work worth doing for theologians? To glance at the literature surrounding panpsychism, it might seem that the growing success of philosophers such as Nagel, Chalmers and Strawson is bad news for Christian philosophy and theology. In recent decades, Christian philosophers such as Alvin Plantinga, Richard Swinburne, Timothy O'Connor and J. P. Moreland have worked tirelessly to build impressive apologetic arguments for the existence of God on the basis of the failure of naturalistic attempts to explain consciousness – the so-called *Argument from Consciousness for the Existence of God*. Although panpsychists and theists are natural allies against materialism, the potential success of panpsychism seems to threaten this apologetic enterprise; theistic substance dualism is not the last man standing. Perhaps Christian philosophers can simply take solace in watching the crumbling edifice of materialism and restrictive naturalism as a broadly religious temperament is readmitted into academic consideration?[132]

We need not settle for so little. The possibility of a new alliance gives more cause for hope than appears at first glance. The resurgence in panpsychism is good news for Christianity – for although panpsychism does not require God to inject minds into the universe at successive intervals, it does stand firmly within the logic of the Cosmological Argument. Panpsychism still needs a Cause or a Reason – a Creator – to bring about and sustain the fundamental level of reality upon which panpsychism's account of consciousness is built. The existence of consciousness in a panpsychist universe may still increase the probability of theism, but it does not do so because there are epistemic or causal gaps in the creation of individual animal minds, such that God becomes a hypothesis in lieu of a scientific explanation. Instead, the argument from consciousness for the existence of God can still be an important part of the apologetic toolbox, but in a manner subsumed perhaps within a cosmological argument to form a deeper and more integrated version of this traditional argument. Not only should we ask 'Why is there *something* rather than *nothing*?' but also 'Why is that something *experiencing something*, rather than *experiencing nothing*?' This is a question to which theists can provide some compelling answers. Front-loading creation with consciousness in this way may turn out to be beneficial to Christian theology in other areas. But, for this alliance to work panpsychists will need to abandon their lingering, unrequited relationship to naturalism; and I encourage them to do so.

132. See Thomas Nagel, 'Secular Philosophy and the Religious Temperament', in *Secular Philosophy and the Religious Temperament: Essays 2002–2008* (Oxford: Oxford University Press, 2010).

Chapter 3

AN INTERLUDE ON GOTTFRIED WILHELM VON LEIBNIZ

The philosophical problems with the emergence of mind from matter, and the theological strain that emergence theologies place upon the transcendence of God, as explored in the first chapter, motivated consideration of contemporary panpsychism as a viable alternative in Chapter 2. The revival of interest in panpsychism by prominent philosophers of mind provides an opportunity for renewed theological attention. It would be false to assume from this that panpsychism is nothing but a passing fad or that panpsychism is alien to the venerable tradition of Christian thought and practice.

To the contrary, panpsychism is an ancient theory regarding the place of consciousness in the world.[1] There may also be an argument to be made that the theological benefits of panpsychism have been considered by a minority of notable thinkers such as Gregory of Nyssa, Augustine of Hippo, Francis of Assisi,

---

1. Panpsychism was a widespread and foundational explanatory principle in pre-Socratic, Platonic, Aristotelian and Stoic schools of thought; see David Skrbina, *Panpsychism in the West* (Cambridge, MA: MIT Press, [2005] 2017), 23–58. In particular, panpsychism was employed to explain movement and causation (the argument from *indwelling powers*) most famously expressed by Thales's maxim, 'all things are full of gods', in Aristotle, *De Anima*, I.5; 411a7, trans. J. A. Smith (Oxford: Clarendon Press, 1931) and affirmed by Plato in *Laws*, 899b, trans. Trevor J. Saunders, in *Plato Complete Works*, ed. John M. Cooper (Indianapolis, IN: Hackett, 1997). Panpsychism undergirded the continuity and order within the universe (the argument from *continuity*) such that the *arch*, whether a spiritual ever-living fire (Heraclitus) or the air, breath and soul (Anaximenes), was a form of psyche in all things. Last, the order (argument from *design*) of the universe was explained as the presence of νοῦς – mind, spirit, reason – throughout all things. This would later develop in to the Stoic active principle, *logos*, the intelligent force and 'vehicle of logos', *pneuma*, which are both 'the faculty of man which enables him to think, to plan, and to speak' and is 'literally embodied in the universe at large'. A. A. Long, *Hellenistic Philosophy: Stoics, Epicureans and Sceptics* (Berkley: University of California Press, 1974), 108; See also B. Inwood and L. Gerson, *Hellenistic Philosophy* (Indianapolis, IN: Hackett, 1997), 133. As a common feature within most ancient Greek philosophies, panpsychism can be described as a part of the intellectual foundation upon which European thought and Christian theology have developed.

Pierre Teilhard de Chardin and, as detailed in this chapter, Gottfried Wilhelm von Leibniz. Thus, although few theologians have cared to launch explicit and robust defences of panpsychism, panpsychist ideas nevertheless flow through the tradition. The consideration of panpsychism by contemporary theologians is neither a mere chasing after the winds of fashion nor does it entail conceding ground to process theology.

The employment of panpsychism for the service of Christian theology comes to the surface in the theological argumentation of Leibniz. Leibniz gave panpsychism one of, if not the most, systematic articulations in the modern period, and his influence remains evident upon panpsychist philosophy today. The reception of Leibniz's philosophy has sometimes characterized his panpsychist monadology as 'necessarily atheistic', or as the 'humanistic secularisation of the Christian tradition' through the 'autarchy' and 'self-sufficient individuality of monads' apart from God.[2] First, I will show that such characterizations are false by summarizing Leibniz's panpsychism as expressed in his theory of monads. Second, I will demonstrate how Leibniz's philosophical metaphysic served three interwoven theological arguments – the doctrine of creation *ex nihilo*, the idea of creation as a single comprehensive order and a sacramental ontology. It is not that a theologian must adopt panpsychism in order to hold these three theological positions, but that panpsychism can be, and has historically been, used to reinforce the affirmation of them. These three theological ideas, sown in the soil of a panpsychist philosophy, are the seeds for the constructive arguments of Chapters 4 and 5 for how theological panpsychism can help provide a robust account of special divine action and respond to the environmental crisis.

Monads and panpsychism

Leibniz's mature metaphysics is a system of monads. The word 'monad' is defined in *Correspondence with John Bernoulli*, as 'a substance which is truly one, i.e. not an aggregate of substances'.[3] Monads are not (only) the fundamental individual

---

2. Bertrand Russell, *A Critical Exposition of the Philosophy of Leibniz* (Cambridge: Cambridge University Press, [1935] 1990), 172; James K. A. Smith, *Introducing Radical Orthodoxy: Mapping a Post-Secular Theology* (Grand Rapids, MI: Baker Academic, 2004), 207; Herman Dooyeweerd, *A New Critique of Theoretical Thought: The Necessary Presuppositions of Philosophy v. 1*, trans. David H. Freeman and William S. Young (Jordon Station, Ontario: Paideia Press Ltd., 1984), 230.

3. Gottfried Wilhelm von Leibniz, *Correspondence with John Bernoulli* in *Leibnizens Mathematische Schriften*, herausgegeben von G. I. Gerhardt, 7 vols. (Berlin and Halle: A. Asher/W. H. Schmidt, 1849–63) [hereafter, GM], III, 537. See also *Letter to de Volder*, where a monad is 'a complete simple substance' in *Die Philosophischen Schriften von Gottfried Wilhelm Leibniz*, herausgegeben von G. I. Gerhardt, 7 vols. (Berlin: Wiedmann, 1875–90) [hereafter G], II, 252; and *Gottfried Wilhelm Leibniz: Philosophical Papers and Letters*, a selection translated and edited with an introduction by Leroy E. Loemker, 2nd edn

building blocks of reality found at the bottom of a finite chain of being, but are unities found at every level of reality; a human mind unifying the composite substances of a human body, a dog mind unifying the composite substances of a dog's body, the microbe entelechy unifying the microbe body are all monads.[4] Every monad is said to have an experiential centre, that is a substantial form of either a soul (in humans or animals with memory) or an entelechy (in plants and small creatures without memory).[5] Together with an organic body a monad forms a 'corporeal substance', such that all individual finite substances are embodied as living things. A body, by contrast, is a collection of monads, a composite substance – a community of souls with a single *telos*. A body of a living organism and a clock are both, then, composite substances, but what distinguishes the two is that the former is a 'genuine unity, like what is called ego in us; while a clock is nothing but an aggregate'.[6] Demarcating his view from that of Thomas's hylomorphism, Leibniz argued that there can be no detachment of the soul from the body, even in death.[7] Instead, death is described as the disintegration of the composite unity into an aggregate, but the individual parts continue to exist so long as the universe is sustained by God.[8] Leibniz is clear

(Dordrecht: D. Reidel, 1969) [hereafter, Loemker], 530. In *Monadology*, a monad is defined as 'a simple substance, i.e. one without parts' (G. II, 607; Loemker, 643). Leibniz adopted a preference for the word 'monad', rather than 'individual substance' around the 1690s, coinciding with his public announcement that the true nature of substance is *force*. See Pauline Phemister, *Leibniz and the Environment* (Oxford: Routledge, 2016), 36.

4. Phemister, *Leibniz and the Environment*, 38–9.

5. Leibniz relationship to the scholastic language of 'substantial forms' varied greatly throughout his lifetime. As a young man he rejected this language, as was the fashion of the early modern period, for being more obscure than explanatory. In *Discours*, §11, however, he writes, 'I know that I am putting forward a great paradox in claiming to rehabilitate ancient philosophy to some extent, and to restore the rights of citizenship to substantial forms, which have practically been banished.' In this later work, he uses the term very frequently, and in *New Essay* 317 he seems to suggest that this is due to the bad reputation of the term, rather than any disagreement as to content. See Stuart Brown, *Leibniz* (Sussex: Harvester Press, 1984), 30–1, 137–8.

6. Gottfried Wilhem von Leibniz, 'New System of the Nature of Substances and of the Communcation between Them', §2, in *The Monadology and Other Philosophical Writings*, trans. Robert Latta (Oxford: Clarendon Press, 1899), 321 [hereafter, Latta]. For more on Leibniz's understanding of the embodiment of living beings as 'nested individuals' with a common *telos*, see Ohad Nachtomy, 'Leibniz's View of Living Beings: Embodied or Nested Individuals', in *Embodiment: A History*, ed. Justin E. H. Smith (Oxford: Oxford University Press, 2017), 189–215.

7. Leibniz, *Considerations on Vital Principles and Plastic Natures* (GP VI 545–6; Latta, 590). See Stuart Brown, 'Soul, Body and Natural Immortality', *The Monist* 81, no. 4 (1998): 578–80.

8. Leibniz, *Nature and Grace*, §6 (Latta, 413–14).

that monads are *created* and contingent substances of secondary power, of which every animate and inanimate creature is composed, and which is made to the glory of God.

Although the monads are simple substances they have two properties: *appetition* and *perception*. Appetition is an active tendency, a kind of striving which moves the monads through time, from unconscious perception to the next, in causation from predecessor to successor. According to Leibniz, there is no interaction from one monad to another, so this pattern of appetition contains the total causal history and future of any monad, and it is impressed on God from the beginning as a kind of law. Perception is described by Leibniz as how 'multiplicity is represented in unity'.[9] Each monad has represented within itself the contemporary states of all other monads; it is a 'mirror [of] the whole universe from its own special point of view'.[10] It is this unique point of view of each monad that undergirds Leibniz's account of space – not as extension but as multiple points of view from each monad. Thus, nowhere is 'fallow, sterile, or dead', and everywhere is filled with monads each of which is unique, forming a kind of 'plenum' of living creatures that fill the universe.[11]

Perception also accounts for consciousness, 'which is the internal state of the monad representing external things'.[12] Importantly, this is distinguished from self-consciousness, which Leibniz describes as '*apperception*, which is *consciousness*, or the reflective knowledge of the internal state, something not given to all souls, nor at all times to a given soul'.[13] Leibniz criticizes Descartes for making self-consciousness the paradigm for all mentality and consequently excluding souls from all non-human organisms or phenomena. Instead, Leibniz writes that monads have consciousness like that of a 'prolonged unconsciousness', 'a profound dreamless sleep' or a 'state of stupor'.[14] Perception, thus, stands in continuity with human consciousness but it is not identical to it. It is perception – the unconscious first-person perspective found in even the barest monad – that Leibniz, in his famous mill analogy, argues is 'inexplicable on mechanical grounds'.[15] This Leibnizian argument, that perception as analogous to human consciousness

---

9. Leibniz, *Monadology*, §14 (G. VI, 608–9; Loemker, 644). Leibniz drew upon the traditional concept of humanity as *microcosm*, structurally representing within itself the whole universe, and applied to every monad in the universe. Phemister, *Leibniz and the Environment*, 42.

10. Leibniz, *Monadology*, §57 (G. VI 618; Loemker, 649).

11. Leibniz, *Monadology*, §68–9; Gottfried Wilhem von Leibniz, *G. W. Leibniz: Philosophical Essays*, ed. and trans. Roger Ariew and Daniel Garber (Indianapolis, IN: Hackett, 1989), 222.

12. Leibniz, *Principles of Nature and Grace, Based on Reason*; G VI 600; Leibniz, *G. W. Leibniz*, 208.

13. Leibniz, *G. W. Leibniz*, 208.

14. Leibniz, *Monadology*, §14, §20 and §24; Latta, 224, 230, 231.

15. Leibniz, *Monadology*, §17; Latta, 227–8.

cannot be explained through the interaction of physical parts, is at the forefront of the revival of panpsychism in contemporary analytic philosophy of mind.[16]

Creation ex nihilo *and the fittingness of panpsychism*

The doctrine of creation *ex nihilo* can be summarized as the affirmation that God freely creates the world, without compulsion or necessity, out of nothing (not from pre-existing materials, nor divinely emanating 'god-stuff', nor space-time), such that God also continues to sustain creation in each moment of its existence. The contemporary resurgence in defending and articulating the doctrine of creation *ex nihilo* can be seen as a response to two misinterpretations of this doctrine. The first is an interpretation of this doctrine as a scientific formula (the Big Bang or equivalent), and the second is as the cause of domineering, authoritarian and abusive pictures of God and God's relationship to the world.[17] This latter concern has been most emphatically argued by process and feminist theologians, who are often attracted to forms of panpsychism (or a panexperientialist metaphysic) as a way to stress the value and possible eternality of the creation. Therefore, the historical illustration of a panpsychist affirmation of creation *ex nihilo*, such as is found in Leibniz's writings, holds particular benefit in this current discussion. By undermining any post-modern opposition between panpsychism and creation *ex nihilo*, Leibniz underscores how the doctrine of creation *ex nihilo* can be affirmed without entailing that God is distant, domineering or that creation is emptied of intrinsic value.[18] To the contrary, as is argued in the final two chapters,

16. This is commonly called 'The Mill Argument', because it involves arguing that if the mind is like a mill in which we can only observe 'parts that push one another, and we will never find anything to explain a perception'. Leibniz, *Monadology*, §17; Latta, 227–8. In Chapter 2, I referred to the contemporary form of this argument as The Genetic Argument.

17. For a good defence of the congruity between modern cosmology and what creation *ex nihilo* might be expected to look like from the inside, see Andrew Davison, 'Looking Back toward the Origin: Scientific Cosmology as Creation *ex nihilo* Considered "from the Inside"', in *Creation* ex nihilo: *Origins, Development, Contemporary Challenge*, ed. Gary A. Anderson and Markus Bockmuehl (Notre Dame, IN: Notre Dame University Press, 2018), 367–89. For scientific discussion of this doctrine, see also Paul Copan and William Lane Craig, *Creation Out of Nothing: A Biblical, Philosophical, and Scientific Exploration* (Grand Rapids, MI: Baker Academic, 2004). Authors who reject creation *ex nihilo* because of a concern over the resulting doctrine of God, see Catherine Keller, *The Face of the Deep: A Theology of Becoming* (London: Routledge, 2003); and Thomas Jay Oord, ed. *Theologies of Creation:* Creatio ex Nihilo *and Its New Rivals* (New York: Routledge, 2015).

18. This is not to say one *must* hold to panpsychism in order to respond to contemporary critiques against the doctrine of creation *ex nihilo*. Instead, Leibniz shows that panpsychism can be put to the service of such a defence as easily as it can be employed in such attacks against this doctrine.

panpsychism is a useful ontology for articulating how a radically transcendent God interacts with and empowers the community of creation.

The different concepts of creation as eternal, a necessary emanation from God, formed from primal matter, or created out of nothing are not ultimately concerned with the (temporal) *origin* of creation but with creation's ongoing relationship to the Creator.[19] Creation *ex nihilo* is not a position within ontological debates regarding what is, in effect of God's will, created. The ontology of the creation has remained an open question within Christian thought. Thus, while this doctrine affirmed the creation of matter directly by God, over against Gnostic and Middle-Platonic intermediaries, the development of this doctrine in the second and third centuries was not orientated towards a contrast between materiality and immateriality but between the Creator and all things (immaterial and material creation).[20]

To claim that God creates 'out of nothing' is to imply that the verb 'to create' is predicated of God in a radically different way to how it might be predicated of humanity or any other creature. This doctrinal formulation arises from a Scriptural exegesis on the otherness of Israel's God and the dependency of creation upon the voice of God (in the Psalms in particular), and this is reinterpreted in light of the incarnation and resurrection of Jesus Christ.[21] For God to create out of nothing is

19. This point has been well argued for in Ian A. McFarland, *From Nothing: A Theology of Creation* (Louisville, KY: Westminster John Knox Press, 2014); and Kathryn Tanner, *God and Creation in Christian Theology: Tyranny or Empowerment?* (Oxford: Blackwell, 1988).

20. To that end, Janet Soskice suggests that while the current revival of creation *ex nihilo* is undoubtedly indebted to the historical work of Gerhard May, his portrayal has resulted in 'too much emphasis on the creation of matter', and so underplayed the createdness of the soul as emphasized, for example, in the Athanasius's *De Incarnatione*. Soskice's astute comment on contemporary scholarship allows her to endorse closer analysis of the potential compatibility between Galen Strawson's panpsychism and Christian theology. Janet Soskice, 'Why *Creatio ex nihilo* for Theology Today?', in *Creation* ex nihilo: *Origins, Development, Contemporary Challenges*, ed. Gary A. Anderson and Markus Bockmuehl (Notre Dame, IN: Notre Dame University Press, 2018), 49, 50–1. See Gerhard May, *Creation* ex Nihilo: *The Doctrine of 'Creation Out of Nothing' in Early Christian Thought*, trans. A. S. Worrall (Edinburgh: T&T Clark, 1994).

21. The progenitor of this doctrine, Theophilus of Antioch, clearly expresses the relationship between the doctrines of creation and resurrection when he defends Christian hope in the resurrection on the basis that 'God created man out of nothing, in that he formed him from a tiny drop of seed which did not exist before'. Such reference to a 'seed' suggests a stronger link than has yet been recognized between Theophilus and the Gnostic defender of creation *ex nihilo*, Basilides, who argued that the world was created from absolutely nothing in the form of a cosmic seed of not-yet being, i.e. potentiality. This is *contra* May, *Creation ex nihilo*, 68–70, 84, 163. Theophilus of Antioch, *To Autolycus* 1.4, in Patrologia Graeca (hereafter PG), 6:1029B, quoted in McFarland, *From Nothing*, 1, 6–8. Gregory of Nyssa, over a century later, also drew heavily upon the notion of 'the seed of all things' such that souls are within matter and both are created 'at the beginning' and allowed to develop 'little by little' by progressing 'from the least perfect to the most perfect'. *In*

to suggest that God has ultimate power and sovereignty over that which is created, and for the creation to be conditioned by nothing but the generosity of God's will. Creation as a *gift*, as a work of grace, cannot be separated from Christian teaching on redemption. Creation *ex nihilo* is, therefore, a 'distributed doctrine' manifesting across Christian treatments of the whole divine economy.[22]

We now turn to consider how Leibniz's panpsychism, as outlined above, served his understanding and affirmation of creation *ex nihilo*. Many of Leibniz's arguments are motivated by the Principle of Sufficient Reason, and this is no different for his panpsychism. This famous principle is outlined in the *Discours* as 'for every contingent fact there is a reason why that fact is so and not otherwise'.[23] In a letter to Arnauld on 14 July 1686, Leibniz describes this as 'my great principle', namely that 'there must always be some foundation for the connexion of the terms of a proposition which is true, and this foundation must be in the notions of the terms'.[24] Put more simply, 'Nothing happens without it being possible to give a reason why it happened as it did and not in another way'.[25] As Leibniz notes in *Principles of Nature and Grace*, 'The first question we are entitled to put will be – *Why does something exist rather than nothing?*'; it follows from the Principle of Sufficient Reason for Leibniz that the 'ultimate reason of things is called *God*'.[26]

From this explication of Leibniz's thought, it may seem then that The Principle for Sufficient Reason grounds the doctrine of creation *ex nihilo*, and in that sense conditions the activity of God in some way.[27] If there must be a sufficient reason for

---

hexaem. I, 77 D, quoted in, von Balthasar, *Presence and Thought*, 58; cf. *De op. hom.* 8; I 148 B; PG 44, 125–256 and *De op. hom.* 22; I, 177 A; PG 44, 125–256. As such, Gregory could affirm that 'creation is self-contained, without experiencing the need for a new intervention and without diminution, as it continues in its arrangements'. *In inscriptiones Psalmorum*, ed. McDonough, GNO V; I, 610 BC. This lack of a need for intervention in the creation of humanity or souls is a theological strength of panpsychism argued for by Leibniz, as we shall see later in this interlude.

22. John Webster, '"Love Is Also a Lover of Life": *Creatio ex nihilo* and Creaturely Goodness', *Modern Theology* 29, no. 2 (April 2013): 156.

23. Leibniz, *Discours de Métaphysique*, §13; G., IV, 436–9; Loemker, 310–11.

24. Leibniz, G., II, 56; Loemker, 337.

25. Leibniz, G., II, 56; Loemker, 337. Elsewhere Leibniz defines sufficient reason as 'in virtue of which we hold that there can be no fact real or existing, no statement true, unless there be a sufficient reason, why it should be so and not otherwise, although these reasons usually cannot be known by us'. Leibniz, *Monadology*, §32; Latta, 235.

26. This is the general thrust of Leibniz's Cosmological Argument for the Existence of God, touched upon in the previous chapter. Leibniz, *The Principles of Nature and Grace, Based on Reason* (1714), G. IV., 598–606, Loemker, 1038–9.

27. Some scholars have interpreted Leibniz as abandoning the doctrine of creation *ex nihilo* for the Platonic notion of emanation. Catherine Wilson (and Philip Clayton) suggest that Leibniz was covering up his true emanatist leanings out of fear of a church inquisition. Catherine Wilson, *Leibniz's Metaphysics: A Historical and Comparative Study* (Princeton, NJ: Princeton University Press, 1989), 84–86, citing G 3:575; and Philip Clayton, *The*

the universe taken as a whole, one must posit a being with ultimate creative power who acts with intentionality, namely God.[28] Once this is achieved, the question arises as to why God chose and willed to create this particular world from, in

Problem of God in Modern Thought (Grand Rapids, MI: Eerdmans, 2000), 233–4, 244. Christia Mercer also argues that Leibniz believed that 'there is a single, unified, and perfect Supreme being who *chooses* to emanate its being and perfection into creatures and who nonetheless remains transcendent while all its creatures contain an imperfect instantiation of its essence'. The confluence of emanation and volition complicates the traditional lines in the debate between emanation and creation as in some sense to do with creation as an act of will, an emanation as a necessity. Christia Mercer, *Leibniz's Metaphysics: Its Origins and Development* (Cambridge: Cambridge University Press, 2001), 216. This is in direct contrast to the interpretation I am here presenting, which argues that Leibniz constructed a system of panpsychism on the foundation of the doctrine of creation *ex nihilo*. Scholars who argue for an emanationist reading of Leibniz often point to three texts where Leibniz uses the language of emanation. In *Discours*, Leibniz writes that 'created substance depend on God, who preserves them and who even produces them continually by a kind of emanation, just as we produce our thoughts' (*Discours*, par. 14). In the *Theodicy*, Leibniz writes that God prevents suffering, 'insofar as the perfection of the universe, which is an emanation from him, permits it' (*Theodicy*, par. 167). Finally, in the *Monadology* Leibniz writes that monads 'are generated, so to speak, by continual flugurations of the divinity'. Robert Latta helpfully describes Leibniz's choice of the word 'fluguration' as 'a middle term between creation and emanation' and thus between Descartes's and Spinoza's philosophies (Latta, 243–4, n.75). In all three of these instances of emanation language, Leibniz's was, perhaps, not as clear as one might wish. However, given the central argumentative place that the concept of creation *ex nihilo* plays within the structure of many of his arguments from sufficient reason and the best of all possible worlds, perhaps Leibniz did not think he needed to be terminologically precise on this point. Moreover, having emptied the emanation scheme of any mediating role, the term 'emanation' may have presented itself as useful terminology for the uniqueness of the causal relation. As Kathryn Tanner writes, 'Emanationist imagery … is often retained in creation *ex nihilo* accounts … but with significant warping.' Tanner points out that across the tradition, emanation is often used to counterbalance personal and intentional language of God's choice to create to avoid an untoward anthropocentricism that makes the act of creation an arbitrary choice by a bored little deity. Since avoiding such arbitrariness is one of Leibniz's most pressing concerns in the Principle of Sufficient Reason and throughout his writings, it seems likely that the same counterbalancing of terminology provides a more sufficient explanation for Leibniz's use of emanation language, rather than revealing his true heterodox colours. See Kathryn Tanner, 'Creation *ex nihilo* as Mixed Metaphor', *Modern Theology* 29, no. 2 (April 2013): 148. For evidence that Leibniz rejects 'the universe as a stairwell' view of an emanating creation, see Gottfried Wilhelm von Leibniz, *Nature Itself*, in *Philosophical Texts*, ed. R. S. Woodhouse and Richard Francks (Oxford: Oxford University Press, 1998), §6; Smith, *Introducing Radical Orthodoxy*, 210, n.82.

28. Leibniz, *On the Ultimate Origination of Things* (1697); Latta, 337–54.

Leibniz's words, all the other 'possible universes' which God might have chosen to create.[29] This logic results in Leibniz's much maligned, teleological notion that this is the best of all possible worlds. However, one can also understand the relationship between Leibniz's 'great principle' and theology in quite the reverse manner; The Principle of Sufficient Reason stands only because God is perfectly good and rational and so does not act without reason. It follows from the doctrine of creation *ex nihilo*, for Leibniz, that everything about this world as a whole and everything within this world has a sufficient reason for being as it is at all times. The relationship between Leibniz's Principle of Sufficient Reason and his affirmation of creation *ex nihilo* can be seen, therefore, to be circular or mutually reinforcing.

Directly flowing from his theistically endowed Principle of Sufficient Reason and creation *ex nihilo*, Leibniz gives his first theological argument for panpsychism. We might refer to this as Leibniz's Argument from Perfection or Fittingness. He wrote that it is 'in conformity with the greatness and beauty of the works of God for him to produce as many substance[s] are there can be in this universe ... it is a perfection of nature to have many [souls]'.[30] Since this is the best of all possible worlds, Leibniz argues, it is fitting that 'there is nothing fallow, nothing sterile, nothing dead in the universe, no chaos, no confusion, save in appearance'.[31] Moreover, 'since every mind is like a mirror' then many minds mean that 'there will be greater light, the mirrors blending the light not only in the [individual] eye but also among each other. The gathered splendour produces glory'.[32] The perception of monads means that 'the universe is in some way multiplied as many times as there are substances, and the glory of God is likewise multiplied by as many entirely different representations of his work'.[33] It is a panpsychist universe that Leibniz suggests brings greatest glory to God by reflecting the divine light at every point of creation, from every possible perspective.

Elsewhere Leibniz describes a panpsychist universe as 'the simplest in hypotheses and richest in phenomena'.[34] He would make this more explicit in *Monadology* where he wrote,

> I believe that ... it is consistent neither with the order nor with the beauty of the reason of things that there should be something vital or immanently active only in a small part of matter, when it would imply greater perfection if it were in all. And even if ... intelligent souls ... cannot be everywhere, this is no objection to the view that there should everywhere be souls, or at least things analogous to souls.[35]

29. Leibniz, *Monadology*, §53; Latta, 247. Leibniz, *Theodicy*, trans. E. M. Huggard, ed. Austin Farrer (London: Routledge & Kegan Paul, 1951), §44, 98–9, §173, 234–5, §196, 249.

30. Leibniz, 'To Arnauld (30 April 1687)'; Leibniz, *G. W. Leibniz*, 87.

31. Leibniz, *Monadology*, §69; Latta, 257.

32. Leibniz, *Elements of Natural Law*, §5; Loemker, 214.

33. Leibniz, *Discourse on Metaphysics*, §9; Leibniz, *G. W. Leibniz*, 42.

34. Leibniz, *Discourse on Metaphysics*, §6; Loemker, 470.

35. Leibniz, *On Nature Itself*, §12; Loemker, 820.

Importantly, in this passage, not only does Leibniz argue that panpsychism 'shows up the greatness of God in an appropriate way' but reinforces that this glory-reflecting panpsychism allows for the distinction between intelligent souls and non-intelligent souls or 'at least things analogous to soul'.[36] It is not only the intellectual rationality of the human mind that brings glory to God, but the basic property of experience found across the universe as well.

In many ways, Leibniz's Argument from Fittingness dovetails with the affirmation that the doctrine of creation *ex nihilo* means that God's 'perfect power does not absorb, exclude or overwhelm and dispossess other dependent powers and agents, but precisely the opposite: omnipotent power creates and perfects creaturely capacity and movement'.[37] Leibniz, at least, argued that the maximum fulfilment of this *ex nihilo* principle – the maximum amount of secondary causation, contingent creaturely power and goodness – results in a panpsychist universe. In a panpsychist universe, at every point of the universe, God has bestowed indwelling powers of action and subjectivity of intrinsic value.

Three arguments for panpsychism from a comprehensive created order

Leibniz's second great principle is the Principle of Predicate-in-Notion.[38] This principle is the main explanatory principle in *The New System* but finds its clearest definition in the earlier *Discours*: 'In every true proposition, necessary or contingent, universal or singular, the notion of the predicate is contained in some way in the subject. If not, I do not know what truth is.'[39] This principle that 'it is the very nature of substance that the present is great [pregnant] with the future and that everything can be understood out of one [that is, the future can be inferred from the present], at least if God does not intervene with a miracle', is a crucial principle for Leibniz's panpsychism.[40] It is because every individual substance is known by God as a 'complete concept', that each monad 'contains' within it all truths about itself, past, present and future.[41] It is in defence of a theological conviction, that the universe has a comprehensive order and so reflects the unity, rationality and omniscience of the Creator, that motivates Leibniz's *Argument from Continuity*, the *Argument from Indwelling Powers* and the *Argument from Non-Emergence* for panpsychism. We shall examine in turn how Leibniz formulated each of these arguments for panpsychism and used each for the service of theology.

---

36. Leibniz, *Monadology*, §59; Latta, 249 and §19; Latta, 230.

37. John Webster attributes this affirmation to both Thomas Aquinas and Karl Barth. Webster, 'Love Is Also a Lover of Life', 170.

38. C. D. Broad, *Leibniz: An Introduction*, ed. C. Lewy (Cambridge: Cambridge University Press, 1975), 6–10.

39. Leibniz, *Discours*, §8; G. II, 56; Loemker, 337.

40. See 'Leibniz to Des Bosses', Hanover 19 August 1715'; G. II, 502–5; Loemker, 999.

41. See Phemister, *Leibniz and the Environment*, 35–45.

Theologically, the Principle of Predicate-in-Notion means that when 'God at first created the soul or any other real unity', God did so in such a way 'that everything must arise in it from its own inner nature'.[42] All integrity and causal powers are given 'from the beginning'.[43] Leibniz argues that God loaded all properties, events and powers for all time into the first act of creation. This is a result of Leibniz's commitment to the wisdom and foreknowledge of God that no later additions or corrections should be required. The act of creation *ex nihilo* stands unique and sufficient. In this way, Leibniz holds to the continuity of all things, such that 'the nature of things is uniform, and our [human] nature cannot differ infinitely from the other simple substances of which the whole universe consists'.[44] There are no latter additions of new substances, which would introduce a dualism of discontinuity into the universe. Leibniz declares proudly that 'it is one of my great and best confirmed maxims that *nature never makes leaps*. I call this the *Law of Continuity*.'[45] Thus, the mentality or the potential for mentality found in humans must also be found in the simplest monads of the universe. These are the bones of a theological argument for panpsychism from continuity.

The Argument from Indwelling Powers for panpsychism is important for this theological assessment of panpsychism because it underpins Leibniz's view of providence. Leibniz's panpsychism grounds his articulation of double agency and the distinction between primary and secondary causation, in contrast to many of the trends in philosophy in his lifetime which sought to move away from this medieval theological schema. In his correspondence with Arnauld, Leibniz writes that 'all [a substance's] actions come from its own depths, except of its dependence on God'.[46] Primary causation is each monad's dependency on God for continued existence; secondary causation is the actions and forces which come from within the monad which God sustains. Leibniz's panpsychism is an articulation of the creation as a plenum of secondary powers, created, sustained and harmonized by God.

Leibniz rejected Descartes's account that emptied the non-human world of any indwelling powers or teleology, because Descartes then had to suppose that God recreated each atom and the whole universe entirely afresh from moment to moment. Robert Boyle's *Free Inquiry* and *On Nature Itself* expanded Descartes's view to argue that external divine laws were the sole cause governing all things.[47]

---

42. Leibniz, *New System*, §14; Latta, 313.

43. Leibniz, *New System*, §15; Latta, 315; *Third Explanation*; Latta, 333.

44. Leibniz, *Correspondence with De Volder*, 30 June 1704; G. II, 270; Loemker, 876.

45. Gottfried Wilhelm von Leibniz, *New Essays on Human Understanding*, trans. P. Remnant and J. Bennett (Cambridge: Cambridge University Press, 1982), 56; G. VI.vi.56.

46. Gottfried Wilhelm von Leibniz, *Correspondence with Arnauld*, in *The Leibniz-Arnauld Correspondence*, trans. and ed. H. T. Mason (Manchester: Manchester University Press, 1967), 170; G II.136. Cf. *Theodicy*, §10, in Huggard and Farrer, 80.

47. Robert Boyle's *Free Inquiry into the Vulgarly Received Notion of Nature* (1682) and the subsequent *On Nature Itself* (1688) were defended by J. C. Sturm's 'Defence' (appended to *Elective Physics*), which Leibniz responds to in *Nature Itself* (1698).

Leibniz was concerned that this would make nature into a kind of idol since the objects of the world were direct and immediate manifestations of the Divine will. For similar reasons, Leibniz also rejects the occasionalism of Malebranche as requiring a 'perpetual miracle', in favour of his own view of 'harmony pre-established'.[48]

Leibniz's monads owe their origin to God and require God's perpetual concurrence as a necessary condition for their continued existence – they are dependent upon God at all times – but all things have genuine secondary causal powers of their own as 'an inherent law, impressed by divine Decree'.[49] As such, there can be no competition between God's agency and the indwelling powers in Leibniz's panpsychist universe. Although 'monads have no windows' to allow causation between created objects, 'we might say that, for Leibniz, God can walk through walls'.[50] Leibniz can affirm the reality of miracles, albeit that God foresaw and pre-established their need, since these are not violations of natural laws but 'something which exceeds the power of created things', or goes beyond the 'God-given nature of things' for a particular purpose.[51] Further discussion on this topic of panpsychism and special divine action is given in the next chapter.

Leibniz also employed the Argument from Non-Emergence for panpsychism. In his *New Essays on Human Understanding*, Leibniz responds to Locke's philosophy, critiquing what he sees as a 'pervasively materialist tendency'.[52] Leibniz clearly disagreed with Locke's assertion that matter 'is evidently in its own nature void of sense and thought'.[53] What is more intriguing, however, is Leibniz's careful refutation of Locke's statement: 'I see no contradiction in [that God] should, if he pleased, give to certain systems of created senseless matter … some degrees of sense, perception, and thought.'[54] Skrbina describes this moment in Locke as one that 'could lead to a version of panpsychism' if the author were not such a thoroughgoing sceptic and empiricist.[55] Why, then, does Leibniz vehemently disagree with a passage where Locke seems to allow for the possibility of Leibniz's own position? It is because the similarity is superficial and the differences profoundly theological.

---

48. Leibniz, *New System*, §12–13; Latta, 312; *Third Explanation*, Latta, 333. See also, *On Nature Itself*, §10; Loemker, 816–17.

49. Leibniz, *On Nature Itself*, §12; Loemker, 819. Brandon C. Look, 'Gottfried Wilhelm Leibniz', in *Stanford Encyclopaedia of Philosophy* (spring 2014 edition), ed. Edward N. Zalta, https://plato.stanford.edu/archives/spr2014/entries/leibniz/, accessed 11 August 2020.

50. Smith, *Introducing Radical Orthodoxy*, 221. See Leibniz, *Monadology*, §7; Leibniz, *G. W. Leibniz*, 214.

51. Leibniz, 'Response to Bayle', GP IV 520; Loemker, 494.

52. Nicholas Jolley, *Leibniz and Locke: A Study on* New Essays on Human Understanding (Oxford: Clarendon Press, 1984), 7.

53. Jolley, *Leibniz and Locke*, 7.

54. John Locke, *An Essay Concerning Human Understanding* (Dent: Dutton, [1689] 1964), IV.3.vi.

55. Skrbina, *Panpsychism in the West*, 92.

Leibniz distinguishes Locke's imagined possibility, where God gives thought to matter as a kind of miracle, from his own view of conceivable modification of the principles given to matter from creation. In his response to Locke, we have Leibniz's clearest articulation of the Argument from Non-Emergence for panpsychism. It is almost identical to contemporary arguments in philosophy of mind, but with more explicit theological concerns and reasoning.

Consistent with the principle of predicate-in-notion, Leibniz argues that changes in nature must arise from what is natural to the genus of a thing.[56] He states that 'God is not arbitrarily free to give to substance one set of qualities or another indifferently' for God has already freely bestowed objects certain natures, and so God 'will never give them any [modifications] but those which are natural to them, that is to say, which can be derived from their [God-given] nature'.[57] Leibniz here is not trying to limit God's power or freedom but denying the implication that God would act arbitrarily, that is 'without rhyme or reason' and either make modifications to substances which had not been foreseen and prepared for in the creation of the universe. It is not that Leibniz denies the possibility of miracles; to the contrary he continually qualifies statements to allow for the possibility, but he holds 'that God should *usually* perform miracles would certainly be without rhyme or reason'.[58] Leibniz argues that miracles should not be built into our systematic or scientific understandings of nature, for this is to make a kind of category error. Leibniz writes that to fail to distinguish the natural and conceivable from the inexplicable and miraculous 'would be to maintain something worse than occult qualities and accordingly to renounce philosophy and reason, and to provide refuges for ignorance and idleness'.[59] Any modifications which do occur, then, must be 'conceivable, if we were admitted into the secret of things'.[60] That is, we may not be able to explain consciousness precisely, but we must hold the form of an explanation that is conceivable. For something to obtain a new property, quality or capacity – say the capacity for thought – it must have hidden within its nature something which makes such a modification conceivable and natural to it. Leibniz is arguing for panpsychism, against theistic emergent dualism whereby God intermittently creates each animal mind from nothing, on the basis of his theology of the uniqueness of creation *ex nihilo* and his commitment to the rationality, power and foreknowledge of God.[61]

56. Leibniz, *New Essays*; Latta, 398.
57. Leibniz, *New Essays*; Latta, 399.
58. Leibniz, *New Essays*; Latta, 399.
59. Leibniz, *New Essays*; Latta, 399.
60. Leibniz, *New Essays*; Latta, 399.
61. These theological concerns manifest through his philosophical principles, the Principle of Sufficient Reason and the Principle of Predicate-in-Notion. One might say that these philosophical principles function as intermediaries between Leibniz's theology and his panpsychism. These principles arise out of Leibniz's doctrine of God and, when put to work in Leibniz's understanding of nature, result in a panpsychist metaphysic.

What we find in Leibniz is a thoroughly panpsychist ontology, motivated by theological concerns guarding the rationality, power and wisdom of God through a single, comprehensive created order. While the principles of sufficient reason and predicate-in-notion are thoroughly philosophical, they are also derived from theological commitments and serve theological ends. Leibniz argues for a theological panpsychism on the basis that a panpsychist universe is most fitting or perfect, by giving maximum glory to God and therefore it is the type of universe that God has sufficient reason to create. The radical uniqueness of the act of creation and foreknowledge of God undergirds Leibniz's version of the argument from continuity as the front-loading of creation. All later developments in the diversity of the natural world are contained in the earliest created monads. A panpsychist continuity between humanity and monads removes any need for additional acts of creation or the addition of new substances to explain human rationality. The indwelling, secondary, powers of a panpsychist creation undergird Leibniz's view of providence as a pre-established harmony. Last, Leibniz disavows the possibility of radical emergence of mind from inert matter not as a metaphysical impossibility, but as contrary to the rationality of God. In all these arguments, Leibniz depicts panpsychism as the ontological conclusion of his theological commitment to a single comprehensive created order, which best reflects the power and goodness of the Creator.

Panpsychism as a sacramental ontology

When panpsychism is moulded to serve the theology of a single comprehensive creation, made from nothing but the free and transcendent will of God, the resulting ontology is thoroughly sacramental. That is, all finite substances symbolize, or point beyond themselves, to their transcendent, supernatural source. This final theological aspect of Leibniz's panpsychism arises out of the amalgamation of the indwelling powers that panpsychism posits throughout reality, and the radical dependency of those powers that the doctrine of creation *ex nihilo* prescribes. The universe is *compatible* with God's presence and in so doing does not stand in competition to God but is sustained as a panpsychist, sacramental, universe.[62] This combination of statements, bolstered by claims of continuity across the created order, results in the view that all points, bodies or subjects of creation are sacramentally open to the indwelling power of God. Panpsychism facilitates a form of sacramentality by suggesting that it is at the point of interiority that all things remain dependent upon and open to the divine presence. Insofar as these indwelling powers of panpsychism also exist on a scale with perception and

---

62. I say *compatible with*, rather than participates in, God as a way to affirm that creation does not share or take on divine qualities, but God in his very presence remains 'at a distance'. See Kathryn Sonderegger, *Systematic Theology: The Doctrine of God* (Minneapolis, MN: Augsburg Fortress, 2015), 108–11, 127.

consciousness, this fundamental mentality allows for a view of creation as filled with praise and with knowledge of the glory of God.[63]

It is, perhaps unsurprisingly, in the unfinished collection of writings known as *Catholic Demonstrations* that Leibniz's sacramentalism comes through strongest. Leibniz wrote that the real presence in the Eucharist reveals that God is 'diffused through everything'.[64] God is present to the world through the sensory accidents that are not God.[65] Drawing upon the more Platonic stream in Christian theology, Leibniz saw creation as the 'Ideas of God' such that 'an act of God is in the creature although God is everywhere'.[66] Moreover, the substance of a thing is an idea in the concurrent mind of God, such that all of creation stands in union with God.[67] Therefore, humanity need not escape the world in order to know God, but 'the beatific vision or the intuition of God, face to face, is the contemplation of the universal Harmony of things', for the beauty and harmony of all things is a reflection of the Invisible God.[68] Christia Mercer argues from this that God, for Leibniz, is found as much in the diversity as in the unity of creation, 'like an infinite melody played in infinitely complex ways'.[69] Whether the metaphor is auditory, as an 'Echo', or visual as a 'mirror', Leibniz depicted the minds of creation

63. The idea of all creation as a community that offers praise to God is most famously expressed in Francis of Assisi's *Canticle of the Creatures*. However, one finds the idea of a sacramental and doxologically ordered universe in conjunction with panpsychist thinking scattered throughout the Christian tradition.

64. Leibniz, *On transubstantiation*, VI i. 511; quoted in Mercer, *Leibniz's Metaphysics*, 224.

65. According to Hans Boersma, a recent version of this sacramental, eucharistic ontology is found in Henri de Lubac. See Hans Boersma, 'Sacramental Ontology: Nature and the Supernatural in the Ecclesiology of Henri de Lubac', *New Blackfriars* 88, no. 1015 (2007): 242–73. For a similar contemporary proposal, see Catherine Pickstock 'Thomas Aquinas and the Quest for the Eucharist', in *The Radical Orthodoxy Reader*, ed. John Milbank and Simon Oliver (London: Routledge, 2009), 270–1.

66. Leibniz, *Notes on the Eucharist* (supplement); Loemker, 184.

67. Leibniz, *On transubstantiation*, Loemker, 179, 183; Leibniz, *Notes on the Eucharist*, Loemker 184.

68. Leibniz, *Conspectus*, quoted in Mercer, *Leibniz's Metaphysics*, 213; GW, VI, i. 499. Later, around 1690 in *On the True Theologia Mystica*, Leibniz would write, 'The divine perfections are concealed in all things, but very few know how to discover them there' because 'only the inner light which God himself kindles in us has the power to give us right knowledge of God.' See Loemker, 608.

69. Mercer, *Leibniz's Metaphysics*, 215. She notes that Philo made the same argument centuries earlier when he wrote that 'our whole system, like a melodious chorus of men, may sing in concert one well-harmonized melody of different sounds well combined'. Her analysis, however, suggests that God is not the worshipped, but the music itself. Philo, *On the Migration of Abraham*, XVIII 104, in *The Words of Philo*, trans. C. D. Yonge (Peabody, MA: Hendrickson, 1993), 263.

as a 'reflection and refraction or multiplication' of God.[70] The minds, as the active principle of substance, of Leibniz's ontology are 'the instrument of God', that is God's active presence in the world and so are 'unified with God'.[71]

Leibniz employed his panpsychist metaphysic to depict a universally sacramental ontology, in an attempt to pacify the divisions between Lutherans, Reformed and Roman Catholics over the Eucharist. Leibniz's idea was that when Christ proclaims the words 'this is my body', then the mind, which is the substantial form and principle of action, in the elements is replaced by the mind of Christ. It is because Leibniz argues that *all* substances must be united with a mind (and this is one of Leibniz's arguments for the existence of God) that all bodies and ideas are a sacramental 'union of God with creature'.[72] Transubstantiation occurs when the sustaining and concurrent mind to which a substance is unified is changed from the mind of God (as primary act) to the mind of Christ. This constitutes a real multipresence, a substantial change without altering the accidents, that makes the elements numerically the same substantial form (numerically the same body) as the crucified and glorified body of Christ.[73] Leibniz's understanding of the sacrament of Eucharist is founded upon a wider sacramental panpsychism.[74]

Conclusion

The benefit of Leibniz's metaphysical system for contemporary theology is argued for by James K. A. Smith. Smith describes Leibniz's thought (read through the eyes of Deleuze) as containing 'the resources for countering a Platonic and modern disenchantment of the world through the re-enchantment of nature, emphasizing the creational character of reality by an affirmation of the integrity of immanence'.[75] Smith urges the proponents of the Radical Orthodoxy movement in particular to adopt a Deleuze-interpreted Leibnizian ontology, in order to articulate their idea of the 'suspension of matter' through participation in God.[76] In envisioning

70. Quoted in Mercer, *Leibniz's Metaphysics*, 218, taken from the second note for the *Elements of Nature Law*, VI i 438.

71. Leibniz, *On the incarnation*, VI.i.534; quoted in Mercer, *Leibniz's Metaphysics*, 221.

72. GW, VI, i., 508–12 (I.8), Loemker, 179.

73. Irena Backus, *Leibniz: Protestant Theologian* (Oxford: Oxford University Press, 2016), 18–20.

74. This is rather differently expressed, but without significant theological changes, in Leibniz's complex exchange with Des Bosses over the role of the *vinculum*, as Christ as the substantial bond of union, in transubstantiation. G. W. Leibniz, *The Leibniz-Des Bosses Correspondence*, ed. and intro. Brandon C. Look and Donald Rutherford (New Haven, CT: Yale University Press, 2007), lvii–lxxii.

75. Smith, *Introducing Radical Orthodoxy*, 207.

76. Radical Orthodoxy is a contemporary theological movement seeking to rediscover the idea that 'if matter is to be more than inert, and even capable of subjectivity and meaning, then it must be innately more than a spatially or mechanically limited substance'.

what is required for the future of Radical Orthodoxy, John Milbank too has called for a 'nuanced version of panpsychic vitalism in which a self-organising power operates with different degrees of intensity at every level of physical reality from the inorganic to the consciously rational'.[77] The rediscovery of panpsychism as a sacramental ontology by the proponents of Radical Orthodoxy is one possible future articulation of a theological panpsychism, which could draw upon the historical resources fronted in this chapter and be clearly distinct from either pantheist or process thought.[78]

This historical interlude has explored the way that Leibniz's system of monads, as one idiosyncratic version of panpsychism, was employed to serve theological arguments amenable to a broad understanding of Christian orthodoxy. Leibniz is not alone in this endeavour, but his panpsychism certainly ran deeper and was expressed more explicitly than in most, and as such Leibniz served the purposes of this interlude well. Panpsychism was both derived from Leibniz's commitments to the transcendence, foreknowledge and rationality of God and employed to bolster his affirmation of creation *ex nihilo*, the view of creation as a complete and comprehensive order, and a sacramental ontology. These three theological claims remain important theological principles in the remaining chapters, which explore the benefit of panpsychism for contemporary discussions in divine action and ecological theology.

John Milbank, 'Materialism and Transcendence', *Theology and the Political: The New Debate*, ed. Creston Davis, John Milbank and Slavoj Žižek (Durham, NC: Duke University Press, 2005), 394–5.

77. John Milbank, 'The Grandeur of Reason and the Perversity of Rationalism: Radical Orthodoxy's First Decade', in *The Radical Orthodoxy Reader*, ed. John Milbank and Simon Oliver (London: Routledge, 2009), 377.

78. Insofar as Kathryn Sonderegger's 'theological compatibilism' (see n.62) provides a stronger affirmation of the Creator-creature distinction than Radical Orthodoxy's theology of participation, this may be preferable. But, panpsychism would be a helpful ontological resource for both models.

Chapter 4

INDWELLING CREATION: PANPSYCHISM AND DIVINE ACTION

Divine action is one of the most discussed topics in recent theology, and it is common to assert that it is a discussion in crisis.[1] Located at the heart of the gospel, many have noted that 'the very idea of God stands or falls with the idea that God acts in relation to the world'.[2] Moreover, theologians must do more than claim that God acts in a vague and ubiquitous manner, since unless some historical events are more decisive than others for understanding who God is, then 'all is thrown back on man rather than on God'.[3] What is required is a suitably differentiated account of the variety of divine acts that forms the basis of the biblical and ecclesial witness to who God is.[4] An interweaving plurality of models of divine action may be required to represent the diverse ways God is depicted as interacting with the world by the biblical authors.

It would be foolhardy to claim that by reconceiving the creation as a panpsychist universe all the questions surrounding divine action can be solved; panpsychism is not a *deus ex machina*. The acts of God affirmed by the Christian tradition are too varied and the resulting questions to be asked too wide-ranging for any one single solution.[5] However, philosophy of mind has long been considered a

---

1. This is the oft-cited conclusion in Nicholas Saunders, *Divine Action & Modern Science* (Cambridge: Cambridge University Press, 2002), 215.

2. Brian Hebblethwaite and Edward Henderson, eds, *Divine Action: Studies Inspired by the Philosophical Theology of Austin Farrer* (Edinburgh: T&T Clark, 1990), 1.

3. Colin E. Gunton, *Being and Becoming: The Doctrine of God in Charles Hartshorne and Karl Barth* (London: SCM Press, 2001), 47.

4. It is customary to organize the various acts of God into typologies, such as distinguishing between general and special divine action, or between preservation, concursus and gubernation. Since these given categories do not always map on as neatly as one might hope to the events of divine action given in Scripture and personal testimonies, and instead tend to collapse non-identical acts into a single treatment, this chapter's own construction avoids relying on these overarching typologies and will seek to refer as specifically as possible to the divine action in question. This is not to say that such typologies are not helpful in some circumstances.

5. This point is well made by William J. Abraham who writes that it is wrong to suggest 'that there is something like "the problem of divine action" … there is no one problem of

parallel discourse to divine action, such that when exploring the implications of a particular ontology for Christian theology, divine action is a pertinent area of investigation. There are two conclusions from this chapter's enquiry. First, panpsychism is a flexible metaphysical backdrop that would be of benefit to a range of theological proposals in the area of divine action. Second, panpsychism's distinctive contribution allows for a greater emphasis upon the presence of the Holy Spirit as the ongoing interaction between God and all God's creatures, which is to be held in conjunction with other manifestations of divine agency.

In order to establish these conclusions, this chapter is best understood as having four tasks, or investigating four questions: (1) What is the perceived problem in discussions of divine action? (2) Given this problem, what solutions are currently offered by theologians? (3) How might panpsychism help make these specific solutions more satisfactory? (4) Finally, what is it that panpsychism brings to the overarching area of divine action? The first three sections of this chapter each discuss questions one to three in the context of different theological projects. The fourth question is discussed independently thereafter.

The first task is to understand what the problem of divine action is understood to be in contemporary theology; why is it that Christianity's claims to believe that God acts in the world today are often met with manifest scepticism (even by many Christians and theologians)? This chapter characterizes the current difficulty facing the proclamation of divine action as the effect of a shadow. If God's actions are like lights shining onto this world, but articulating this idea raises issues in different areas, then these issues can be depicted as casting a shadow over the Christian witness to divine acts. This shadow is identified as the resistance to invoking the language of *intervention* in describing how God acts in the world. Millard Erickson, for example, simply states that 'God resides outside the world and intervenes periodically within the natural processes through miracles.'[6] This seems to be a straightforward conception of divine action, so why does the crucial verb, 'intervenes', throw the proclamation of God's action into murk for many? The first three sections of this chapter categorize the issues of intervention into scientific objections, ethical concerns and theological dilemmas. Together these issues, insofar as they are perceived to be real and legitimate challenges for theology, have placed significant constraints upon contemporary accounts of divine action.[7]

divine action or divine agency; there is a cluster of issues that overlap in complex ways and that require both careful delineation and reintegration if we are to make progress'. William J. Abraham, *Divine Agency and Divine Action: Exploring and Evaluating the Debate*, vol. 1 (Oxford: Oxford University Press, 2017), 12–13.

6. Millard J. Erickson, *Christian Theology* (Grand Rapids, MI: Baker Book House, 1985), 304.

7. The widespread resistance to the language of intervention has been challenged by Alvin Plantinga. Alvin Plantinga, 'What Is "Intervention"?', *Theology and Science* 6, no. 4 (2008): 369–401. Writing on divine action after this publication certainly requires theologians to be clearer about what the problem with intervention language is taken to be, which is the first task of this chapter.

The challenge has been – and continues to be – articulating a model of God's redemptive personal engagement with the world without invoking the language of intervention. The second task of this chapter is to evaluate three prominent answers, each of which is written as a response to a different aspect of the shadow of interventionism: Robert J. Russell's response to scientific objections by use of quantum indeterminacy, David Ray Griffin's answer to ethical concerns through a process account of divine persuasion and Kathryn Tanner's account of double agency as the best way to hold together theological claims of power, grace and freedom.

The third task of this chapter is to consider if and how panpsychism could be a beneficial metaphysic for each of these three theologians to adopt in their effort to dispel the shadow of interventionist language. This is not a syncretistic argument since the three models of divine action are constructed as incompatible alternatives by their various proponents. This variety is deliberate since it serves to show the theological flexibility of panpsychism. The intention is not to construct a single, new, all-inclusive panpsychist model of divine action – a task which I neither have the space to achieve, nor does panpsychism *alone* provide the theological resources to accomplish. To construct a new single panpsychist model of divine action would be to portray panpsychism as a *theological* alternative, rather than a metaphysical view of creation that may be of benefit to various theological positions. Due to my prior affirmation of the doctrine of creation *ex nihilo* and resistance of naturalism, I am only able (or willing) to engage in the latter sort of investigation and subsume this metaphysical ontology of panpsychism within different theological proposals, not *vice versa*.

The fourth task, considered in the final section, is to gather together the various strands of this argument to identify panpsychism's distinctive contribution to discussions of divine action. In so doing, we are left with the conclusion that what panpsychism uniquely offers is a robust way to articulate an interactive divine presence. By envisioning an interior depth to all created beings, panpsychism allows theologians to extend the concept of the presence of the Holy Spirit as the means of divine action in the life of the believer to the whole of creation. In this way, panpsychism dispels a bit more of the gloom cast by the shadow of interventionism.

Scientific objections and quantum solutions: Robert J. Russell

Robert J. Russell defines divine intervention as when 'God performs such acts by intervening in or suspending the laws of nature'.[8] This definition presupposes theological *incompatibilism*, such that divine action and creaturely action compete

8. Robert J. Russell, 'Introduction', in *Chaos and Complexity: Scientific Perspectives on Divine Action*, ed. Robert John Russell, Nancey Murphy and William R. Stoeger, SJ (Vatican City State/Berkeley, CA: Vatican Observatory/Centre for Theology and the Natural Sciences, 1997), 10. This definition is often traced back to David Hume's rejection of miracles as the 'transgression of a law of nature by a particular volition of the Deity'. David Hume, *An*

as alternative explanations for events. The central question raised by this common definition of divine intervention is, what do we mean by 'laws of nature' such that they seem to compete with God? Natural laws can be understood in a variety of ways; do natural laws prescribe or describe the activity of nature or are they just useful in scientific models such that we cannot be sure they refer accurately to reality at all?[9] Due to commitments to epistemological realism and the contingency of the natural order, many theologians reject the anti-realist, instrumentalist or prescriptive interpretations of natural laws. Instead, contemporary theologians working in the dialogue between science and religion typically support the view that natural laws describe the regularities that exist in the created world. However, these regularities may be neither ironclad nor identical to our scientific descriptions, which reduce to deterministic equations.[10]

This understanding of natural laws already introduces a measure of ambiguity and flexibility into the mechanistic description of the natural world offered by Newtonian physics. And yet, theologians still find themselves doing conceptual gymnastics to avoid implying that God's actions 'break' natural laws or intervene in nature. Why? There is nothing within science itself that prohibits God's action over and above the causal powers of the creation and our description of how they usually function. Yet, the fear of interventionist language remains because the idea that God suspends nature's regular processes seems to threaten some of the core philosophical presuppositions upon which scientific research proceeds, as well as some of the most long-standing and celebrated ways of construing harmony between the natural sciences and belief in God. I will briefly outline the theological foundations and philosophical presuppositions of these scientific objections to divine intervention, and then explore the non-interventionist model of divine action proposed by Robert J. Russell.

The concept of natural laws in Western thought was developed upon the theological foundation of belief in a divine lawgiver. One of the most celebrated ways of construing harmony between science and theology is the argument that the search for underlining principles in the natural order in the early modern period

Enquiry Concerning Human Understanding and Concerning the Principles of Morals, ed. L. A. Selby-Bigge (Oxford: Clarendon Press, 1902), 115–16. John Wilkins, one of the founding members of the Royal Society, was another early voice in defining miracles as 'violation' or 'disordering' the 'universal laws of nature'. Peter Harrison, 'Newtonian Science, Miracles, and the Laws of Nature', *Journal of the History of Ideas* 56, no. 4 (1995): 535.

    9. See Rom Harré, *Laws of Nature* (London: Duckworth, 1993).

    10. A good example of this discussion is found in William R. Stoeger, 'Contemporary Physics and the Ontological Status of the Laws of Nature', in *Quantum Cosmology and the Laws of Nature: Scientific Perspectives on Divine Action*, ed. Robert J. Russell, Nancey Murphy and C. J. Isham (Vatican City State/ Berkeley, CA: Vatican Observatory/Centre for Theology and the Natural Sciences, 1996), 207–34. See also John Polkinghorne, 'The Laws of Nature and the Laws of Physics', in *Quantum Cosmology*, 429–40.

was only made possible because of the widespread belief in a rational, faithful and all-powerful Creator.[11] The regularities of the natural order serve as testament to the 'faithful and trustworthy action' of God.[12] In the preface of the second edition of Isaac Newton's *Principia Mathematica*, Roger Cotes wrote that from 'the perfectly free will of God ... those laws, which we call the laws of Nature, have flowed'.[13] As the medieval distinction between created processes as secondary causation, and God's primary action which sustains and directs creation, faded from view, God's relationship with the discoveries of science became more immediate. In his correspondence with Leibniz, Samuel Clarke argued, 'What men commonly call "the course of nature" ... is nothing else but the will of God producing certain effects in a continued, regular, constant, and uniform manner.'[14] Not only does the regular uniformity of natural laws manifest the constancy of God's character and the rationality of God's will, but since natural laws are finitely inviolable – they cannot be broken or made void by finite beings – they point to the power of God. Although the fallible laws of physics constructed by the scientist may not be identical to the infallible laws of nature made by God, decoupling the two is not a straightforward matter. As such, the descriptions of science often appear in the place of the pronouncements of God.

This is all well and good, until one turns to consider the particular divine acts to which Scripture and tradition witness. These claims go beyond God's original creation and preservation of the world to describe events that stand apart from scientific descriptions of nature's usual processes. Wesley Wildman summarizes the concern of many that 'the idea of God sustaining nature and its law-like regularities with one hand while miraculously intervening, abrogating or ignoring those regularities with the other hand struck most members [of VO/CNTS project, see below] as dangerously close to outright contradiction'.[15] One could respond, as Alvin Plantinga has done, that the objection that God's intervention would be inconsistent presupposes that God could not have any good reasons for acting in a twofold way.[16] God's actions, eschatologically conceived, might be seen as consistently working to bring about the same intended end.[17] Who are we to judge

---

11. This paragraph is indebted to Alvin Plantinga, *Where the Conflict Really Lies: Science, Religion, and Naturalism* (Oxford: Oxford University Press, 2012), 275–7.

12. Robert J. Russell, *Cosmology. From Alpha to Omega: The Creative Mutual Interaction of Theology and Science* (Minneapolis, MN: Fortress Press, 2008), 119.

13. Roger Cotes, *Newton's Philosophy of Nature: Selections from His Writings* (New York: Hafner Library of Classics, 1953), 132–3.

14. Samuel Clarke, *A Demonstration of the Being and Attributes of God*, ed. Ezio Vailati (Cambridge: Cambridge University Press, 1998), 149.

15. Wesley Wildman, 'The Divine Action Project, 1988–2003', *Theology and Science* 2 (2004): 38.

16. Plantinga, 'What Is "Intervention"?', 373.

17. Colin E. Gunton, *The Triune Creator: A Historical and Systematic Study* (Grand Rapids, MI: Eerdmans, 1998), 176–7.

the consistency between God's acts? Moreover, the inconsistency objection often follows Clarke in implying that God not only mercifully sustains but also directly wills natural laws. Clarke's view should be questioned, since it leaves little scope for articulating the idea of creation as in need of redemption or as fallen in some way. These responses notwithstanding, it remains the case that objections from within the science and religion dialogue against the language of intervention are linked to an association between natural laws as signs of God's rationality, constancy and power, such that any contradiction of these laws implies irrationality, inconsistency and weakness on the part of God.

A subtle shift in the conceptual framework underpinning the natural sciences, from theological foundations to philosophical presuppositions, slowly transpired throughout the modern period. In the early part of the twentieth century this transference became manifest in the arguments of some prominent theologians against belief in divine intervention. Rudolf Bultmann, for example, identified divine action with 'myth' because supernatural causation is 'not capable of objective scientific proof'.[18] Bultmann is discussing the epistemology, or inability for objective (empirical) verification, of special divine action. In contemporary terminology we might refer to this as methodological naturalism, a term first coined by theologians seeking to protect theology against expansionist tendencies of scientism.[19] However, the presupposition that science can provide an accurate and complete description of the world apart from divine action rests upon another questionable presupposition – the principle of causal closure. Causal closure is defined by John Macquarrie as the assumption 'that whatever events occur in the world can be accounted for in terms of other events that also belong within the world'.[20] If God is spoken of at all in conjunction with causal closure/physical

---

18. Rudolf Bultmann, *Jesus Christ and Mythology* (New York: Charles Scribner's Sons, 1958), 61. This disenchantment led to the two-language problem in theologies of divine action, famously criticized by Langdon Gilkey, 'Cosmology, Ontology and the Travail of Biblical Language', *Journal of Religion* 41 (1961): 194–205. Robert J. Russell's work in founding the VO/CNTS project and providing scientific solutions to theological questions can be seen as a response to Gilkey's paper, as is clear in the title of Russell's article, 'Does "The God Who Acts" Really Act?', *Theology Today* 54 (1997): 44–65.

19. Harry Lee Poe and Chelsea Rose Mytyk, 'From Scientific Method to Methodological Naturalism: The Evolution of an Idea', *Perspectives on Science and Christian Faith* 59, no. 3 (September 2007): 213–19.

20. John Macquarrie, *Principles of Christian Theology*, 2nd edn (New York: Scribner's Sons, 1977), 248. Nicholas Saunders summarizes, 'The causally closed view of science in which every event leads to another seems to many to leave no room for God at all.' Nicholas Saunders, 'Does God Cheat at Dice? Divine Action and Quantum Possibilities', *Zygon: Journal of Religion and Science* 35, no. 3 (2000): 518. As such, Benedikt Göcke argues that causal closure 'is neither a consequence, nor a presupposition of science itself. Instead, it is a philosophical assumption that belongs to an atheistic and naturalistic worldview'. Benedikt Paul Göcke, 'The Many Problems of Special Divine Action', *European Journal for Philosophy of Religion* 7, no. 4 (Summer 2015): 32.

determinism, it is to metaphysically prop up the causal structure that the natural sciences describe, to sustain but never transform or interact with creation.[21] These naturalistic presuppositions leave theological concepts barren and vacuous.

These objections to divine intervention, arising from the theological and philosophical underpinnings of the natural sciences, have been responded to (but not critiqued) in a tremendous joint effort from the Vatican Observatory and the Centre for Theology and the Natural Sciences (VO/CNTS). The resulting publications from this project, which each bears the subtitle *Scientific Perspectives on Divine Action*, explore the fecundity of different areas in the natural sciences where God (or human minds) may objectively be said to influence the causal nexus *in a manner consistent with the scientific description of events*. This model is often referred through the acronym 'NIODA' – non-interventionist, objective, divine action.

The importance of specific scientific theories, which posit that some events 'have necessary but not sufficient natural causes' so that the future is 'influenced but underdetermined by the factors of nature acting in the present', cannot be overstated for this approach to divine action.[22] This is because proponents of NIODA accept methodological naturalism, causal closure, that most events are physically determined, and Clarke's view of natural laws as manifestations of God's direct will. As such, the language of interventionism is taken as a very serious threat to the dialogue between science and religion. It is believed that insofar as Christianity stakes its claims upon accounts of divine intervention, it places itself in conflict with the natural sciences. It is predicted that this is a war that theology is unlikely to win. If the policy is one of appeasement, then the terms of peace are seen in the search for indeterministic openings within our current scientific theories that 'make room' for God to act in a non-interventionist manner.

One of the most popular models emerging from the VO/CNTS project is the engagement with quantum mechanics (accounting for more than twenty-five of the ninety-one published chapters).[23] The leading architect of the quantum approach to special divine action is Robert J. Russell, and his efforts have been supported by Nancey Murphy, George Ellis and Thomas Tracy. Russell summarizes his model:

---

21. See William Alston's analysis of this problem, 'Divine Action, Human Freedom, and the Laws of Nature', in *Quantum Cosmology*, 185–206.

22. Thomas Tracy, 'Particular Providence and the God of the Gaps', in *Chaos and Complexity*, 289–324; Russell, *Cosmology*, 156.

23. See Robert J. Russell's table summarizing the contents of the whole project. Russell, 'Challenge and Progress in "Theology and Science"', in *Scientific Perspectives on Divine Action*, 9–17. Theological engagement with quantum mechanics for articulations of divine action goes back to the 1950s in the work of William G. Pollard, *Chance and Providence: God's Action in the World Governed by Scientific Laws* (New York: Charles Scribner's Sons, 1958); and Karl Heim, *Transformation of the Scientific World View* (London: SCM Press, 1953). Heim lent towards a more panpsychist interpretation of quantum phenomena.

If quantum mechanics is interpreted philosophically in terms of ontological indeterminism (as in one form of the Copenhagen interpretation), one can construct a bottom-up, non-interventionist, approach to mediated, objective, and direct divine action in which God's indirect acts of general and special providence at the macroscopic level arise in part from God's direct action at the quantum level.[24]

The indeterminacy of quantum phenomena, Russell suggests, provides 'intrinsic, naturally occurring gaps' in which God may act without intervening.[25] The main advantage of this model of special divine action is the fundamental and ubiquitous nature of quantum events/particles/waves: 'God is active everywhere in space and time in relation to ψ [the wave function] as it extends throughout space and evolves in time.'[26] Locating divine action in quantum events means that this one model can account for the pervasiveness of divine action in the 11 billion years of cosmic history prior to the phenomenon of life, and God can be just as effective at the far reaches of the universe as on planet earth. But what does God actually *do* at the quantum level?

I am not trained in the area of quantum physics, but an illustration can be helpful in conveying what Russell proposes. A common example of an underdetermined quantum event is the decay of uranium into thorium, which occurs by the emission of an alpha particle. In a sample of uranium atoms, there appears to be no determining sufficient physical cause for when the alpha particle will be admitted from each atom, only probabilities (known as a 'wave function').[27] Similar probabilities occur throughout the subatomic realm, which is then characterized as full of open potentiality (Heisenberg interpretation). Russell suggests that, because quantum events are underdetermined, there is space for God to act at this subatomic level *by changing the probability* (collapsing the wave function) of when the decay of uranium occurs.

If we are looking for a 'causal joint', a mechanism in the natural world where God can act 'immediately in nature', without interrupting sufficient and determinist causal networks, then Russell has clearly identified such a place – the wave function of quantum mechanics.[28] The idea is that by 'direct action' at the subatomic level, God's will can be brought about indirectly at other levels of reality (biological, historical, etc.); 'God can act providentially to determine the future course of the

---

24. Russell, *Cosmology*, 151.

25. Robert J. Russell, 'Quantum Physics and the Theology of Non-Interventionist Objective Divine Action', in *The Oxford Handbook of Religion and Science*, ed. Philip Clayton and Zachary Simpson (Oxford: Oxford University Press, 2006), 584.

26. Russell, *Cosmology*, 184.

27. Russell, *Cosmology*, 156.

28. Russell, 'Introduction', 12. Cf. Robert J. Russell, 'Cosmology from Alpha to Omega', *Zygon: Journal of Religion and Science* 29, no. 4 (December 1994): 567–8.

world through the openness of quantum reality'.[29] For the purposes of showing the flexibility of panpsychism for discussions in divine action, this section argues that Russell's proposal faces significant challenges on its own terms, which a panpsychist interpretation of quantum mechanics would resolve. However, this is not to endorse the presuppositions explored above that have led to the search for non-interventionist openings in nature. Indeed, a panpsychist interpretation of quantum mechanics moves Russell's account of divine agency away from the problematic assumptions of incompatibilism and naturalism, towards a more adequate theological picture.

Russell's theological incompatibilism inclines him towards the Copenhagen interpretation of quantum indeterminacy because it posits causal gaps in the natural order; God need not interrupt the causal nexus, because God created spaces in the causal chain at the quantum level. This leaves Russell's proposal vulnerable to the 'God-of-the-gaps' objection, where God's actions are limited to the (potentially temporary) phenomena science cannot explain.[30] Russell responds to the god-of-the-gaps accusation by drawing a strong distinction between epistemological gaps in our current knowledge and ontological gaps that arise from what we do know. This distinction, however, is not as clear-cut as Russell suggests since quantum mechanics remains a mysterious scientific field (full of epistemological gaps) and the reality of indeterminacy is highly debated.[31] Russell's distinction between 'epistemic gaps' and 'ontological "bubbles"' slips easily through our fingers.[32]

Panpsychism is closely associated with two of the other interpretations of quantum mechanics (the mind-dependent views of von Nuemann, Wigner, Wheeler and Stapp and Bohm's theory of 'hidden variables'). As such, theologians invested in quantum models of special divine action should consider the implications of panpsychism.[33] Moreover, these interpretations reject the gappy view of nature posited by Heisenberg's interpretation; one might even say that consciousness is employed to plug the apparent gap of indeterminacy. A panpsychist interpretation of quantum divine action could depict God as working with or within the psyche of quantum phenomena.

Interestingly, this more panpsychist-compatibilist approach is gestured towards by Russell in response to the challenge, launched by two VO/CNTS colleagues,

---

29. Russell, 'Cosmology from Alpha to Omega', 567–8.

30. Veli-Matti Kärkkäinen, *Creation and Humanity: A Constructive Christian Theology for a Pluralistic World*, vol. 3 (Grand Rapids, MI: Eerdmans, 2015), 180. See more on 'god-of-the-gaps' in Chapter 3, Section 'Three arguments for panpsychism from a comprehensive created order'.

31. As physicist Richard Feynman famously quipped, 'Nobody understands quantum mechanics.' Richard Feynman, *The Character of Physical Law* (Cambridge, MA: MIT Press, 1967), 129.

32. Russell, 'Cosmology from Alpha to Omega', 567–8.

33. I have developed this line of enquiry in Leidenhag, 'The Revival of Panpsychism and Its Relevance for the Science-Religion Dialogue', *Theology & Science* 17, no. 1 (2019): 90–106.

to specify the extent of God's involvement at the quantum level. If God acts directly in all quantum events, this leads dangerously close to 'omnideterminism'.[34] Alternatively, if God is only acting in some quantum measurements (because only a few quantum events are indeterminate), then John Polkinghorne has argued that this leads to a woefully 'episodic account of providential agency' by a 'hole-and-corner deity, fiddling around at the rickety roots of the cosmos'.[35]

In response to this challenge, Russell follows Nancey Murphy in arguing that God is active in all quantum events, but not in an all-determining fashion. Instead, he writes that this model involves 'a continuous creative (divine) presence within each (quantum) event, co-determining the outcome of these elementary physical processes'.[36] This is an elegant and promising solution. However, there is a large question mark over the words 'within' and 'co-determining' here. How is the 'within each (quantum) event' to be understood? It seems unlikely, given the non-material nature of divine presence and from what we know of quantum particles/waves, that this can be interpreted in a purely spatial way. A better interpretation would be to posit that quantum particles/waves have a 'within' by virtue of having experiences, since this is how we use the word 'within' when referring to God's presence within human beings – 'a subjective inwardness rather than an inner receptacle'.[37] But this, of course, is panpsychism.

Furthermore, any implication for Russell's and Murphy's account of cooperation between elementary physical processes and Divine agency can only be metaphorical. It is unclear that 'co-determining' as used here sufficiently avoids the charge of determinism when there is only one active agent, as incompatibilism prescribes. Again, it seems that panpsychism, which posits a genuine 'within' and the possibility of genuine cooperation (in so far as there are indwelling powers, but not rational volition) at the quantum level, may aid Russell in this regard.[38]

If quantum indeterminacies are interpreted as the result of gaps (or openings) rather than of fundamental interiority, then Russell must say that God *only* works

34. Russell rejects Karl Heim's and E. L. Mascall's employment of quantum indeterminacies to support divine omni-determinism. Russell, *Cosmology*, 153–4.

35. John Polkinghorne, *Science and Creation: The Search for Understanding* (London: SPCK, 1988), 58; John Polkinghorne, *Science and Providence: God's Interaction with the World* (West Conshohocken, PA: Templeton Press, 2005), 27–8; John Polkinghorne, *Reason and Reality: The Relationship between Science and Theology* (London: SPCK Classics, 2011), 40–1.

36. Russell, *Cosmology*, 156.

37. Ian T. Ramsey, *Models for Divine Activity* (London: SCM Press, 1973), 12.

38. Nancey Murphy implies an indwelling powers concept when she describes God 'activating or actualising one or another of the quantum entity's innate powers at particular instants'. Nancey Murphy, 'Divine Action in the Natural Order', in *Chaos and Complexity*, 340.

directly at the quantum level, since it is only here that such openings appear.[39] But is the emission of an alpha particle (or similar subatomic events) a sufficient basis for God to achieve transformation or effect change at the level which human persons interact with and are concerned with? The formal argument against divine action through quantum events on these grounds has become known as 'the amplification problem'. This is the argument that 'whatever God might do at the quantum level, nature by and large prevents those actions from affecting the macroscopic realm'.[40] The reason that nature prevents the amplification of quantum events to have macroscopic effects is because of emergent 'protectorates', which make higher-level fluctuations less sensitive to lower-level changes.[41] Therefore, even if the subatomic world is truly indeterministic, this indeterminism seems to level out into deterministic regularities at the atomic and molecular level.[42]

If quantum indeterminacy is the only means through which God could act within the universe, then the amplification problem would be a fatal blow to the power and effectiveness of divine agency. However, Russell and other theologians invested in this model limit their claim to arguing that 'quantum physics contributes a necessary – though not a sufficient – piece to the explanatory puzzle of how God acts in the world'.[43] Russell makes additional appeals to concepts of strong emergence in particular. There is an unrealized tension in this move. Strong emergence is based on the idea of causal irreducibility and often makes appeals to emergent protectorates, which prevent the different levels of reality from collapsing

39. The concern that Russell only leaves room for divine action at the quantum level is furthered by his argument that as consciousness evolves in complex organisms God must 'increasingly refrain' from acting. Accordingly, and contrary to the majority of the Christian tradition, God, for Russell, is less involved in human affairs and interpersonal relationships, and more invested in mechanistic changes of events. This does not seem like a promising conclusion for Russell's view of divine action. Russell, *Cosmology*, 189.

40. Jeffrey Koperski, 'Divine Action and the Quantum Amplification Problem', *Theology and Science* 13, no. 4 (2015): 379. See also Timothy Sansbury, 'The False Promise of Quantum Mechanics', *Zygon: Journal of Religion and Science* 42 (2007): 111–21.

41. Robert W. Batterman coined the term 'Protectorates' in 'Emergence, Singularities, and Symmetry Breaking', *Foundations of Physics* 41, no. 6 (2010): 1031–50. See also Robert B. Laughlin and David Pines, 'The Theory of Everything', *Proceedings of the National Academy of Sciences of the United States of America* 97, no. 1 (2000): 28–31.

42. There are some good examples of amplification, such as individual photons falling onto the retina of a mammal or determining a genetic mutation. Russell makes a great deal of these examples of amplification in his account of theistic evolution. Russell, *Cosmology*, chapter 6.

43. Robert J. Russell, 'Christian Discipleship and the Challenge of Physics: Formation, Flux, and Focus', *Perspectives on Science and Christian Faith* 42, no. 3 (1990): 150.

by restricting the 'traffic' between them.[44] By contrast, this quantum model relies upon reductionism in claiming that God's direct action at the micro level can have indirect effects at the macro level through amplification. Put simply, if emergent phenomena do not reduce down, then quantum events do not amplify up.

While quantum-based and mind-based accounts can be developed in parallel, Russell states that 'we will eventually need to work out the detailed relations between these models by integrating them into a consistent and coherent, adequate and applicable metaphysical framework'.[45] It seems that this may be an impossible task if the philosophy of mind employed is strong emergence theory. Instead, panpsychism, which shares with this quantum model the view that microscopic entities (minds at the micro level) play an important constituting role in macroscopic entities (animal minds); they amplify up. Panpsychism might be a better ally for Russell in understanding how God's action includes, but also goes beyond, interaction with quantum phenomena.

Adapting quantum-based accounts of divine action to work with panpsychist interpretations of quantum mechanics remains compatible with Russell's commitment to non-interventionism and provides a way to integrate his theory with more mind-based and personal approaches. However, the language of non-interventionism seems increasingly unnecessary as panpsychism draws Russell towards a more compatibilist view of divine action; God acts in and with the minds of quantum phenomena in a way that neither replaces, suspends, nor fills in the causal gaps of natural processes. Quantum-based models of divine action should be retained in so far as they are useful for highlighting God's omnipresence. However, they fail in this task if they limit God to the microscopic realm. By integrating mind-based and quantum-based models of divine action in a more compatibilist fashion, a panpsychist model of divine action is as effective in articulating God's presence at the interpersonal level of reality as at the quantum level of reality. God competes with neither free human action nor scientific explanations, for God sustains and indwells the agencies and powers of the natural world.

Ethical concerns and the process of persuasion: David Ray Griffin

The section above explored the shadow of interventionist language in the theology-science dialogue and investigated how the Copenhagen interpretation of quantum mechanics has been used to find a non-interventionist workaround. Although the definition of intervention, as breaking natural laws or interfering in a closed causal network, may arise from the dialogue with natural science, the pejorative tone of this language is sourced from elsewhere. That is, while language

---

44. This is clear for example in the work of William C. Wimsatt. See *Re-Engineering Philosophy of Limited Beings: Piecewise Approximations to Reality* (Boston, MA: Harvard University Press, 2007).

45. Russell, *Cosmology*, 159.

of intervention has been deemed problematic on (supposedly) scientific grounds, it is judged as incriminating largely on moral grounds. The moral ambiguity of interventionist language relates to both the implied *manner* and the *occasionality* of divine intervention. The following section evaluates the process theology of David Ray Griffin, which is pitched as the moral alternative to interventionism. It is argued that the panexperientialism adopted by process metaphysics is less suited than its subject-based counterpart (subject panpsychism) to deal with the ethical concerns of process theologians. It is also argued that the doctrine of God that process theology offers does not provide the balm needed to meet the needs of a suffering world.

The first moral concern that many theologians have with the language of intervention as a description of the manner in which God acts in the world is revealed by the frequency to which 'violation' and 'coercion' are employed as synonyms of intervention.[46] Process theology has been particularly vocal in rejecting the language of divine intervention as a 'divine intrusion into a manipulation of the world'.[47] Intervention, it seems, has malicious overtones that imply that any such action from God, regardless of the outcome, would entail an abuse of creation in some way. Process theologians place an emphasis on the integrity of the world as something that must be respected, even by God. From this emphasis, the concern follows that any unilateral action by God within or upon nature would be intrusive, violent or akin to the invasion from a foreign power; indeed, 'military intervention' is a powerful connotation for this verb.

In contemporary scholarship, I suspect that the identification between intervention and violation arises not only from this military metaphor but also from another powerful metaphor – that is the association between nature and the female body. Ecofeminist theology has brought this association into the forefront of the contemporary imagination through the powerful linkage between ecological violation and the violation of female bodies.[48] The gendering of God

46. David Ray Griffin, *Two Great Truths: A New Synthesis of Scientific Naturalism and Christian Faith* (Louisville, KY: Westminster John Knox Press, 2004), 2, 4, 23, 50, 88; David Ray Griffin, *Reenchantment without Supernaturalism: A Process Philosophy of Religion* (Ithaca, NY: Cornell University Press, 2001), 5, 27, 40, 43, 52, 54, 78, 116, 124, 133, 136, 148, 152, 153, 292; David Ray Griffin, *Panentheism and Scientific Naturalism: Rethinking Evil, Morality, Religious Experience, Religious Pluralism, and the Academic Study of Religion* (Claremont, CA: Process Century Press, 2014), 51, 62, 72, 116, 187, 208, 230, 274; David Ray Griffin, *God, Power, and Evil: A Process Theology* (Louisville, KY: Westminster John Knox Press, 2004), 4–9.

47. Norman Pittenger, *The Lure of Divine Love: Human Experience and Christian Faith in a Process Perspective* (Edinburgh: Pilgrim Press, 1979), 97.

48. See the pioneering article, Sherry Ortner, 'Is Female to Male as Nature Is to Culture?', *Woman, Culture and Society*, ed. M. Z. Rosaldo and L. Lamphere (Stanford, CA: Stanford University Press, 1974), 67–87. For collections of ecofeminist writings, see Judith Plant, *Healing the Wounds: The Promise of Ecofeminism* (Philadelphia, PA: New Society, 1989);

and nature, as spotlighted in ecofeminism, has clearly problematized the language of intervention. In his defence of miracles, and divine intervention in nature, C. S. Lewis writes, 'If Nature brings forth miracles then doubtless it is as "natural" for her to do so when impregnated by the masculine force beyond her as it is for a woman to bear children to a man.'[49] Lewis would never have intended to describe God as acting abusively or criminally, but the language of intervention has, nevertheless, been tainted with resonances of theological sexism. The legacy of androcentric depictions of God and gynocentric caricatures of nature has created an often unspoken, almost subconscious, concern that the language of intervention implies a male god violating a female world.[50] As a result, language of divine action as the empowerment of creation through cooperation, and even the need for creation to *consent* to God's action, has become a central part of theological rhetoric in recent discussions.[51]

A second moral concern arises from the apparent occasionality of God's intervening. This objection is distilled from the cry of suffering that asks, 'how could God let this happen?' Put more formally, why does a good and powerful God intervene to prevent some instances of suffering and allow others? This seems the sharp pastoral edge of the larger philosophical question regarding the existence of evil.[52] It has been argued that if God is willing and able to intervene at certain points and places, then it is morally unacceptable that God has not acted more often to prevent instances of grievous and meaningless suffering.[53] The point has been pushed further to argue that an interventionist God should be considered directly culpable for all the suffering in the history of the universe, because when God could have intervened to prevent it God chose to simply spectate.[54] A God who only occasionally intervenes to prevent evil or heal suffering is seen by many to be arbitrarily cruel, unjust and prone to favouritism.[55]

and Irene Diamond and Gloria F. Orenstein, *Reweaving the World: The Emergence of Ecofeminism* (San Francisco, CA: Sierra Club Books, 1990).

49. C. S. Lewis, *Miracles: A Preliminary Study* (London: Centenary Press, 1947), 75; cf. 33–5, 72.

50. For the theological discussion of the female-nature association, see Rosemary Radford Ruether, *Sexism and God-Talk: Toward a Feminist Theology* (London: SCM Press, 1983), 72–85, 259–67. Ruether describes 'the sin of intervention in nature' as a product of 'male culture' (76).

51. It is perhaps for this reason then that process feminism has been one of the strongest strands of process thought.

52. I suspect that although issues of evil and suffering clearly overlap, they should not be collapsed into one another and may in the end require slightly different theological responses.

53. Brain Hebblethwaite, *Evil, Suffering, and Religion*, rev. edn (London: SPCK, 2000), 93, 97.

54. Griffin, *Reenchantment without Supernaturalism*, 222–3.

55. James A. Keller, *Problems of Evil and the Power of God* (Aldershot: Ashgate, 2007), 57–61. George Ellis writes, intervention 'suggest[s] a capriciousness in God's action, in

An exposition of process metaphysics and the problematic doctrine of God in process theology was given in the Introduction. It was argued that process theology's acceptance of the naturalistic principle, the decision to subsume God under an all-expansive metaphysic, was a fatal error.[56] What has not yet been discussed is the motivation for adopting naturalism and the appeal that process theology continues to have for many.[57] I would wager that the central attraction of process theology for many is its provision of a constructive alternative to the two ethical concerns arising from interventionist accounts of divine action.

Process theology makes two distinct moves in constructing an alternative account of divine action. First, rather than positing reasons that justify God's permittance of suffering (such as John Hick's Irenaean defence or Alvin Plantinga's free-will defence) process theology delimits the power of God. According to process theology, God could not create a world without suffering and 'God *cannot* unilaterally prevent all evil'.[58] There is no divine favouritism or injustice because God is always doing everything in God's power to prevent suffering and maximize flourishing, but often God's efforts are not enough.[59] This first move responds to the second ethical concern regarding the apparent occasionality of God's intervention to prevent suffering.

God's efforts are not attempts to coerce, intervene or overpower evil, but to *persuade* creatures (actual occasions) to 'act' (or, rather to 'become') in a way that promotes individual flourishing, environmental harmony and brings about greater levels of freedom and value in the universe overall.[60] We see the importance of creaturely *consent* since it is creation that is the primary agent in the transformation of the universe, and God's action is restricted to the repertoire of persuading, informing, guiding, luring and inspiring. This second move is process theology's response to the first ethical concern regarding the manner of divine action; God's

terms of sometimes deciding to "intervene" but mostly deciding not to do so'. George Ellis, 'Ordinary and Extraordinary Divine Action', in *Chaos and Complexity*, 384.

56. As David Ray Griffin writes, it is the placing of God within an overarching metaphysics as one formative principle, among others, 'that makes this a naturalistic, as distinct from a supernaturalistic, theism'. Griffin, *Reenchantment without Supernaturalism*, 223.

57. David Ray Griffin defines naturalistic theism, of which he sees process theism as the best variant, as any theory of God that denies interventionism. Griffin, *Reenchantment without Supernaturalism*, 21.

58. Griffin, *Reenchantment without Supernaturalism*, 224.

59. 'God does the best job he can in trying to persuade the recalcitrant matter to receive the impress of the divine forms'. Pittenger, *Lure of Divine Love*, 97.

60. Whitehead famously stated that Plato's insight that 'the divine element in the world is to be conceived as a persuasive agency and not as a coercive agency. This is one of the greatest intellectual discoveries in the history of religion'. Alfred North Whitehead, *Adventures of Ideas* (New York: Free Press, [1933] 1967), 166.

action does not override the power of creatures but depends upon it.[61] In this way, process theology's panexperientialism is fundamental to its account of divine, human and other creaturely action. It is only because all things have the capacity of experience and spontaneity that they can feel the lure of God and allow God to impact the world. In what follows, I evaluate David Ray Griffin's response to these moral concerns and argue for how the adoption of subject-panpsychism may aid process theology in providing a stronger model.

The process model of divine action states that God's perfect knowledge of all possibilities (Primordial Nature) offers or informs the subjective aim of each actual occasion with ideals. These ideals are the best available self-determination, the best version of itself, within the scope of novelty appropriate to each actual occasion. That is, the reality of an actual occasion is a self-determining choice, based equally on the constraints of its past self and the novelty that God offers to it. This self-determining choice is, in fact, the only type of 'action' available to actual occasions, just as luring is the only action available to God. Panexperientialism, as opposed to panpsychism, gets process theology into difficulty here. 'Action', in process thought, cannot be predicated of agents, since there are no enduring subjects or agents but only streams of experience (or streams of action). The question remains open as to whether we can make sense of 'action' without any agents, not to mention the difficulties this creates for notions of justice or moral responsibility.[62] If process theologians were, instead, to posit enduring subjects as fundamental then they would avail themselves of both action and relational predicates, which must be predicates of agents or subjects.

It is also important to judge how successful process theology is, when evaluated as a response to the evil and suffering in the world. Philip Hefner, in a review of David Ray Griffin's monograph presenting process theology's response to the problem of evil, writes the following:

> Griffin's explanation of evil amounts, at the end, to saying that evil is a consequence of the way the worldly machinery operates ... Presumably because

---

61. As Lewis Ford summarizes, 'God proposes and the world disposes.' Lewis Ford, *The Lure of God: A Biblical Background for Process Theism* (Minneapolis, MN: Fortress Press, 1978), 21. Griffin writes that 'power is always shared power', such that an increase of power in one place necessitates the decrease of power in another; thus, God's power is in competition with the power of creatures. Griffin, 'Creation out of Nothing, Creation out of Chaos, and the Problem of Evil', in *Encountering Evil: Live Options in Theodicy*, ed. Stephen T. Davis (Louisville, KY: Westminster John Knox Press, 2001), 122.

62. The deficiency of agential (and therefore person-based) categories in process thought was, to my knowledge, first critiqued in William Hill OP, 'The Two Gods of Love: Aquinas and Whitehead', *Listening* 14 (1976): 262–3. See also Abraham, *Divine Agency and Divine Action*, vol. 1, 139–40; J. P. Moreland, 'An Enduring Self: The Achilles' Heel of Process Philosophy', *Process Studies* 17 (1988): 193–9.

process metaphysics is *descriptive* it cannot answer [the question 'why does it have to be this way?']; it can only accept what it is and describe it.[63]

Hefner's conclusion here is that the moral concern with intervention is expressed in a question that demands an agential, personal answer and to which process theology provides an answer in terms of metaphysical necessity – thus nullifying the question rather than answering it. The only comfort that process theology provides, in light of such metaphysical necessity, is that God (necessarily) suffers too. This is the Consequent Nature of God, where all the experiences of the world are received into God and inform the ongoing lure of God. Thus, the suffering of actual occasions is not lost, nor is it meaningless. However, it does seem hopeless. Process theology provides no guarantee that God's desire for good will have victory over evil. Even if every actual occasion in the universe were, for an instant, to respond positively to the lure of God the threat of great evil not only remains in the next instance but actually increases. There can be no final rest from the threat of (ever-increasing) suffering within process theology.

Process theology finds a place for suffering and evil within its metaphysical system; this is a task that traditional Christian theology continues to struggle with. However, as Ian McFarland sagely warns, 'The temptation to explain evil is the first step to empowering it.'[64] This is the result in process thought, where evil has (at least) equal power as God in influencing creatures – who alone are the majority shareholders in determining the future. To explain suffering as a metaphysical necessity over which God has little or no power is one way to respond to the injustice of suffering, but, of course, it gives no real explanation as to why suffering appears to be so unequally distributed and it takes away any grounds for hope for the future. Although the sensitivity of process theology to the moral difficulties with interventionist language is to be admired, it serves no one to handicap God in response.

The first move in the process account of divine action, to limit the power of God, therefore appears counterproductive. A panpsychist theology does not necessarily, by virtue of its ontology, accept or reject the limitation of God's power. This is an important part of the reason why I have argued for the compatibility of panpsychism and the doctrine of creation *ex nihilo*, and so disentangled panpsychism from process theology. The limitation of God's power is a separate move to the process theologian's panexperientialist proposal that God acts

---

63. Philip Hefner, 'Is Theodicy a Question of Power? Review of *God, Power and Evil: A Process* Theodicy by David Ray Griffin', *Journal of Religion* 59, no. 1 (January 1979): 90. It is for this reason that Kathryn Tanner's work, discussed below, argues that the transcendence of God is a necessary belief if theology is to criticize and act against the status quo, rather than simply describe it as a form of necessity. Kathryn Tanner, *The Politics of God: Christian Theologies and Social Justice* (Minneapolis, MN: Augsburg Fortress, 1992), 32, 67–8.

64. Ian A. McFarland, *From Nothing: A Theology of Creation* (Louisville, KY: Westminster John Knox Press, 2014), 131–2.

through persuasion. It would be possible, and I argue advisable, to combine a persuasive account of divine action with an affirmation of God's sovereignty and power. This is to leave unanswered the question as to why God allows suffering. Such reticence might be necessary in order to think again about what kind of answer is required from this injustice, and to affirm the hope that God's justice will finally end all pain.

Theological dilemmas and double agency: Kathryn Tanner

The objections from science and the ethical concerns explored above both make what Kathryn Tanner might call a shared grammatical mistake. The mistake is that in seeking to overcome the threat of invoking interventionist language, they both fall prey to naturalistic logic – namely, the logic that created causes – natural regularities or the self-determination of actual occasions – can be contrasted with God's agency. As such, God's activity is constrained by the activity of creatures. This is seen clearly in that, for Russell, God must find indeterminist openings in creation where there is an absence of created causes. Or, if there are no such openings, as in Griffin's process ontology, God must attempt to influence creatures to use their own agency as intermediaries for good.[65] In both cases, to suggest that God could do otherwise would be to depict a coercive, irrational or tyrannical intervention. The presenting issue in discussions of divine agency for Tanner is that this language of intervention *and* non-intervention is improper grammar for theological speech.[66] For Tanner, the shadow of interventionist grammar is a threat to the coherency of theology's claims about who God is as Creator and what God has done as Saviour.

As seen in the evaluation offered above, I support much in Tanner's critique of the grammar of interventionist and non-interventionist language. However, my concluding concern is that her proposal of total metaphysical discontinuity between God and creation leaves no room for an account of what God is doing as Sanctifier in interaction with creatures. That is, the model of divine action known as 'double agency' is an important part of the theologian's repertoire in providing an account of God's activity, but it cannot be the whole story; additional complementary models need to be woven together.

It is worth probing further into the theological dilemma of interventionist language as Tanner conceives of it. The motivation behind Tanner's exposition of the proper grammar of divine action is, to my mind, a soteriological dilemma.[67]

---

65. Kathryn Tanner, *God and Creation in Christian Theology: Tyranny or Empowerment?* (Oxford: Blackwell, 1988), 164–5, cf. 45–6.

66. While Tanner presents her project as one of grammar, it is clear that these grammatical rules are grounded in material and referential beliefs. Cf. Tanner, *God and Creation*, 11, 50.

67. Tanner's choice of examples, one biblical and the other from the tradition, to articulate the problem of expressing coherently the relation of divine agency to created

How can theologians make sense of the twofold claim that salvation is attributable wholly to God as an act of grace, and that salvation is performed, chosen or worked-out by the human as an act of freedom? There seem to be two agents, both of whom are described as being sufficient causes for one event; the problem is the overdetermination of salvation.[68] Tanner suggests that the in-church battles, emphasizing either the sovereignty of God or the integrity of creatures, make Christian theology seem incoherent.[69] Faced with the question of how to proclaim salvation as entirely a work of God's power achieved in the freedom of creaturely activity, Christian discourse about God's action has begun to 'splutter'.[70] The employment and over-zealous avoidance of interventionist language are both forms of such spluttering.

Tanner's aim is not merely one of internal coherence and ecumenism, but she seeks to bring the grammar of the Christian faith to bear upon the political arena of the modern world.[71] The historical transition from deriving political authority from direct divine appointment to the freedom of the democratic process remains an important part of the collective identity of Western (post-Christendom) societies. This modern political economy is part of the story of how the language of divine intervention became a kind of blasphemy. Since 'intervention' implies that God's power is a rival political force to the freedoms of democracy, an intervening God is perceived to be a destabilizing power operating without any checks and balances.[72] In addition to the soteriological dilemma outlined above, the politics of theological language is of concern to Tanner.

agents reveals salvation as the driving issue. The first is Philippians 2:12–13: 'Work out your own salvation with fear and trembling, for God is at work in you, both to will and work for his good pleasure.' The second is the quote from Bernard of Clairvaux (d. 1274): 'Free will accomplishes the entire work and grace performs the entire work; in such a way, however, that the entire work is in the will precisely because the entire work is from grace.' Tanner, *God and Creation*, 19, 92. Moreover, Tanner uses the 'Pelagianism' or 'Pelagian structure' as shorthand for when the proper grammar of theological discourse about God's agency breaks down, again revealing the importance of the Augustine-Pelagian debate for her proposal. Tanner, *God and Creation*, 18, 122ff., 136, 144, 146, 155, 157–61.

68. Owen Thomas describes this as 'the key issue in the general problem' of divine action. See 'Recent Thought on Divine Agency', in *Divine Action: Studies Inspired by the Philosophical Theology of Austin Farrer*, ed. Brian Hebblethwaite and Edward Henderson (Edinburgh: T&T Clark, 1983), 46.

69. Tanner, *God and Creation*, 4.

70. Tanner, *God and Creation*, 17.

71. Tanner, *Politics of God*, vii. This is fitting since to speak of 'grammar' is to discuss the *public* rules of discourse, and to set the limits of what one is permitted to say, and therefore what one is able to imagine and do; grammar is never apolitical.

72. This view was famously put forward by Richard Rorty, who described religious institutions as 'dangerous to the health of democratic societies' because appeals to religious

Tanner illuminates this history in terms of the bifurcation of language describing the activity of the Holy Spirit in sixteenth- and seventeenth-century England. The first view of the work of the Spirit, represented by non-conformist enthusiasm, claims that the Spirit works – God intervenes – with 'immediacy, interiority, privacy, singularity, and the bypassing of the fallibility and sinful corruption of the human'.[73] The Spirit is perceived to intervene, to overthrow ordinary natural processes and human institutions, to bypass the methods of reflective self-criticism in a self-evident manner. Tanner concludes that such spiritual fervour becomes 'a simple recipe for ongoing bloodshed' between opposing viewpoints, as occurred in the English Civil War.[74] This history casts a long shadow and continues to thwart many efforts for coherent (non-oppressive) theological speech in the public square.

In the second view, members of the established church described the Spirit as making 'do with the fallibility, corruption, and confusion of human life' by acting through 'historical process, mediation, publicity, surprise within the course of the commonplace'.[75] This second method is favoured by Tanner as the more aligned with contemporary science and the more suitable Christological model.[76] The Spirit acts 'in and through all human agencies and natural events', not against them, nor in place of them, as the language of intervention and non-intervention have come to imply.[77]

Tanner refers to this in-and-through model of divine action as 'God's universal providential agency', whereby God works directly and immediately in every part of creation.[78]

Tanner writes,

> A created cause can be said to bring about a certain created effect by its own power, or a created agency can be talked about as freely intending the object of its rational volition, only if God is said to found that causality of agency directly and *in toto* – in power, exercise, manner of activity, and effect.[79]

Tanner's proposal can be summarized as the claim that God creates free human actions. God's agency is manifest neither violently, nor intermittently, nor in some

knowledge and divine authority are 'a conversation-stopper'. See the discussion between Richard Rorty and Nicholas Wolterstorff; Richard Rorty, 'Religion as Conversation-Stopper', *Common Knowledge* 3, no. 1 (1994): 1–6; Nicholas Wolterstorff, 'An Engagement with Rorty', *Journal of Religious Ethics* 31, no. 1 (2003): 129–39; and Richard Rorty, 'Religion in the Public Square: A Reconsideration', *Journal of Religious Ethics* 31, no. 1 (2003): 141–9.

73. Kathryn Tanner, *Christ the Key* (Cambridge: Cambridge University Press, 2010), 274.

74. Tanner, *Christ the Key*, 288.

75. Tanner, *Christ the Key*, 288.

76. Tanner, *Christ the Key*, 274–5, 296, 299.

77. Tanner, *Politics of God*, 31, 99.

78. Tanner, *Politics of God*, 100.

79. Tanner, *God and Creation*, 86.

places and not others, nor persuasively, nor under limitation at all. Instead, Tanner asserts, God is as maximally involved with the world as it is possible to express, 'in the form of a productive agency extending to everything [in] an equally direct manner … [as the] immediate source of being of every sort.'[80] Tanner follows 'the Latin default' position in Western theology and conceives of action on two levels, because 'agency' is predicated of God and creatures differently, or analogically.[81] Creatures act and are acted upon on a horizontal plane, and God creates this plane in every moment, vertically. This works in much the same manner as the (neo-)Thomistic framework of double agency, where God is the primary cause of all secondary causes; 'created beings are the executors of the order for the world that God ordains but only as God's creative agency is at work every step of the way by which such an order is produced.'[82] This is a compatibilist model of divine action where God and creatures both act to bring about the same events.

How does Tanner's proposal escape the challenge of overdetermination? Overdeterminism is the charge levelled against scholars who posit two sufficient and independent causes for the same event. This violates, what Jaegwon Kim has called, the causal exclusion principle: 'Two or more complete and independent explanations of the same event of phenomenon cannot coexist.'[83] One can posit two (or more) partial causes both contributing to a single and sufficient set of causal conditions to bring about a single event – such as when two people push a broken-down car – but one cannot give multiple *exhaustive* explanations for a single event without making one explanation obsolete. The perceived danger in theology of this move is that one of these two causes becomes superfluous and epiphenomenal, such that either God's power or creaturely freedom could be removed and the events in the world would remain unchanged.

Tanner resists the threat posed by overdeterminism by employing, what she calls, two rules of grammar. The first rule states that the agency of God and the agency of creatures exist in a 'non-competitive relation' – that is, not in a relation of inverse proportionality such that for one to increase the other must decrease.[84] This is made possible by the second rule, Tanner argues, 'a radical interpretation of divine transcendence' such that there can be no comparison and no contrast between God and creatures.[85] It is the 'loss of such an account of transcendence … [that is] responsible in great part for the dualistic, mutually exclusive alternation between

---

80. Tanner, *God and Creation*, 46.

81. David A. S. Fergusson, *The Providence of God: A Polyphonic Approach* (Cambridge: Cambridge University Press, 2018), 59–109, esp. 69.

82. Tanner, *God and Creation*, 92.

83. Jaegwon Kim, *Supervenience and the Mind: Selected Philosophical Essays* (Cambridge: Cambridge University Press, 1993), 250.

84. Kathryn Tanner, *Jesus, Humanity and Trinity: A Brief Systematic Theology* (Minneapolis, MN: Fortress Press, 2001), 2.

85. Tanner, *Jesus, Humanity and Trinity*, 2.

deistic, interventionist God and pan(en)theism so common in modern Christian thought'.[86] It is by remembering *who* this divine agency belongs to, namely the Creator and Saviour of all things, that Tanner rejects *both* interventionist language *and* the constraints that this rejection might place on divine action discourse.

Since the creature exists in utter dependence upon God, divine agency cannot be described as epiphenomenal; but since God creates freedom and genuine agency in creatures, creation's agents cannot be regarded as illusions either.[87] God's agency is here primarily manifest in the doctrine of creation *ex nihilo*; God alone creates agents and their effects in actuality. It might seem that this means that God is the sole agent, but divine transcendence is also refracted through the incarnation where God takes one creature as God's own, and thus reveals that the integrity of the creation stands in a non-competitive relationship to God. This model of divine action is theologically robust, and so while it stands incomplete it should not be abandoned.

How far does Tanner's emphasis on non-contrastive transcendence diffuse the shadow of interventionist language? Certainly, her emphasis on the radical transcendence of God should be affirmed against the tendency of naturalism to subsume transcendence into a natural or created category. God's power to create *ex nihilo* is a necessary articulation of God's patient and generous sustaining of all things, as well as an assurance of God's final victory over darkness. Does this suffice for an articulation of God's agency and actions? There are two points to make here. First, it seems odd to take creation *ex nihilo* as the paradigm for all God's engagement with the world.[88] The implication of this paradigm is that the

---

86. Kathryn Tanner, 'Creation *ex nihilo* as Mixed Metaphor', *Modern Theology* 29, no. 2 (April 2013): 138.

87. I am not claiming to fully understand double agency, only to give it the best hearing that I can. Fortunately, Austin Farrer, one of double agency's chief proponents in the twentieth century, described the position as a 'paradox' whereby we must 'refuse the challenge' to speak further. Austin Farrer, *Faith and Speculation: An Essay in Philosophical Theology* (New York: New York University Press, 1967), 62.

88. Abraham describes how this move in contemporary neo-Thomism more widely traces back to the motivating question, 'why is there something rather than nothing?' If this philosophical question is the foundation of all theology, then it is apparent why creation *ex nihilo* provides the cornerstone for reflection on divine agency. Abraham, *Divine Agency*, vol. 1, 165–87, 188, 199. However, as Austin Farrer writes, 'Thought of God is a summary of a tale that narratives the actions of God', and as such theology has to be more than a philosophy; 'no personal knowledge without personal intercourse; no thought about any reality about which we can do nothing but think'. Farrer goes on to say that what is needed for any theology of divine action is 'some notion of mutually engaged activity, or (for short) of interaction, applicable to the case of man and God and merely requiring more exact definition by the addition of specific marks'. I am unsure if Farrer's integrated theory of double agency and an interactive existentialism is successful, but it shows the importance of the experience of God for theories of divine agency. Farrer, *Faith and Speculation*, 22, 37.

only act that God is doing, on Tanner's proposal, is creating – creating agents, creating creaturely actions, creating effects, creating circumstances.[89] Second, and more importantly, what is missing from this account is any interaction between God and God's creatures. In dispelling the murk of interventionism, the light of double agency is blinding and we are left with a picture lacking in either shape or colour.

Tanner states quite clearly that what the framework of double agency and the radicalization of transcendence prohibits is 'talk of God's working with created causality in any way' because 'God's agency is not to be talked about as partial, or as composed or mixed with created causality'.[90] It follows from this that God cannot interact with creatures at their level; God cannot choose to appear to creatures in and among them.[91] This seems to present a challenge to notions of inspiration, God's speaking, and the experience of God's Spirit as guiding, comforting or convicting. It is telling that Tanner locates her concern for the political implications of theologies of divine action in pneumatology – for it is through the Spirit that God is commonly described as coming alongside, providing aid and making God's will known today. Instead, for Tanner, 'where created happenings follow God's will for them, they do so unconsciously, without knowingly and willingly doing so; this is a blind following'.[92] God's action is beneath the creature and so hidden from them. God cannot *affect* the operations of creatures, as creatures do among themselves, for God already and only *effects* everything.

The concern is that, when all God's action is grammatically structured in accordance with non-contrastive transcendence, any experience of God's presence to which a creature may testify to having felt must then undergo heavy 'translation'.[93] God may create experiences in the mind of the creature, which the creature interprets as created by God for the purpose of facilitating a relationship; but, strictly speaking, this is not an experience of God's action in any different

89. 'The rule in this case is just an instance of a more general one; predicates that diversify divine agency should be able to be ascribed to only the effects of divine agency ... Qualifiers that seemed to diversify divine agency may indicate only a real difference in that agency's effects: the operation of divine agency remains constant – simple and undifferentiated.' Tanner, *God and Creation*, 103.

90. Tanner, *God and Creation*, 94.

91. Tanner, *Jesus, Humanity and the Trinity*, 3. Thus, Tanner's account of the incarnation is one that emphasizes the full humanity of Jesus which God creates immediately and directly like every other creature's, but then is uniquely different because God claims this human life as God's own life. 'Jesus performs divine works in a human way', but 'the assumption of the human as a divine act does not take place on the human plane'. Tanner, *Jesus, Humanity and the Trinity*, 21, 19.

92. Tanner, *Jesus, Humanity and the Trinity*, 44.

93. Tanner, *God and Creation*, 102–3.

way to the experience of other created phenomena.[94] For example, in her account of petitionary prayer, Tanner writes that we can affirm that God responds to prayer because God has decided to create certain situations only after God has also brought about certain prayers.[95] When God and creatures relate on two different levels such that there is no 'commonality of a field of agency', then any notion of being brought closer to God or of falling further away, and any hope of distinguishing 'different types of union between God and what is not God', is lost to the relation of total dependence.[96] Tanner's move to radical transcendence zooms out the picture of God's action so far that the picture has flattened, and the dynamics of personal piety or relationship with God in the life of the believer seem hard to articulate. If double agency is taken as an exhaustive or sufficient account of divine action, then when we turn to narrate God's interaction with God's creatures, we are still left spluttering.

How does positing a panpsychist universe aid Tanner's project? After all, Tanner claims that her two rules of grammar apply regardless of the ontology of the creation.[97] More critically, panpsychism cannot be used to imply that spirit or mind is a necessary intermediary between God and matter. A theologian should not adopt panpsychism out of the misguided concern that without ensouled creatures God could not interact with matter. This would be a mistake. The proposal developed below is not to contradict Tanner's two 'rules' but is offered in conjunction with her non-contrastive understanding of divine transcendence. The hope is that a panpsychist view of creation allows for greater interaction between God and creatures, and a more robust understanding of the work of the Spirit, than is currently offered by Tanner.

First, it is clear that a panpsychist universe overlaps with Tanner's proposal as an ontology aligned with a powers-based view of causation.[98] As we have seen

94. Similarly, there is nothing unique about miracles from God's perspective; it is simply that God chooses not to also create the additional secondary causes sufficient for an event, only the primary causes. Tanner, *God and Creation*, 98–9.

95. Tanner, *God and Creation*, 97–8.

96. Frank G. Kirkpatrick talks of 'a commonality of a field of agency' as necessary for interaction in *The Mystery and Agency of God: Divine Being and Action in the World* (Minneapolis, MN: Fortress Press, 2014), xiv. Tanner, *Jesus, Humanity and the Trinity*, 2, 35. As David Fergusson concludes, 'In short, double agency, on the classical construction, either offers too much, or not enough, or not the sorts of things that Scripture and the life of faith attest'. Fergusson, *Providence of God*, 228.

97. Tanner, *God and Creation*, 89.

98. Philip Goff defines the theory of causation, *Power Realism*, to mean that 'for any law L which governs the universe, the fact that L governs the universe is, ultimately, grounded in the causal powers of some fundamental entity or entities'. Goff, *Consciousness and Fundamental Reality* (Oxford: Oxford University Press, 2017), 249. Power's causality makes laws of nature a manifestation of the indwelling powers, which God may create or sanctify through the interactive presence of the Holy Spirit. Although, there was insufficient space to

in previous chapters, the Christian panpsychist might say that God creates the indwelling powers of the universe.[99] On panpsychism, as on Tanner's model, every point of creation exists as a point of power, a point of something analogous to agency, radically dependent upon God. Creation is not a series of points of mere (empty) extension, but a network of points of secondary power created by God and distinct from God. Second, it might be felt that panpsychism, as a discourse that 'fractures anew the language of the ordinary' by subverting the dualisms of mind and matter or human and non-human, is broadly in line with her vision of tolerance of all creatures before God.[100] The transcendence of God relativizes all other differences in the universe, such that – as a panpsychist would affirm – there are no absolute divisions within creation, only contrasts; the only non-contrastive and absolute difference lies between God and creation. These two general points of congruence point towards a deeper thesis.

If we express the following through metaphysics as grammar, as Tanner does, we might say that panpsychism teaches us to speak of God's relation to all of creation as one of interior depth, not exterior force. This would be the first rule. Panpsychism does not only posit indwelling secondary powers throughout creation but also view these powers as the seeds of mentality. Therefore, the second grammar of a panpsychist account of divine action is the gracious possibility of reciprocity between God and all creation, in a manner analogous to human–divine interaction. This rule might be that there can be no absolute contrast, but only a scalar difference, between how God relates to human beings and how God relates to other creatures.[101] The interior depth in which God is intimately present to the creature is *both* a hidden source of being and the realm of experience.[102] For the indwelling powers of the universe to be the seedlings of mentality or soul is to suggest that, while allowing for the distortive effects of sin and imperfection, every

develop a panpsychist interpretation of natural laws in this chapter, this points towards an interpretation of laws of nature that dispels much of the scientific objections to intervention discussed above.

99. As Tanner writes, 'One might say that God brings forth the operations of created causes by working interiorly, in their depths ... God operates from within created causes, in the very place from which their operations arise.' Tanner, *God and Creation*, 95.

100. Tanner, *God and Creation*, 169.

101. But we cannot rule out, using the same logic, that God may interact with baptized Christians who are *en Christo* and indwelt by the Spirit permanently in a different manner to the rest of creation (human and non-human). I leave this question open.

102. Aquinas, in his consideration of how double agency was a vital but insufficient model for divine action, also turns to the experiential dimension of reality and employs the language of the human person as the temple of the Holy Spirit to compensate. Aquinas, *Summa Theologiae, Questions on God*, ed. Brian Davies and Brian Leftow (Cambridge: Cambridge University Press, 2006) I, q.43, a.3. I propose, similarly, to complement the model of double agency with the Spirit's presence, but (unlike Aquinas) I extend this throughout creation.

creature is given, as a gift, the capacity to experience God's Spirit in their own way. God can *interact* with creation just because these creatures exist continually in radical dependence upon God. It may not be a rational knowledge of God as humans grapple for, but panpsychism can suggest that every creature may feel God's presence as a pull towards God's Kingdom. Here, the adoption of panpsychism significantly extends Tanner's thesis further than she has been willing to go, but without abandoning the rules of transcendence and non-competitive agency she lays down.

Panpsychism and the presence of the Holy Spirit

The shadow of interventionist language has been responded to in three very different ways by Robert J. Russell, David Ray Griffin and Kathryn Tanner. In each of the sections above, brief suggestions were made as to how a panpsychist ontology of creation may strengthen each of these proposals. The goal of this section is to step back, gather these suggestions together and discern the overarching contribution that panpsychism makes to discussions of divine action. In what follows, I will summarize the ways panpsychism was seen to aid the three proposals explored above. Thereafter, I will argue that panpsychism's main benefit is that it enables theologians to extend discussions of the indwelling of the Holy Spirit, as God's active and transformative presence within Christian believers, to speak of a comparable inner presence of the Spirit throughout creation.

The first section, 'Scientific objections and quantum solutions: Robert J. Russell', discussed the work of Robert J. Russell. In order to avoid depicting God as breaking natural laws, Russell restricts God's direct action in the world to places where the natural sciences posit indeterminacy, most prominently in quantum mechanics. It was argued that Russell's theory would benefit from adopting a panpsychist interpretation of quantum physics, since this would allow Russell to give a more compelling account of God acting cooperatively 'within' quantum phenomena (and everything else in the universe). It would also facilitate Russell's expressed desire to combine his quantum-based account with mind-based accounts that enable discussion of God acting at the level of personal interaction. Here, it is already clear that panpsychism's contribution is a metaphysical space, a 'within' all things, an interiority of experience analogous to that which humans call the mind. An account of divine action in this 'space' corresponds to theological notions of the inner presence of the Holy Spirit.

The second section, 'Ethical concerns and the process of persuasion: David Ray Griffin', explored the ethical concerns regarding both the coercive manner and unjust occasionality of divine intervention, as voiced by process representative David Ray Griffin. Process theology responds to these concerns by limiting, not the location of divine action since God already indwells every occasion in process theology's panexperientialist universe, but the range and effectiveness of actions predicated of God. God is said to influence, as a contributing factor, the self-determination of actual occasions. I argued, against process theology, that limiting the power of God was counterproductive to their pastoral concern. Although the persuasive activity of God is an important, interactive way that a theology may wish to speak of God's sanctifying presence within the universe, there is no reason to limit God's action to this one mode. It was also argued that the event-based metaphysic, which denies the reality of enduring substances, agents or subjects, undermined the ability of process metaphysics to employ action predicates in a meaningful way. As such, the adoption of a subject-panpsychism would aid process theologians in articulating more fully the persuasive activity of God.

The third section, 'Theological dilemmas and double agency: Kathryn Tanner', focused on the theological dilemma of affirming both creaturely freedom and divine sovereignty in both soteriology and the public square. Kathryn Tanner sought to dissolve this dichotomy by adopting a radical 'grammar' of divine transcendence, such that God's power and creaturely freedom are not inversely proportionate. It was argued that while this non-contrastive account of God's transcendence is a necessary component within discussions of divine action, it cannot alone be sufficient. This is because the non-competitive account of God acting solely through primary causation cannot articulate any interaction between God and creatures, which can only occur if God sometimes acts in metaphysical continuity with creatures. This chapter will now go on to discuss the inner presence of the Holy Spirit as a mode of God's engagement with creatures at the level of secondary causation. For the interactive presence of the Holy Spirit to reach beyond human subjects, subjectivity must be extended throughout the universe. Panpsychism, it is argued, thus provides a way to construe God's omnipresence as not only a directly present creative force but also as an intimately relational and transformative Person.

It is a central claim of the Christian faith that the Holy Spirit is present to individual human beings, in the church and even hidden throughout the natural world. It is often on the basis of the Spirit's presence that claims of either special divine action or divine concursus are based.[103] As Anthony Thiselton summarizes, 'The Spirit of God is clearly a mode of God's activity, whose nature and identity are inseparable from God. Indeed, many begin to define or to explicate the Spirit as "God in action."'[104] 'Spirit' does not refer to the stuff God is made of and it is then not the divine substance in creatures. Instead, '*discourse about the Spirit is a way*

---

103. Eugene TeSelle, 'Divine Action: The Doctrinal Tradition', *Divine Action: Studies Inspired by the Philosophical Theology of Austin Farrer*, ed. Brian Hebblethwaite and Edward Henderson (Edinburgh: T&T Clark, 1990), 89–90.

104. Antony C. Thiselton, *The Holy Spirit – in Biblical Teaching, through the Centuries, and Today* (Grand Rapids, MI: Eerdmans, 2013), 13. Cf. Ernst Käsemann, 'Geist und Geistesgaben im NT', in *Die Religion in Geschichte und Gegenwart*, ed. H. F. von Campenhausen et al., 3rd edn (Tübingen: J.C.B. Mohr, 1958); Hendrikus Berkhof, *The Doctrine of the Holy Spirit: The Annie Kinkead Warfield Lectures, 1963–1964* (Richmond, VA: John Knox Press, 1967), 14, 94; Alan Richardson, *An Introduction to the Theology of the New Testament* (New York: Harper & Row, 1958), 104–5.

of being articulate about God's initiating activity and our responsive activity'; when theologians are articulating models of divine action, they are operating within the doctrinal locus of pneumatology.[105]

Historically, the relation of indwelling between God (the Holy Spirit) and humanity has received little philosophical or sustained theological attention. In recent years, more serious consideration has been given to the relation of indwelling, due largely to the practical and pastoral importance of elucidating how indwelling facilitates personal sanctification in the life of the believer (which can be considered one example of divine action). By adopting panpsychism one can extend these recent discussions of indwelling beyond the human believer and give an analogous account of God's transformative, sanctifying presence throughout the universe.[106]

William Alston's essay 'The Indwelling of the Holy Spirit' has defined recent discussions of this topic. Alston identified two issues of primary concern with regard to specifying indwelling as a mode of God's action.[107] The first issue regards the division of labour between the Holy Spirit and the created subject in bringing

---

105. Ramsey, *Models for Divine Activity*, 7.

106. Austin Farrer makes a passing indulgence into 'a little mythology' to this effect. He writes,

> Let us endow the ultimate component of natural force – the Whatever-it-is in Itself behind the electron – with a Christian soul. The minute creature may then be supposed to stand in the same relation to God's action by way of nature, as does the Christian to God's action by way of grace. It can throw itself on a creative purpose which carries it beyond itself; but has (presumably) as little concern as we have with the causal touch through which the divine action embraces, directs or extends that of the creature. Now let us cancel the mythical supposition. The minute entity has neither mind nor will; yet the causal or quasi-causal relation between it and infinite purpose may be thought the same in principle as the causal dependence of our action upon the divine. (Farrer, *Faith and Speculation*, 78)

In this 'mythic' thought experiment, Farrer considers electrons with Christian souls, and argues that in such an ontology they would have the same direct relation to God as a human being, such that any notion of a causal joint or mechanism of causal influence becomes irrelevant. With this understanding of how panpsychism may contribute to models of divine action, I entirely agree. However, I would disagree that when he cancels the mythical supposition and reverts back to a physicalist notion of electrons as entirely lacking in an ontological analogue to a human soul, the picture remains unchanged. The reason the thought experiment is useful is because it is immediately apparent to us, as ensouled human believers, that God's action in the soul is direct and needs no further mechanism. To then suggest that the same God–creature interaction can work without any soul or subjectivity within the creature seems to contradict the basis of this thought experiment.

107. Alston's main concern for this relation is how it brings about *sanctification*. He refers to this as the transformation of the 'motivational structure' of an individual; 'that is, it has

about transformation. For Alston, this particular type of special divine action requires that the two agents (Holy Spirit and created subject) both be involved and interacting in order to bring out the desired effect. This first issue highlights that the presence of the Holy Spirit articulates God's interaction with creatures on the level of secondary causation. The second issue regards the internality of the Holy Spirit's presence, which Alston argues should be contrasted with a general account of God's omnipresence, or the general creative and sustaining activity of creation.[108] Similar to how Nancey Murphy and Robert Russell depicted God as acting cooperatively within quantum events, the inner presence of the Holy Spirit (or 'indwelling' in Christian believers) specifies an internal and interactive mode of God's action.[109]

Alston examines three models of indwelling, rejecting the first two and affirming the third. Alston's first model is the fiat model, whereby God simply produces new dispositions within the human being or infuses the believer with specific virtues. Alston views this model as being both insufficiently interactive, because nothing is required from the creature, and insufficiently distinct from God's general creation and preservation of creation. Moreover, Alston suggests that the fiat model is morally problematic in the same way that accounts of interventionism were seen by some theologians as violations or coercive. The second model is the 'interpersonal' model whereby God is 'influencing the human being as one person influences another'.[110] Although sufficiently interactive, this model is rejected by Alston for being insufficiently *internal*. It is based upon an analogy to the moral influence between human beings who always remain, he argues, separate and distinct persons. N. T. Wright has emphasized that 'in biblical thought heaven and earth – God's sphere and our sphere – are not thought of as detached or separate. They overlap and interlock.'[111] Such overlapping and interlocking is what Alston takes from the biblical language of 'filled, permeated, pervaded' by the Spirit to suggest the interweaving of subjectivities between the Spirit and the creature. He calls this 'mutual inter-penetration of the life of the individual and the divine life' the 'sharing' model.[112]

---

to do with changes in one's tendencies, desires, values, attitudes, emotional proclivities, and the like ... The issue is as to just what role the activity of the Holy Spirit has in such changes as these'. William P. Alston, *Divine Nature and Human Language: Essays in Philosophical Theology* (Ithaca, NY: Cornell University Press, 1989), 229.

108. Alston, *Divine Nature and Human Language*, 227.

109. I take this inner presence of the Holy Spirit to include, but not exhaust, what is achieved in the Spirit's indwelling of Christian believers. That is, 'inner presence' is the basis for, but not identical to, the indwelling relation.

110. Alston, *Divine Nature and Human Language*, 236.

111. N. T. Wright, 'Mind, Spirit, Soul and Body: All for One and One for All; Reflections on Paul's Anthropology in His Complex Contexts', http://www.ntwrightpage.com/Wright_SCP_MindSpiritSoulBody.htm (accessed 26 November 2013).

112. Alston, *Divine Nature and Human Language*, 242, 244.

The sharing model states that God transforms the creation from within by accessing the internal powers, dispositions and subjectivity of the creature and then sharing God's own dispositions and desires within it.[113] In the case of volitional subjects, it remains the responsibility of the creature to act in accordance with these dispositions and appropriate them as her own in order for the transformation to be wholly effectual.[114] This is how the believer may 'work out your salvation with fear and trembling' (Phil. 2:12) and say with Paul that this was done by 'I, yet not I, but the grace of God was within me' (1 Cor. 15:10). As with process theology, Alston's 'sharing model' depicts creatures as having an active role in building the Kingdom of God, but with neither the rejection of subjects as ontologically primitive nor severe restrictions on God's power. On panpsychism, there is no metaphysical reason why Alston's sharing model might not be extended throughout the cosmos, such that a comparable inner presence is added to the arsenal of models of divine action possible at all times and places.[115]

Marylin McCord Adams points in the direction of how such an extension to other creatures might be articulated. Adams uses the doctrine of the indwelling of the Holy Spirit to attack 'any notion that ego-centred autonomy is normative' or 'the final stage of personal development'.[116] Adams goes on to suggest that, rather than viewing the Holy Spirit's influence as a kind of information input of divine

113. Eleonore Stump has developed a similar model, which depicts indwelling as a second-personal presence which the believer can experience through empathy and mind-reading. However, Stump strongly relies upon some (highly speculative) theories about neurological mechanisms which support empathy and mind-reading in the human brain, namely mirror-neurons, in her model of indwelling. As such, her model of indwelling is unable to be extended to other creatures, and even may exclude some humans (she explicitly discusses persons with autism) from being indwelt and sanctified by the Holy Spirit. Eleonore Stump, 'Omnipresence, Indwelling, and the Second-Personal', *European Journal for Philosophy of Religion* 5, no. 4 (Winter 2013): 29–53.

114. Alston, *Divine Nature and Human Language*, 246, 249–50.

115. I emphasize that there is no *metaphysical* reason for an extension of this concept, since there is theological discussion to be had around depicting indwelling as 'a new-birthright, not a creatureright', which may limit the Holy Spirit presence to baptized humans only. It is to show sensitivity to this theological issue that I speak of an inner presence of the Holy Spirit in all things, whereby leaving open the possibility that 'indwelling' refers to a distinct relation between the Holy Spirit and the baptized human person. Alston, *Divine Nature and Human Language*, 241.

116. Marilyn McCord Adams, 'The Indwelling of the Holy Spirit: Some Alternative Models', in *The Philosophy of Human Nature in Christian Perspective*, ed. Peter J. Weigel and Joseph G. Prud'homme (New York: Peter Lang, 2005), 97. This she notes is contrary to 'the American political ideal and with autonomous self-government that is the Aristotelian and Kantian ethical norm'. We might also say that this is contrary to Leibniz's 'windowless monads'.

dispositions, or an infused capacity of virtues, we should view the indwelling of the Holy Spirit as 'being built into the functional dynamics of the created person, so that it is no longer the individual's ego that centres the personality but rather a lived partnership with the Godhead'.[117] The presence of the Holy Spirit refers to a lived partnership with God, and such a lived partnership is simply what it means to be God's creature.[118] In so far as this partnership defines creaturehood, it seems a natural extension of contingency and the radical transcendence of God depicted in double agency, where God is intimately involved with creatures at the centre of their operation.

The benefit of Adams model of indwelling is that, as well as avoiding the reduction of the divine presence to a kind of information, it provides a way for God to work interactively with creatures to bring about the transformation of the universe and, in the process, transform the agents and powers themselves. In dialogue with panpsychism, this model also prevents theologians from sneaking in a stronger form of consciousness and agency at the fundamental level than has been argued for in previous chapters. If the Holy Spirit works within the experiential processes themselves, rather than manifesting as an experiential quality that requires a high level of cognitive capacity to receive (such as rationality, self-consciousness or volitional willing), then the idea that the inner presence of the Holy Spirit is a means of, and a type of, divine action that can be extended to more basic subjectivities throughout creation.

Subjects, Adams suggests, are meant to engage in intersubjective relationships. As discussed in Chapter 2, the success of panpsychism relies upon finding a solution to the combination problem. This solution will require a view of subjects that are at least partially or potentially open, rather than absolutely private and closed. As such, there seems to be an alliance of interest with regard to philosophical discussions of combination or the union of minds in panpsychism and theological discussions regarding indwelling and theological anthropology; the mind does not have high walls of isolation.

The inner presence of the Holy Spirit is a model for divine–creature interaction, whereby God can act in the world to transform not only the events of the world but also the motivational structures of the agents that bring about these events. Oliver O'Donovan writes that the importance of the inner presence of the Holy Spirit is that

the renewal of the universe touches me at the point where I am a moral agent, where I act and choose and experience myself as 'I'. It means that in the redemption of the world I, and every other 'I', yield myself to God's order and freely take my place within it.[119]

117. Adams, 'Indwelling of the Holy Spirit', 96.
118. Adams, 'Indwelling of the Holy Spirit', 96.
119. Oliver O'Donovan, *Resurrection and Moral Order: An Outline for Evangelical Ethics* (Grand Rapids, MI: Eerdmans, [1986] 1994), 23.

The inner presence of the Holy Spirit means that 'far from God's intervention reducing the scope of [human] free will, it is the precondition for it' and the only way creatures can confront 'the real challenge of the divinely created order'.[120] Again, the Spirit empowers, and does not coerce, creatures to act in new ways. If this is adopted as part of the repertoire of articulations of divine action, then God would be seen to transform the world not only by acting *upon* creation but also by acting with and *within* creatures. God is not acting in creation as yet another external factor in the life of a creature, but by dwelling within the internal life of each mind, each created individual. Moreover, God can draw incomparably close to creatures, even entering into their experience, without compromising either God's transcendence and utter Otherness or the creature's finitude or integrity. To adapt Sonderegger's phrase, God 'has set up for Himself a temple, a house, in the land' of creaturely subjects.[121]

In a statement, highly resonant of this panpsychist extension of the Spirit's inner presence that I am proposing, Jürgen Moltmann writes,

> Through his Spirit God himself is present in his creation. The whole creation is a fabric woven and shot through by the efficacies of the Spirit. Through his Spirit God is also present in the very structures of matter. Creation contains neither spirit-less matter nor non-material spirit; there is only *informed* matter.[122]

If the psychosomatic ontology of the human person is not radically discontinuous with the rest of creation, then the Spirit's presence as felt by psychosomatic persons might not be either.[123] The Spirit can be conceived as informing the subjectivities in matter in a way analogous to how Alston and Adams have depicted the Spirit informing the psychic life of believers. That is, by dwelling within the panpsychist subjects the Spirit engages in a partnership with creatures and so sanctifies the creaturely dispositions and intrinsic powers to cooperatively bring about the kingdom of God.

120. O'Donovan, *Resurrection and Moral Order*, 23.

121. Kathryn Sonderegger, *Systematic Theology: The Doctrine of God* (Minneapolis, MN: Augsburg Fortress, 2015), 105.

122. Jürgen Moltmann, *God in Creation: An Ecological Doctrine of Creation* (London: SCM Press, 1985), 212. Emphasis in original.

123. To be clear, I am not suggesting that God is the Soul of the universe or that creation is the body of God, although these are both images that Moltmann readily employs. Not only would this imply a *lack* (rather than an abundance) of created subjectivities, but such a view would risk undermining the transcendence of God and leading theology into the rabbit warren of theological determinism. The presence of the Holy Spirit throughout creation is an internal presence, not defined in terms of extension or embodiment, but testified to in terms of experience. The testimony of creatures is discussed more fully in the next chapter.

It would be a mistake to interpret this proposal as a return to theological subjectivism. God's action is not reducible to our interpretation of ordinary events. On the contrary, mental action is as real and objective as material causation (if the two can even be separated, which in panpsychism they cannot). Therefore, God can be said to make a genuine causal difference in the universe, whether we recognize it or not, through the mentality that is fundamental throughout the universe. It is also important to recognize that intersubjective *interaction* need not be the only mode of the divine presence; omnipresence and incarnate presence may be articulated in different ways. It is only an interactive sanctification, whereby the Holy Spirit in humility comes into the experiential awareness of creatures that is under discussion here. This means that divine action is hidden from third-person knowledge; God cannot be put under a telescope, pointed at, verified or falsified in repeated tests. However, divine action is not entirely hidden in the first-person form of knowledge, but hidden throughout creation and so intermingled with our experience of 'I' and everything else. This can be experienced, felt and responded to, although not with infallible certainty. And, importantly, this means that divine action can also be known in a second personal form of knowledge. It can be witnessed to, communicated and testified about, as we see in scriptural and aural forms of Christian testimony.

Conclusion

This chapter explored how the claim that God intervenes in creation has been met by scientific objections, ethical concerns and theological dilemmas. These challenges have cast a powerful shadow and have constrained theological accounts of God's action in the world. Panpsychism, nor any other metaphysic, cannot answer all the puzzles regarding God's action in the world. The panpsychist account of the inner presence of the Holy Spirit that I have given should not be taken as an exhaustive account of divine action. Most significantly, this account gives no aid to articulations of creation, incarnation or resurrection, which are the three most central claims of God's action in the Christian faith. Yet, neither are these three claims the total sum of God's action within Christian theology. There is no reason to suppose that the variety of God's effects in the world can be understood as the outcome of only one type of action, whether creating, persuading or adjusting quantum probabilities.

What panpsychism does offer is a way to extend discussions of the Holy Spirit's presence and dwelling within the human person throughout the cosmos. As a location, a metaphysical 'space' for God's action, this proposal can help to deflate the scientific objections discussed in the section 'Scientific objections and quantum solutions: Robert J. Russell' without limiting God's action to quantum indeterminacies. As one mode of divine action, and in response to the ethical concerns raised by the seeming external and violating connotations of 'intervention', the presence of the Holy Spirit emphasizes the internal, interactive and persuasive agency of God. This, then, complements God's creative sustaining of creation and the unique act of assumption as the person of Jesus Christ.

Chapter 5

THE VOICES OF CREATION: PANPSYCHISM AND ECOLOGY

Contemporary articulations of the doctrine of creation face two main challenges. The first, tackled in the previous chapter, is to provide a realistic and flexible account of divine action. I concluded with a model of the inner presence of the Holy Spirit as calling all creatures into greater union with God. The antiphon, the response of creation, is the focus of the present chapter. This is the second challenge for contemporary theology, a doctrine of creation in a time of ecological crisis.

Lynn White Jr's infamous judgement, that Christianity is 'the most anthropocentric religion the world has ever seen', arose from the analysis that Christian theology upholds 'man's effective monopoly on spirit in this world'.[1] White also noted that this monopoly is diametrically opposed to the 'panpsychism of all things, animate and inanimate, designed for the glorification of their transcendent Creator' – a view that White attributes to Francis of Assisi.[2] While the aetiology of the environmental crisis cannot be laid solely at the feet of Christianity, White's article highlighted the importance of both panpsychism and the Christian imagination for contemporary ecology.[3] In the fifty-years of debate

---

1. Lynn White Jr, 'The Historical Roots of Our Ecologic Crisis', *Science* 155, no. 3767 (10 March 1967): 1205.

2. White, 'Historical Roots', 1207. Later White argued that the solution for Christianity was 'to find a viable alternative to animism', which is exactly what a theologically robust panpsychism can offer. Lynn White Jr, 'Continuing the Conversation', in *Western Man and Environmental Ethics: Attitudes toward Nature and Technology*, ed. Ian G. Barbour (Reading, MA: Addison-Wesley, 1973), 55–64.

3. Christian theology is not to blame for the ecological crisis, but it remains the case that the metaphysical models and paradigms of Christian thought have served as theological justifications for, and so been complicit in normalizing, the ecologically destructive greed of the human heart. Although an ecologically sensitive articulation of Christianity is necessary for pragmatic purposes and the survival of the planet, the Christian faith should not be utterly abandoned or reconstructed to fit specific practical ends, even one as severe as this. The practical urgency of this crisis does not define the truth claims of theology, but it does raise awareness of the texts and ideas that have, historically, received insufficient attention. Although it is possible to adopt panpsychism solely on eco-pragmatic grounds, this is

that followed, it seems that only process theologians took up White's challenge to employ panpsychism in conjunction with Christian theology. This chapter constructs an alternative Christian panpsychism, which remythologizes Scriptural texts and recalibrates the traditional metaphors of theological anthropology, in response to the ecological crisis.

The first section of this chapter, 'Panpsychism and ecological philosophy', considers and offers a theological critique to the role that panpsychism already plays within eco-philosophy as the ground for intrinsic values. The second section of this chapter, 'How a mental monopoly distorts doctrine', argues that humanity's monopoly on the mind has had the same distorting tendency across a variety of otherwise rich and elegant theological discussions. Traditional depictions of humanity's place in creation require a panpsychist corrective to offset this distortive monopoly.[4] After exploring the thickets in both eco-philosophy and theology, the third section of this chapter, 'Panpsychism and theological imagination: A proposal', maps out a path that employs panpsychism within a robustly theological response to the ecological crisis. This entails defending a panpsychist hermeneutic for interpreting the Scriptural passages that depict non-human voices in creation. This is used as a basis to open up the boundaries of the church and to include the entire creation as a congregation of praise, a cosmic ecclesial body of Christ and a temple of the Holy Spirit. An intriguing implication from this final chapter is that Christian panpsychism is not solely a rational philosophical position worthy of theological consideration but also an ontological theory that arises out of the praxis of faith in a truly cosmic context.

Panpsychism and ecological philosophy

While panpsychism has been cast as the understudy to physicalism in recent philosophy of mind, and to dualism in Christian theology, panpsychism is the leading lady of ecological philosophy. The prominence of panpsychism in the history of ecological thinking can be highlighted by pointing to figures such as Fredrich von Schelling, Henry Thoreau, John Muir, Aldo Leopold and Albert Schweitzer who, David Skrbina argues, were 'panpsychists all of them'.[5] The

---

not the thrust of this books central thesis, which has argued philosophically (Chapter 2), historically (Chapter 3) and theologically (Chapter 4) for more careful consideration of a panpsychist doctrine of creation. The argument from pragmaticism and ethics should be understood in this wider context.

4. 'Anthropocentrism' is the tendency to view humanity as ontologically and axiologically distinct from other creatures, conceptually facilitating the harmful utilization of other creatures for human benefit.

5. David Skrbina, *Panpsychism in the West* (Cambridge, MA: MIT Press, [2005] 2017), 223–34. Cf. David Skrbina, 'Ethics, Eco-Philosophy, and Universal Sympathy', *Dialogue and Universalism* 4 (2013): 68.

employment of panpsychism in ecological philosophy largely arises as a solution to what is perhaps the field-defining problem – how to understand and ground intrinsic values. It is worth wandering down this well-trodden path in order to understand precisely the appeal of panpsychism in ecological philosophy, and thus its potential for a theological response to the ecological crisis.

Ethics, as an intellectual discipline, is the reflection upon values and upon the resulting duties, rights and appropriate behaviour of agents in recognition of values. Values can be categorized into two kinds: intrinsic values and instrumental values.[6] Instrumental values are fairly easy to understand; they are the value that something has for something else. For example, I might value my house for the warmth and protection it provides, but if it failed to provide me those things it might no longer be of value to me and I might move. In environmental ethics, instrumental values seem to make nature nothing more than a resource for human comfort, thereby licensing a purely utilitarian relationship between our species and our environment. This does not necessarily lead to a view of the planet as disposable, since the instrumental value of our environment may be extended across the globe and to future generations, it might even extend to other life forms.[7] Such an extension of instrumental values is often employed in public campaigns attempting to motivate ethical urgency for the protection and comfort of future human generations – a 'sustain it, or lose it' approach. Yet, for many, the idea that the universe possesses solely instrumental value for human beings, such that humans have no responsibilities or duties to other creatures or to the planet itself, is an unsustainable idea. It not only entails that nothing of value existed for billions of years on this planet or across the light years of space, but it also fails to account for the responsibilities that many people feel intuitively towards animals, plants and the landscape.

Intrinsic values are a little harder to define. Any intrinsic property is a property 'that can be had by something regardless of whether it is accompanied or unaccompanied by any other contingent being.'[8] Therefore, intrinsic values are values that can be had by something, in and of itself, irrespective of its relationship to other contingent beings. By virtue of being a *value*, not merely any old property, intrinsic values give an ethical structure to relations between things. In truth, instrumental values are parasitic on intrinsic values.[9] An object has instrumental

---

6. There are, of course, other kinds of value – systemic value, aesthetic value, sentimental value and sacramental value to name a few – but we can keep things simple for now.

7. An interesting discussion on obligations to future generations is found in Tim Mulgan, 'What Is Good for the Distant Future? The Challenge of Climate Change for Utilitarianism', in *God, the Good, and Utilitarianism: Perspectives on Peter Singer*, ed. John Perry (Cambridge: Cambridge University Press, 2014), 141–59.

8. Rae Langton and David Lewis, 'Defining Intrinsic', *Philosophical and Phenomenological Research* 58 (1998): 333–45.

9. Frederick Ferré, 'Personalistic Organicism: Paradox or Paradigm?', in *Philosophy and the Natural Environment*, ed. Robert Attfield and Andrew Belsey (Oxford: Oxford University Press, 1994), 69.

value because there is an intrinsic value that it serves. To use the example again, I might value my house instrumentally, because I value my survival and comfort intrinsically. We need to have some working understanding of intrinsic values if instrumental values, and the larger network of ethical relations, are to be properly grounded.

The question then arises, what kinds of things have intrinsic values? Here, we might look around for an example of something with unassailable intrinsic value: 'I'. I know, beyond reasonable doubt, that I have intrinsic value because I value myself, my survival and my own happiness. As a subject I value many things, but the one thing that I can value intrinsically without reference to other contingent beings is myself. This well-worn track in ethical theory gives rise to two important presuppositions from which many have proceeded. First, value is the result of a valuing mind or a valuer; 'value, like a tickle or remorse, must be felt to be there'.[10] This need not collapse into full subjectivism, such that values are nothing but the projections onto objects by valuing minds. To the contrary, subjective values can have objective existence. It may only be that values have to be felt to be operative or actualized, and that minds are necessary for the discovery (rather than the creation) of objective values.[11] Second, intrinsic value only exists in things that have minds, that can be both valuer and valued simultaneously – to be 'entirely devoid of significant subjectivity [is to be] therefore empty of intrinsic value'.[12] We have, thus, relocated the problem of intrinsic values into the problem of other minds.

If human beings are the only valuing agents, the only subjective minds in the universe, then this line of thinking creates a severe problem for environmental ethics.[13] The implication would be that humans alone carry intrinsic value, and all else can be used as instruments for human benefit. It is in this way that mechanistic

10. Holmes Rolston III, 'Values in Nature and the Nature of Value', *Royal Institute of Philosophy Supplement* 36 (1994): 29; Freya Mathews, *The Ecological Self* (London: Routledge, [1991] 1994), 117; Keith Ward, *More than Matter? Is There More to Life than Molecules?* (Grand Rapids, MI: Eerdmans, 2010), 89; Skrbina, 'Ethics, Eco-Philosophy and Universal Sympathy', 62.

11. The objectivity of values has been defended by Holmes Rolston III, *Philosophy Gone Wild: Essays in Environmental Ethics* (Amherst, NY: Prometheus Books, 1986); and Holmes Rolston III, *Environmental Ethics: Duties to and Value in the Natural World* (Philadelphia, PA: Temple University Press, 1988).

12. Ferré, 'Personalistic Organicism', 69.

13. Thus, it has become common for ecofeminists in particular to trace the philosophical roots of the current ecological crisis to Cartesian dualism, although this is not an unchallenged genealogy. See Genevieve Lloyd, *The Man of Reason; 'Male' and 'Female' in Western Philosophy*, 2nd edn ([London: Methuen, 1984] London: Routledge, 1993); and Carolyn Merchant, *The Death of Nature: Women, Ecology and the Scientific Revolution* (San Francisco, CA: Harper & Row, [1980] 1989). This is challenged by Cecilia Wee, 'Cartesian Environmental Ethics', *Environmental Ethics* 23, no. 3 (2001): 275–86.

ontologies, the idea that the non-human world is a mindless mechanism lacking in any teleology or feeling, are seen as the swiftest path to anthropocentrism; all things are valued in reference to humanity. If humanity's needs and desires are the sole measure of value, then nothing is to prevent us from remaking the world as best serves our species alone, paying no heed to the cost or damage this might have for other species or things; if there are no other values, there are no other costs to consider. This way of thinking is deeply ingrained in modern society and forms the assumption of many of our collective practices, institutions, scientific truth-making practices and financial systems; it will take both hard work and time to change.[14] The name of the game in environmental ethics, therefore, is 'constructing an adequate theory of intrinsic value for nonhuman entities and for nature as a whole'.[15]

One option is to accept that human beings, and perhaps a few other mammals, are the only experiencing subjects in the world and search for an alternative way to ground intrinsic values besides subjectivity. However, many argue that 'this will not be easy, since intrinsic value that is not valuable for any experiencing valuer is a vacuous concept'.[16] Or, at least, it appears at present that the burden of proof for non-experience-based intrinsic values remains unmet. A second option, far simpler for the meta-ethicists but complicated for the philosophers of mind, is to extend the language of rights, which are grounded in intrinsic values, beyond the human sphere by expanding the bounds of subjectivity.[17] This 'expanding circle'

14. Freya Mathews, 'Why the West Failed to Embrace Panpsychism?', in *Mind That Abides: Panpsychism in the New Millennium*, ed. David Skrbina (Amsterdam: John Benjamins, 2009), 341–60.

15. J. Baird Callicott, 'Intrinsic Value. Quantum Theory, and Environmental Ethics', *Environmental Ethics* 7 (1985): 257–75. Two voices, highlighting their minority position, who oppose the grounding of environmental ethics on the notion of intrinsic value are Tom Reagan, 'Does Environmental Ethics Rest on a Mistake?', *The Monist*, 75, no. 2 (April 1992): 161–82; and Anthony Weston, 'Beyond Intrinsic Values: Pragmatism in Environmental Ethics', *Environmental Ethics* 7 (1985): 321–39.

16. Ferré, 'Personalistic Organicism', 73. Similarly, Alfred North Whitehead surmised that 'intrinsic value resides only in the experiencing of value'. Quoted in Susan Armstrong-Buck, 'Whitehead's Metaphysical System as a Foundation for Environmental Ethics', *Environmental Ethics* 8 (1986): 241–59. Timothy L. S. Sprigge claims that panpsychism is the 'only basis' for intrinsic values in nature because 'there cannot be intrinsic value where there is nothing at all akin to pleasure and pain, joy and suffering'. Timothy Sprigge, 'Are There Intrinsic Values in Nature?', in *Applied Philosophy*, ed. B. Almond and D. Hill (New York: Routledge, 1991), 41.

17. Theological ecofeminist Sallie McFague's book *Super, Natural Christians* has the thesis that 'Christian practice, loving God and neighbour *as subjects*, as worthy of our loves in and for themselves, should be extended to nature'. It is clear that it is the designation of 'subject' that gives instrinsic value for McFague. Sallie McFague, *Super, Natural Christians: How We Should Love Nature* (London: SCM Press, 1997), 1ff.

approach to ethical inquiry was famously employed by Peter Singer's argument for animal rights based upon the capacity to experience pain.[18] Singer employed the so-called 'sentience criterion' in order to expand the same moral reasoning employed against racism to argue against 'speciesism' as a form of discrimination.[19] The question then becomes, what are the bounds of sentience and how can we tell?

The appeal of panpsychism for environmental ethics can now come into focus. By positing subjectivity as fundamental to the universe, panpsychism allows intrinsic values to be a ubiquitous, objective feature of reality, without giving up the compelling logic that values require someone to value them (a valuer). Values can be, contra Kantianism, 'anchored in the real', and 'the way the universe *is* determines how man *ought* to behave himself in it', because the universe is flush with experience.[20] This is not to say that the capacity for 'pain', as predicated of nervous systems, is found throughout the universe. Instead, one can find an array of terminology striving to speak of a sufficiently experiential property throughout nature, in a plausibly minimal way. Recent proposals include the capacity of having interests,[21] being a teleological centre of life or having a good of one's own,[22] the capacity for intentionality,[23] being a systematic whole with a *telos* or object-with-will,[24] 'conativity' in the Spinozian sense of an endeavour to persist in its own being[25] or the capacity for feeling or 'prehension'.[26]

18. Peter Singer, *Animal Liberation*, 2nd edn (London: Cape, 1990). Cf. Roderick Nash, *The Rights of Nature: A History of Environmental Ethics* (Madison: University of Wisconsin Press, 1989).

19. Singer, *Animal Liberation*; similarly, Tom Regan used the criterion of being 'subjects of life' to ground animal rights. Tom Regan, *The Case for Animal Rights* (Berkeley: University of California Press, 1983), 245.

20. Charles Taylor, *Sources of the Self: The Making of the Modern Identity* (Cambridge: Cambridge University Press, 1989), 13, 56, quoted in Michael Northcott, *The Environment & Christian Ethics* (Cambridge: Cambridge University Press, 1996), 70. Cf. Oliver O'Donovan, *Resurrection and the Moral Order* (Leicester: InterVarsity Press, 1986), 17.

21. Joel Feinberg, 'The Rights of Animals and Unborn Generations', in *Philosophy and Environmental Crisis*, ed. W. T. Blackstone (Athens: University of Georgia Press, 1974), 43–68.

22. Paul Taylor, *Respect for Nature: A Theory of Environmental Ethics* (Princeton, NJ: Princeton University Press, 1986).

23. Val Plumwood, *Feminism and the Mastery of Nature* (London: Routledge, 1993).

24. Rolston III, *Environmental Ethics*, 109–19.

25. Mathews, *Ecological Self*; Baruch Spinoza, *Ethics*, trans. R. H. M. Elwes (New York: Dover Press, 1951), Part III, Prop. IV, Proof.

26. Charles Hartshorne, 'The Rights of the Subhuman World', *Environmental Ethics* 1 (1979): 49–60; Jay McDaniel, 'Physical Matter as Creative and Sentient', *Environmental Ethics* 5 (1983): 291–317.

By grounding intrinsic values objectively, as a funda*mental* feature of the universe, panpsychism is the strongest metaphysical stance in opposition to the mechanistic utilitarianism of a materialistic culture. This opposition goes beyond solving the philosophical puzzle of how to ground intrinsic values. Panpsychism has also been celebrated for bridging the 'great gulf' established by Cartesian metaphysics between 'the conscious, mindful human sphere and the mindless, clockwork natural one' so that 'nature can be recognized as akin to the human'.[27] Through the shared quality of 'being en-minded', panpsychism is heralded for the potential to change humanity's existential position, 'to know the universe more intimately and find ourselves at home within it'.[28] This is to extend personalist ethics to non-human creatures, as Rosemary Radford Ruether writes, to 'respond to the "thou-ness" in all beings'.[29] The potential of panpsychism to widen the field in which humans can sympathize and even empathize has been emphasized by process thinkers, who have been at the forefront of environmental scholarship.[30]

This shared ontology and sympathy for other creatures need not flatten all differences, ontological or axiological, in the world. Value, like subjectivity, is not an all-or-nothing category. Although some, such as Aldo Leopold and Arne Naess, argue for a total equality between all entities, most emphasize a gradient of values.[31] This is because without such a gradient, or way of comparing and evaluating values, we would be paralysed in a sea of moral obligations, unable to

---

27. Plumwood, *Feminism and the Mastery of Nature*, 5, 137.

28. Skrbina, *Panpsychism in the West*, 4. As John Haught has written, 'As long as we fail to experience how intimately we belong to the earth and the universe as our appropriate habitat, we will probably not care deeply for our natural environment.' John F. Haught, 'Religious and Cosmic Homelessness: Some Environmental Implications', in *Liberating Life: Contemporary Approaches to Ecological Theology*, ed. C. Birch, W. Eaken and J. B. McDaniel (Maryknoll, NY: Orbis Books, 1990), 160.

29. She goes on, 'This is no romanticism or an anthropomorphic animism that sees "dryads in trees" although there is truth in the animist view. The spirit in plants or animals is not anthropomorphic but biomorphic to its own forms of life.' Rosemary Raford Ruether, *Sexism and God-Talk: Towards a Feminist Theology* (London: SCM Press, 1983), 87.

30. Charles Birch and John B. Cobb write that 'if in physical nature also there is experience, then there is a universal community for mutual participation in sympathy'. Charles Birch and John B. Cobb, *Liberation of Life: From the Cell to the Community* (Cambridge: Cambridge University Press, 1985), 134. Cf. McDaniel, 'Physical Matter', 315.

31. Aldo Leopold's description of humanity's place as 'a plain member and citizen' of the land community and Arne Naess's suggestion that '*the equal right to live and blossom* is an intuitively clear and obvious value axiom' seem to imply that all are of absolutely equal value. Aldo Leopold, *A Sand County Almanac* (New York: Oxford University Press, 1966), 219–20; Arne Naess, 'The Shadow of the Deep, Long-Range Ecology Movement: A Summary', *Inquiry* 16 (1973): 96. Such ecological egalitarianism means that *degrees* of sentience are irrelevant to the Deep Ecology movement. See George Sessions, quoted in Ferré, 'Personalistic Organicism', 60.

make any ethical decision.[32] However, by grounding intrinsic value in subjectivity, panpsychism need not face this problem since the complexity and intensity of the subject will quite naturally correspond to the quantity of intrinsic value. As we learnt in Chapter 2, panpsychists typically place an almost inexpressibly basic form of subjectivity as fundamental, and this corresponds to what might be called a 'background value' permeating all things. Freya Mathews writes, 'While this background value evokes a generalized sense of reverence for the physical world … it does not prescribe one kind of action rather than another.'[33] Above this background value, complex unified subjects (organisms) of higher intrinsic value, as well as instrumental values, can be used to structure ethical reflection in a complex world interwoven with value.

It should be noted that a panpsychist eco-philosophy presents a significant challenge to Christian theology. This is not a challenge arising from blame or guilt (although I am sure many panpsychist eco-philosophers would join that chorus), but the more serious challenge of offering a cogent alternative vision of values and of humanity's relationship to the cosmos. Panpsychism, it might be argued, has no need of God, and with a panpsychist ontology, neither does ecological ethics. It is common for Christian theologians engaged in ecological ethics to assert that the mechanism, materialism, alienation and subsequent exploitation of the non-human world arose due to the loss of a sense of transcendence, a separation of grace from nature, an eclipse of the Creator and so of creation.[34] This historical narrative serves an apologetic purpose; it grounds the argument that humanity must return to the Creator and rediscover creaturehood if we are to heal our relationship with non-human creation. It is a powerful plea for the relevance of theology in a culture where many people have never stepped inside a church or opened a Bible. I neither wish to critique the apologetic project nor deconstruct the supporting historical narrative (which I find largely compelling), but only to highlight that panpsychism offers a secularist parallel or alternative. Christian theology must recognize the power of panpsychism and wrestle with it, if their own claims for relevance at this point are to be maintained.

---

32. Midgley astutely recognizes that people resist discussions of humanity's moral duty to other animals not because of a total lack of feeling and not, on the popular level, because of misguided metaphysics, but 'because they see this as likely to lay on them an infinite load of obligation, and they rightly think than infinite obligation would be meaningless. *Ought* implies *can*. Indefinite guilt is paralyzing.' Mary Midgley, *Beast and Man: The Roots of Human Nature* (Hassocks: Harvester Press, 1978), 222–3.

33. Mathews, *Ecological Self*, 83.

34. Louis Dupré, *Passage to Modernity: An Essay on the Hermeneutics of Nature and Culture* (New Haven, CT: Yale University Press, 1993); Peter Scott, *A Political Theology of Nature* (Cambridge: Cambridge University Press, 2003), 3–29; Norman Wirzba, *From Nature to Creation: A Christian Vision for Understanding and Loving Our World* (Grand Rapids, MI: Baker Academic, 2015), 6–18, 39–59; Hans Boersma, *Heavenly Participation: The Weaving of a Sacramental Tapestry* (Grand Rapids, MI: Eerdmans, 2011), 30.

All is not lost, however, because it is possible to critique the claim that a panpsychist eco-philosophy is fully sufficient. The first weakness of the approach outlined above as a meta-ethical ontology is that it presents, what might be called, a maximally selfish universe. Each subjectivity in the universe, which grounds its own intrinsic value and orbiting instrumental values in itself, structures the world in a fundamentally egoist way. While the recognition of the intrinsic value of another creates an interconnecting web of moral restrictions and obligations, values themselves are highly privatized, and thus relativized. There may be a collective society of minds, on this philosophy, but there is little scope for the community or fellowship that is sort, because there is no shared teleology, no shared values. Individual survival is the name of the game, beyond that horizon nothing remains.[35]

This limits the scope of critique that a panpsychist eco-philosophy can place on the exploitative and abusive behaviour of human beings towards the non-human subjects and the level of hope that can be provided for change and healing. The sickness of the human heart, that theology calls sin, is reduced to the disordering of external relations which it falsely appears within our power to change – if only we got our eco-philosophy right! But how to do this appears impossible, for there is no Archimedean point of values and human beings remain on the throne of relative intrinsic values. There can be little hope of genuine transformation on this model, for if humanity, whose power to destroy seems to far outweigh our power to redeem, remains the leading edge of history then all is thrown back on to the image of man as the measure of all things, in an infinite world.

It is in part for the reasons above that many Christian theologians have resisted the temptation to speak too strongly of intrinsic values, or to search for a ground for such values within the cosmos. In the words of Karl Barth, 'The creature is no more its own goal and purpose than it is its own ground and beginning.'[36] Perhaps the most famous, if not notorious, discussion of the question of how to ground values when the universe is understood as *creation* is given by Augustine of Hippo. In book one of *On Christian Doctrine*, Augustine distinguishes between *uti*, translated as 'uses' or sometimes 'means' referring to that which is pursued for (*diligere propter*) some higher thing, and *fruitio*, translated as 'enjoyment' or 'ends' referring to things that are pursued for themselves.[37] Augustine's distinction maps

35. A panpsychist ecological philosophy that strives to avoid this problem through an account of 'relational value' or 'instrumental intrinsic value' can be found in Pauline Phemister, *Leibniz and the Environment* (Oxford: Routledge, 2016), 104. While Leibniz's philosophy is clearly of interest to secular ecology, as Phemister shows, Leibniz's rationale and particularly Leibniz's account of values is incomplete if separated from its theistic point of reference.

36. Karl Barth, *Church Dogmatics* [hereafter, *CD*] III/1, ed. and trans. G. W. Bromliey and T. F. Torrance (London: T&T Clark, 2009), §41.2, 93.

37. '*amore inhaerere alicui rei propter se ipsam*'. Augustine, *On Christian Doctrine*, 1.3–4, quoted in Oliver O'Donovan, '*Usus* and *Fruito* in Augustine *De Doctrina Christiana I.*', *Journal of Theological Studies* 33, no. 2 (October 1982): 361.

sufficiently onto the contemporary categories of instrumental and intrinsic values to warrant further reflection.

Augustine's ethical theory, contrary to the search within contemporary ecological philosophy, does not look for intrinsic values within the natural world – for things to be enjoyed in and for themselves. Instead, Augustine writes that within this temporal dispensation Christians should 'use' creation, and indeed our human friends, as a vehicle or as one might use an instrument. The only proper and final object of enjoyment and love is the Triune God; all else is loved instrumentally as a way to love God.[38] Augustine insists that no one should resent being loved for the sake of God, since this is how we love ourselves.[39] Thus, intrinsic values are replaced, or perhaps reinterpreted, with *sacramental value* – things to be enjoyed in reference and participation of God.[40] This counteracts the problems outlined above, since God provides a transcendent horizon and Archimedean point for value, in which all contingent values can participate and thus be opened up from their privatized survival tactics, to a shared vision and purpose. It is the sacramental nature of subjectively grounded intrinsic values that allows creatures to relate to one another in a common sphere of love and respect.

In so far as this critique hits its mark, it can be claimed that a panpsychist eco-philosophy is not sufficient in and of itself to provide the metaphysical framework for ecological ethics. When the claim of sufficiency is dropped, then panpsychism and Christian theology need not stand in competition to one another, but the deficiencies of each might be offset by the other. This is the hypothesis explored in this chapter, that while panpsychism offers significant ontological resources to ecological philosophy, the naturalist or immanentist frame in which it claims sufficiency undermines its efforts. Conversely, Christian theology offers a transcendental horizon, where creation can be understood as gift, not only of being but the gift of fellowship with both God and other creatures. If this fellowship is to find a sufficient place for non-human creatures, however, then a theologically contextualized panpsychism may still need to be in play; it is to this argument that we now turn.

How a mental monopoly distorts doctrine

It was seen above that although panpsychism plays a leading role in ecological philosophy, it requires a transcendent ground beyond that offered by the naturalistic frame. In a reciprocal fashion, the following section argues that Christian proposals would benefit from a panpsychist ontology, as the complementary immanent

---

38. Augustine, *On Christian Doctrine*, 1.3.3, 1.5.5, 22.20-21, in O'Donovan '*Usus* and *Fruito*', 384.

39. Oliver O'Donovan, *The Problem of Self-Love in Augustine* (New Haven, CT: Yale University Press, 1980), 26.

40. Boersma, *Heavenly Participation*, 24.

expression of values. This serves to counteract the persistent anthropocentric distortion that forms part of our intellectual inheritance. This argument proceeds by considering four prominent metaphors within Christian theology that characterize the relationship between God, humanity and creation. The four metaphors are: (a) humanity as a microcosm, as mediators and as priests of the universe, which is then the material for human worship; (b) humanity as bearers of the image of God, and stewards of God's cosmic household; (c) humanity as conversation partners invited into the Trinitarian dialogue or even protagonists within the divine drama on the stage of creation; and (d) humanity as the recipients of salvation in Jesus Christ, towards which creation serves a pedagogical purpose. These are all theologically powerful constructions and should not be rashly jettisoned. The argument below is intended to be restorative. There is only one rotten thread running through these four intellectual trajectories, which allows them each to be distorted into providing theological justification of the mistreatment of creation by human beings. That distortive thread is the monopoly that humanity has over mind and spirit. If we can unweave this thread and replace it with the democratization of mind that panpsychism offers, then theologians may find a promising way to articulate an ecologically sensitive Christianity, without discarding these precious heirlooms of Christianity's theological imagination.

Humanity as microcosm, mediator and priest

The concept of humanity, soul and body, as *microcosm* of heaven and earth, has been fairly pervasive in the history of Christian thought.[41] In the words of Kallistos Ware, 'Heavenly yet earthly, spiritual yet material, we human persons are each a microcosm.'[42] As the sole creatures of both mind and body, humanity alone reflects the nature of reality. In the theology of Nemesius of Emeasa and Maximus the Confessor, the confluence between humanity as microcosm and as made in God's image took on a vocational meaning; the task of humanity was not just to reflect but also to reconcile the divisions within the universe.[43] As microcosm humanity can be characterized as 'the laboratory in which everything is concentrated and in itself naturally mediates between the extremities of each division' within the created order.[44] Humanity, in this theological imagination, is the lynchpin of

41. This idea is not uniquely Christian but can be traced back to pre-Socratic philosophy and was a central tenet within Stoic and Platonic philosophy. See Lars Thunberg, *Microcosm and Mediator: The Theological Anthropology of Maximus the Confessor* (Lund: Håkan Ohlssons Boktrycheri, 1965), 141.

42. Kallistos Ware, 'Through Creation to the Creator', in *Toward an Ecology of Transfiguration: Orthodox Christian Perspectives on Environment, Nature, and Creation*, ed. John Chryssavgis and Bruce V. Foltz (New York: Fordham University Press, 2013), 98.

43. Thunberg, *Microcosm and Mediator*, 144–5.

44. Andrew Louth, ed., *Maximus the Confessor* (New York: Routledge, 1996), 157; *Ambigua* 41 1305A–B.

creation, the keystone in the arch; the doctrine of creation is incorporated into theological anthropology, rather than the opposite.[45] The risk of this anthropology, although it is not an entailment, lies with humanity being the *normative* pivot of the world. It is not a long jump from humanity's vocation as microcosm to a theological justification for the expansion of human civilization to remake creation in 'his' own image and for 'his' own articulation of praise.

This human vocation is emphasized in many Eastern Orthodox theologies that stress the priesthood of humanity. This logic from microcosm to mediator or priest is captured in the following quote:

> Through man alone the material becomes articulate in praise of God. Because man is body he shares in the material world around him, which passes within him through his sense perceptions. Because man is mind he belongs to the world of higher reality and pure spirit. Because he is both, he is, in Cyril of Alexandria's phrase, 'God's crowned image'; he can mould and manipulate the material and render it articulate.[46]

In this account, the creation appears mute, soulless and even bereft of God's Spirit, until it is utilized to express the praises of humanity. John Zizioulas describes humans as 'the only possible link between God and creation' who therefore have the power to 'either bring nature in communion with God and thus sanctify it; or condemn it to the state of a "thing", the meaning and purpose of which are exhausted with the satisfaction of man'.[47] Zizioulas's intention is that this tremendous responsibility will motivate ethical behaviour. However, the monopoly that humanity has upon mind and spirituality distorts this intention into a motivation towards instrumentalizing nature to serve humanity's spiritual needs.

The concept of humanity acting as priests of creation has been critiqued by Michael Northcott and Richard Bauckham. Bauckham describes this as an 'arrogant assertion', antithetical to Scripture's repeated depiction of God's direct relationship with non-human creatures and the voices of creation raised to God.[48] Similarly, Northcott critiques the priesthood of humanity as

> deeply humanocentric and seems to encourage the remaking and hominisation of the whole biosphere in the human image and for the needs of the human

---

45. Ian A. McFarland, *From Nothing: A Theology of Creation* (Louisville, KY: Westminster John Knox Press, 2014, 80. Cf. Maximus Confessor, *Ambiguum* 41 (PG 91:1305B); *The Church's Mystagogy* 7 (PG 91:684D–685A).

46. Gervase Mathew, 'The Material Becomes Articulate', from *Byzantine Aesthetics*, in *The Creation Spirit: An Anthropology*, ed. Robet van de Weyter and Pat Saunders (London: Darton, Longman, and Todd, 1990), 18.

47. John Zizioulas, 'Priest of Creation', in *Environmental Stewardship: Critical Perspectives – Past and Present*, ed. R. J. Berry (London: T&T Clark, 2006), 290.

48. Richard Bauckham 'Joining Nature's Praise of God', *Ecotheology* 7 (2002): 50.

body. Nature and creation by this metaphor is denied any independent or intrinsic values.[49]

At the heart of Bauckham's and Northcott's critiques is the idea that humanity, as priests, provides the exclusive mediation between God and creation; humanity should not have a monopoly on a living relationship with the Creator. Neither Bauckham nor Northcott unpick the ontological underpinnings of the microcosm idea, whereby humanity holds a monopoly on spirit within the material world, but it is this monopoly that generates the felt need for human mediators. Moreover, the championing of a cosmic priesthood by Orthodox theology is tied to the hierarchical and patriarchal theology of priesthood operative within these denominations.[50] The possibility of reimagining the priestly vocation of humanity (as deacons, ministers, pastors or worship leaders, if you prefer), as expressed within recent Protestant theologies of priesthood, is explored in the final section of this chapter, but it requires the extension of mind to include all creatures who together praise God.

Humanity as steward, creation as household

The crux of much theological anthropology, especially in dialogue with ecology, has been the determination in Gen. 1.26–28:

> Then God said, 'Let us make humanity in our image, according to our likeness. And let them rule over the fish of the sea and the birds of the air. Let them rule over the livestock, over all the earth, and over everything that moves upon the earth.' So God created humanity in his image. In the image of God he created him. Male and female he created them. And God blessed them and said to them, 'Be fruitful and increase, fill, the earth and subdue it. And rule over the fish of the sea and the birds of the air, and over every living thing that moves upon the earth.' (Gen. 1.26–28)

It is hard to overstate either the importance or the controversy of these verses. Most pertinently, ecological ethicists have criticized the way this passage has provided 'intellectual lubrication for the exploitation of nature'.[51] Despite the ethical and interpretative baggage, the *imago Dei* remains an 'indestructible symbol' which

---

49. Northcott, *Environment*, 133–4.

50. Stephen R. L. Clark has suggested that Christian environmentalists who 'speak of man [*sic*] as "the world's high priest"' should likewise remember what priests, in Greece and Israel, actually did'. Stephen R. L. Clark, 'Global Religion', in *Philosophy and the Natural Environment*, ed. Robin Attfield and Andrew Belsey (Cambridge: Cambridge University Press, 1994), 124.

51. Nash, *Rights of Nature*, 90.

every generation must reinterpret and wrestle with, and indeed redeem, for their own context.[52]

A substance- or structural-based interpretation, which defines the *imago Dei* as a human capacity or ontological constitution, has dominated the Christian tradition, most commonly focusing on the rational soul. A representative quote can be taken from Thomas Aquinas, who is quoting John of Damascus, as saying that 'being after God's image signifies his capacity for understanding, and for making free decisions and his mastery of himself'.[53] Even relational and vocational interpretations of the *imago Dei* presuppose this ontological uniqueness as the ground of a unique relationship with God or calling from God. It is this underlying ontological assumption, therefore, in addition to the proposed manifestation of the image, that needs careful handling.

Biblical scholarship has tended to favour functional interpretations; the image symbolizes humanity's stewardship over creation on God's behalf.[54] From the perspective of eco-theology, this vocational interpretation can do either tremendous harm or tremendous good, as it places humanity's relationship to non-human creatures at the centre of what it means to be distinctively human. Yet, much depends on what humanity are seen to be stewards over and what future our stewardship is orientated towards. As part of a response to the ecological crisis it is often emphasized that humanity is not the proprietors of creation, which belongs solely to God. As a method for cultivating sustainable behaviours within Christian communities, this has not been a wholly unsuccessful strategy. Yet, as Michael Northcott writes, 'The fundamental problem with this metaphor is the implication that humans are effectively in control of nature, its managers or, as Heidegger prefers, its guardians.'[55] This is an illusion, since 'so much of recent environmental history teaches us that we are not in fact in control of the biosphere'.[56] Northcott goes on to argues that stewardship

---

52. Paul Ricoeur, 'The Image of God and the Epic of Mart', in *History and Truth*, trans. Charles A. Kelby (Evanston, IL: Northwestern University Press, 1965), 110. See also John Douglas Hall, *Imaging God: Dominion as Stewardship* (Eugene, OR: Wipf and Stock, 1986).

53. Thomas Aquinas, *Summa Theologiae, Questions on God*, ed. Brian Davies and Brian Leftow (Cambridge: Cambridge University Press, 2006), 1a, 93.5.

54. Gerhard von Rad, *Genesis: A Commentary*, trans. John H. Marks, The Old Testament Library (Philadelphia, PA: Westminster, 1961), 56; and Hans Walter Wolff, *Anthropology of the Old Testament*, ed. and trans. Maragaret Kohl (London: SCM Press, 1974).

55. Northcott, *Environment*, 129. John Zizioulas, 'Proprietors or Priests of Creation?', in *Toward an Ecology of Transfiguration: Orthodox Christian Perspectives on Environment, Nature and Creation*, ed. John Chryssavgis and Bruce V. Foltz (Fordham Scholarship Online, 2014), 164.

56. Northcott, *Environment*, 129.

has become associated with instrumentalist attitudes ... with absolute property rights and land ownership patterns in Western civilisation result[ing] in its mutation into a metaphor of human control and mastery over nature.[57]

Despite its usefulness, then, Northcott concludes that the idea of human stewardship 'has become a misleading and potentially harmful metaphor'.[58] The central reason that the metaphor of stewardship is vulnerable to this distortion is because of the assumption that non-human creation is purely material; a steward cares for his master's *property*.[59] As property, albeit God's property, the created world has no rights or values of its own. Moreover, this metaphor can too easily portray the divine proprietor as more like an absentee landlord than a loving and present Creator. Instead, the call to stewardship should be combined with the idea of the cosmos as the home of both humanity and God (Rev. 21:3). Larry Rasmussen, among others, has constructed an *oikos* theology, using the etymological root of economics, ecumenics and ecology to unite various aspect of eco-theology together. Here, 'creation is pictured as a vast public household'.[60] This connotes a sacred space that resists utilitarian views of the earth (and universe) and emphasizes a sense of human belonging in creation against escapist spiritualities or eschatologies. The creation is a *place*, a sacred space, of the divine presence. If all creatures share this home together, then a retrieval of the stewardship metaphor has great potential. However, if creation remains an empty space and the background for shared life of God and humanity, then it is valued as nothing more than the context of the divine–human drama.

Humanity as dialogue partner, creation as theatre

The *imago Dei* has also been used as an organizing principle in more relational approaches to Christian theology. Karl Barth exemplifies this model when he emphasized the phrase in Genesis; 'male and female he created them' in order to

57. Northcott, *Environment*, 180.

58. Northcott, *Environment*, 180. Paul Santmire argues that, while not intrinsically flawed, the notion of stewardship is 'too fraught with the heavy images of management, control, and exploitation of persons and resources'. H. Paul Santmire, *Nature Reborn: The Ecological and Cosmic Promise of Christian Theology* (Minneapolis, MN: Fortress Press, 2000), 120.

59. Laurence Osborn, *Guardians of Creation: Nature in Theology and the Christian Life* (Leicester: Apollos, 1993).

60. Larry L. Rasmussen, 'Theology of Life and Ecumenical Ethics', in *Ecotheology: Voices from South and North*, ed. D. G. Hallmann (Geneva: World Council of Churches, 1994), 118. See also Ernst Conradie, 'The Whole Household of God (Oikos): Some Ecclesiological Perspectives (Part 1)', *Scriptura* 94 (2007): 1–9; and Ernst M. Conradie, 'The Whole Household of God (Oikos): Some Ecclesiological Perspectives (Part 2)', *Scriptura* 94 (2007): 10–28.

draw a parallel between heterosexual relationships, the love between the Father and the Son in the Godhead and the encounter between God and creatures (humans).[61] This view has been criticized for both its binitarian view of God (leaving out the Holy Spirit) and Barth's tendency to underplay the role of non-human creatures in the covenant.[62] Thus, we find Barth argue that all Christian theology and thought 'has to be exclusively and conclusively the doctrine of Jesus Christ as the living Word of God *spoken to us men*'.[63] Humanity alone stands in an 'I-Thou' relationship to God and is conceived of as 'the partner in the covenant of grace which is the whole basis and aim of creation'.[64] Barth's relational interpretation of the *imago Dei* and definition of humanity as persons-in-relation corresponds to a wider turn towards *personalism* within Christian theology in the twentieth century.

The idea of humanity as dialogue partners with God corresponds to a view of creation as a 'beautiful theatre'.[65] We see Barth, for example, describing creation as 'the theatre and setting, the location and background' for the drama of the history of Christ.[66] Calvin's idea of a creation as a theatre was intended to suggest that creation proclaims and reflects God's glory and power, and in that sense witnesses

---

61. Barth, *CD* III/1, §41.2, 188–206.

62. Colin E. Gunton, 'Trinity, Ontology and Anthropology', in *Persons Divine and Human*, ed. Christoph Schwöbel and Colin E. Gunton (Edinburgh: T&T Clark, 1991), 57–8; Andrew Linzey, 'The Neglect of the Creature. The Doctrine of the Non-Human Creation and Its Relation with the Human in the Thought of Karl Barth' (PhD diss., University of London, 1986).

63. Karl Barth, 'How My Mind Has Changed', *Christian Century* 56, nos. 37–8 (13, 20 September 1939): 1132; italics mine.

64. Martin Buber, *I and Thou*, trans. Ronald Smith, 2nd edn (New York: Charles Scribner's Son's, 1958); Karl Barth, *Church Dogmatics* III/2, ed. G. W. Bromiley and T. F. Torrance, trans. Harold Knight et al. (Edinburgh: T&T Clark, 1960), 14. Interestingly, Buber affirmed the possibility of establishing an I–Thou relationship with a tree. Buber, *I and Thou*, 7–8. In reviewing Buber's thought here, Paul Santmire writes,

> At first glance, it might seem helpful to invoke a doctrine of panpsychism at this point. Karl Heim did that, and, in a sense, Teilhard moved in the same direction with his construction of the 'within' of every creature. But a doctrine of panpsychism does not really solve the problem before us. It only postpones the basic questions. For we would then have to ask: in what sense is the tree psychic? In what sense is the tree psychic when one's relation to it lacks the mutuality and the speech that are characteristic of the psychic relation with the human Thou?

Santmire too quickly dismisses panpsychism without considering the possibility of creations 'speech', as I will below. Santmire, *Nature Reborn*, 142, n.21.

65. Jean Calvin, *Institutes of the Christian Religion*, 1.14.20, trans. Henry Beveridge (Peabody, MA: Hendrickson, 2008), 101.

66. Karl Barth, *Church Dogmatics* IV/3.1, ed. G. W. Bromiley and T. F. Torrance (Edinburgh: T&T Clark, 2009), §69.2, 131, 137.

God *to* humanity.[67] Yet, without any non-human subjects, only objects, it is hard to avoid the more negative implication, articulated by Emil Brunner whereby 'the cosmic element in the Bible is never anything more than the "scenery" in which the history of mankind takes place'.[68]

As a framework of Christian theology, personalism is extremely compelling but has the effect of excluding non-personal creatures, typically defined as those without the capacity for speech, from theological consideration. Kevin Vanhoozer defines humans as the 'creatures to whom God relates personally (Gen. 1.28–30), creatures with whom God can speak'.[69] Similarly, Robert Jenson defines humanity essentially and uniquely as 'praying animals' – the animals capable of a communicative personal relationship with the Creator.[70] The turn towards personalism has sought to build Christian theology upon the axis of a (private) conversation between God and humans. For the rest of creation to stand in an analogous relationship to God, it follows that creation would require an analogous subjectivity and to be extended the right to speak; this is where panpsychism can aid theologians in expanding the dialogical axis of theology to include all creatures.

Mary Midgley highlights that language, as the signification of subjectivity, has been 'the keys to the castle' of human superiority.[71] However, she argues that this is 'simply a piece of bad metaphysics, namely, Descartes' dualistic view that the world is divided sharply, without remainder, into lifeless objects on the one hand and human, fully rational, subjects on the other'.[72] Panpsychism rightly threatens our own self-importance, because it bestows a moral status to other creatures as *subjects*. Importantly, panpsychism, therefore, implies that language and consciousness are 'not, any more than reason, a yes-or-no business, [they are not] a hammer that you are holding or not holding, a single, indivisible, sacred heirloom guaranteeing supremacy'.[73]

Whether humanity is conceived of as microcosmic priests, as stewards, or God's dialogue partners, it is humanity's monopoly on consciousness and subjectivity that distorts each of these models into excessive anthropocentricism.

67. Cornelis van der Kooi, 'Calvin's Theology of Creation and Providence: God's Care and Human Fragility', *International Journal of Systematic Theology* 18, no. 1 (January 2016): 47–65.

68. Emil Brunner, *Revelation and Reason* (Philadelphia, PA: Westminster Press, 1946), 33n.

69. Kevin Vanhoozer, 'Human Being, Individual and Social', in *The Cambridge Companion to Christian Doctrine*, ed. Colin E. Gunton (Cambridge: Cambridge University Press, 1997), 178.

70. Robert Jenson, *Systematic Theology* vol. 2: *The Works of God* (New York: Oxford University Press, 1999), 59, 63.

71. Midgley, *Beast and Man*, 215.

72. Midgley, *Beast and Man*, 217.

73. Midgley, *Beast and Man*, 226.

Without some subjectivity dispersed throughout the creation, it is hard to avoid the implication that the non-human creation has no purpose, intrinsic value, or relationship with the Creator apart from its utility for human beings. A theological response to the ecological crisis need not reject the metaphors and the heritage that they represent, but only employ panpsychism as a guard against such distortion.

The centrality of the incarnate saviour, the periphery of creation

Christian discourse must return again and again to one name, and with that name to the claim that God saves the world by becoming incarnate, living, dying and being resurrected as a particular human being. Christian theology cannot properly speak of creation, humanity or God without speaking of Jesus Christ as 'the image of the invisible God, the firstborn of all creation' (Col. 1:15). As such, this chapter cannot avoid consideration of the centrality of both Christology and soteriology. Animal theologian, David Clough captures the challenge presented by the incarnation of Christ for the doctrine of creation:

> Here, it seems, is the final and decisive evidence that God is concerned with one species, rather than the multitude of creatures … and that Christianity will never be able to escape a blinkered preoccupation with only one kind of animal.[74]

The humanity of God presents a distinct challenge for theological engagement with wider ecological (and animal) concerns. The question is, how does a Christological foundation relate to the doctrine of creation; how do we relate the centre to the periphery?[75] In the case of human beings, Christian theology has traditionally claimed that the effects of salvation are manifest either through a common human nature or through the indwelling of the Holy Spirit in the soul of the believer. However, if non-human creatures do not have souls, then both these solutions exclude non-human creatures. Again, the human monopoly on

---

74. David L. Clough, *On Animals: Volume One: Systematic Theology* (London: T&T Clark, 2012), 81–2.

75. A parallel might be drawn, in epistemological method only, between the focus on Jesus Christ in theological anthropology and on the individual human self in panpsychism. In both instances, the basis of their respective truths claims (the reality of salvation or reality of consciousness) arises from one, single human centre; we are necessarily 'self-centred' and there is a positive sense to this term. From here, the investigator has a choice; limit the truth claim to the specific individual (Jesus/the self), limit the claim to those who stand in some apparent physiological continuity with the individual (Jews, males or all humanity) or expand this discovery out to include the widest possible collective on the basis of a universal monism or universal creaturehood. In panpsychism, and in theologies that emphasize the cosmic scope of salvation, the latter option is adopted. See Mary Midgely, 'The End of Anthropocentricism?', in *Philosophy and the Natural Environment*, ed. Robin Attfield and Andrew Belsey (Cambridge: Cambridge University Press, 1994), 103–12.

mind, soul or spirit lies at the heart of the problem. This monopoly has led to some recent theological gymnastics over the issue of Christology and creation. While some over-particularize the effects of the incarnation and discuss the possibility of multiple incarnations for different species, others underplay the particularity of Jesus of Nazareth in order to speak of a 'deep incarnation' of the whole universe, or the incarnation as the taking of non-specific 'flesh'.[76] Both the theory of multiple (species-specific) incarnations and the idea of one cosmic incarnation relate the doctrine of the incarnation to the wider creation through the medium of a common nature. Neither, however, seems suitable for articulating the cosmic importance of this particular God-human person, Jesus Christ. As such, it may be wise to return to the communication of salvation through the indwelling of the Holy Spirit to solve this riddle.

While I do not wish to develop a panpsychist deep incarnation, but instead offer a cosmic or 'deep' view of the presence of the Spirit of Christ (see Chapter 4), Niels Henrik Gregersen's argument is correct in emphasizing the universal and immediate relation of union between Jesus Christ and all creation.[77] The

76. Oliver Crisp, 'Multiple Incarnations', in *Reason, Faith, and History: Philosophical Essays for Paul Helm*, ed. Martin Stone (Aldershot: Ashgate, 2008), 219–38; Paul Tillich, *Systematic Theology*, vol. 2: *Existence and the Christ* (Chicago: University of Chicago Press, 1957), 95–6; Brian Hebblethwaite, 'The Impossibility of Multiple Incarnations', *Theology* 104 (2001): 323–34; Clough, *On Animals*, 82–3; Niels Henrik Gregersen, 'Cur deus caro: Jesus and the Cosmos Story', *Theology & Science* 11, no. 4 (2013): 370–93. Niels Henrik Gregersen, 'The Cross of Christ in an Evolutionary World', *Dialog: A Journal of Theology* 40, no. 3 (2001): 192–207; Niels Henrik Gregersen, 'Deep Incarnation and *Kenosis*: In, with, under, and as: A Response to Ted Peters', *Dialog: A Journal of Theology* 52, no. 3 (2013): 251–62. Although it is not always clear, I interpret Gregersen's stress on the interconnectedness of embodied existence as offering something stronger than a traditional denial of Docetism, although it is certainly possible to interpret him in the weaker sense. The danger with presenting the Son as hypostatically connected to the whole universe through the humanity of Jesus of Nazareth is that it seems to weaken the claim that this particular human life reveals and saves and to which Christianity must again return in worship. The description of the incarnation as the assumption of a non-specific flesh is favoured by animal theologians, Andrew Linzey, Denis Edwards and process theologian John Cobb Jr. See Andrew Linzey, 'Is Christianity Irredeemably Speciesist?', in *Animals on the Agenda: Questions about Animals for Theology and Ethics*, ed. Andrew Linzey and Dorothy Yamamoto (London: SCM Press, 1998), xvi; Denis Edwards, 'The Redemption of Animals in an Incarnational Theology', in *Creaturely Theology: On God, Humans, and Other Animals*, ed. David Clough and Celica Deane-Drummond (London: SCM Press, 2009), 81–99; John Cobb Jr, 'All Things in Christ', in *Animals on the Agenda: Questions about Animals for Theology and Ethics*, ed. Andrew Linzey and Dorothy Yamamoto (London: SCM Press, 1998), 173–80.

77. Holmes Rolston III has criticized the theology of deep incarnation on the grounds that it requires a panpsychist ontology to underpin it, although Gregersen does not discuss the implicit metaphysical ontology of his position. This may follow if a two-minds Christology is presupposed. Rolston gestures in this direction by implying that only subjects

salvific impact of Jesus's life arises from neither a common nature nor biological interconnection, but from the divine character of this life as the life of the second Person of the Trinity.[78] On the panpsychist ontology I am proposing, all are included into this divine life because all can receive Christ's Spirit, who as an equal member of the Godhead shares in that same divine life. The effects of salvation are universal in scope because of the universal range of the presence of Christ's Spirit, not a single common nature that we all share. Panpsychism facilitates a clear articulation of the inner omnipresence Spirit who is active in the deep fundamental nature of reality. This prevents distorting Christology, either by undermining the cosmic significance of Christ as a species-specific Saviour or by underemphasizing the particularity of the incarnate life of Jesus of Nazareth.

The beating heart of the Christian faith is the promise of salvation, and even Christology might be characterized as reflection upon the One who saves. The tunnelling effect of a human Saviour who only saves other humans is captured by the idea that 'saving trees and wetlands is a distraction from saving souls, building the church, and shoring up the approved moral issues'.[79] In matters of salvation the human monopoly on the mind has led, not primarily to the active negation of creation's good, but to its neglect as not an issue of ultimate concern.[80]

One traditional way to incorporate creation into soteriology is through perceiving the providence of God as a school or training ground for human development. Early church father, Basil of Caesarea, wrote,

> You will finally discover that the world was not conceived by chance and without reason, but for a useful end and for the great advantage of all beings, since it is really the school where reasonable souls exercise themselves, the training ground where they learn to know God.[81]

can possibly be considered candidates for incarnation, although he does not develop the point. Holmes Rolston III, 'Divine Presence – Causal, Cybernetic, Caring, Cruciform: From Information to Incarnation', in *Incarnation: On the Scope and Depth of Christology*, ed. Niels Henrik Gregersen (Minneapolis, MN: Fortress Press, 2015), 256.

78. Kathryn Tanner, *Jesus, Humanity and the Trinity: A Brief Systematic Theology* (Minneapolis, MN: Fortress Press, 2001), 54.

79. Steven M. Studebaker, 'Spirit in Creation: A Unified Theology of Grace and Creation Care', *Zygon: Journal of Religion and Science* 43, no. 4 (2008): 948.

80. The prioritization of souls over bodies in soteriology arises from the hope for a post-mortem endurance of the soul, in contrast or prior to the resurrection of the body. However, it is only if humans alone are perceived as ensouled creatures that the differing mechanisms of salvation become a tendency towards instrumentalism within Christian theology.

81. Basil, *Hexaemeron* I.6, in *Nicene and Post-Nicene Fathers*, ed. Philip Schaff and Henry Wallace, 2nd series, vol. 8 (Peabody, MA: Cosimo, 1995), 55.

Beneath the metaphor of creation as school is a soteriology of ascent, which became particularly popular in the twelfth and thirteenth centuries.[82] Humanity's vocation and hope lay in employing the rationality of the mind to contemplate the meaning within other creatures and (implicitly) to graduate from this worldly classroom.[83] Creation, in this view, may either be an empty sign, disposable after its pedagogical role is complete, or an active and living witness speaking of and to God; the latter is close to the panpsychist view developed below.

In early modern Protestantism, the pedagogical role of creation was maintained but the hermeneutic for reading the book of nature changed. The maximization of the doctrine of providence drained creation of power and agency in exchange for the assurance that natural processes were all direct signs for God's people and of God's sovereign control.[84] In the words of Christian Wolff,

> The world is accordingly a machine ... Consequently, the world and all things in it are God's instruments by means of which, since they are machines, he executes his intentions. From which it becomes evidence that they become a work of God's wisdom through the very fact that they are indeed machines.[85]

This is an argument for divine sovereignty, wisdom and providence on the basis of mechanistic philosophy. Here, the view of creation as a mindless and valueless machine is not an unintended distortion, but an apologetic strategy within Christian theology. Norman C. Habel, a leading figure within ecological hermeneutics, astutely writes that Western theologians have 'generally read the text to hear the voice of God not the voice of the Earth, God speaking through the whirlwind, not the whirlwind itself'.[86] As we shall see below, one need not deny God's speech through creatures in order to affirm creation's own speech, and to do so is to employ a panpsychist hermeneutic to hear and to join the voices of creation.

This section has argued that a human monopoly of spirit or mind distorts a wide spectrum of theological articulations of the relationship between God, humanity and creation. This monopoly is not an exhaustive account of the challenges facing eco-theology, but it is powerful enough to cripple other noble efforts to build a

---

82. Bonaventura, *The Soul's Journey to God, the Tree of Life, the Life of St. Francis*, Classics of Western Spirituality (Mahwah, NJ: Paulist Press, 1978), esp. 59.

83. Paul H. Santmire, *The Travail of Nature: The Ambiguous Ecological Promise of Christian Theology* (Minneapolis, MN: Fortress Press, 1985), 182.

84. As seen in Chapter 4's discussion of natural laws. Rupert Sheldrake, *The Rebirth of Nature: The Greening of the Science of God* (London: Rider, 1990), 20–1.

85. Christian Wolff, 'Reasonable Thoughts about God, the World, and the Human Soul' (1719), quoted in Jürgen Moltmann, *God in Creation: An Ecological Doctrine of Creation* (London: SCM Press, 1985), 314.

86. Norman C. Habel, 'The Challenge of Ecojustice Readings for Christian Theology', *Pacifica* 12 (2000): 133.

theology that will counteract the sinful tendency to exploit creation for our own benefit. If this monopoly is a common toxic thread through these theologies, then democratizing mentality by adopting panpsychism is one clear and powerful way to correct this distortion. The remainder of this chapter employs panpsychism to remythologize various biblical texts and to retrieve the theologically rich metaphors of the Christian tradition outlined above. The result is a panpsychist account of creation that can form the basis of a Christian environmental ethic.

Panpsychism and theological imagination: A proposal

The first section of this chapter, 'Panpsychism and ecological philosophy', outlined the benefit of a panpsychist ontology in the field of ecological philosophy but concluded that a naturalistically framed panpsychism is insufficient as a basis for environmental ethics. The second section, 'How a mental monopoly distorts doctrine', then focused on ways that Christian theologians have depicted the relationship between God, humanity and the wider creation and argued that when human beings are the sole creatures endowed with subjectivity, then otherwise rich theological metaphors are distorted. It remains the task of this final section to draw the pieces together and construct a proposal for how panpsychism may remythologize creation in the theo-dramatics of the Christian imagination. To speak of 'remythologizing theology' is to follow Kevin Vanhoozer in 'rendering explicit the implicit "metaphysics" of the biblical *mythos*'.[87] As such, the first stage of this proposal is a panpsychist interpretation of Scriptural passages that depict nature as speaking. The second stage is to recast non-human creatures, not as the theatrical scenery on humanity's stage, but as the active chorus of God's theo-drama, a created congregation of praise. This lends itself to, in the third stage, an attempt to rehabilitate the priestly and stewarding roles of humanity into a more egalitarian model of priesthood or interpersonal model of stewardship, better referred to as a minister or worship leader.

Metaphysics and the biblical mythos: Nature's voices

How Scripture is read and interpreted is always and already influenced by theological commitments and dispositions, even as Scripture then informs theological content and articulation as both source and norm. Given this symbiotic relationship, it is unsurprising that the tendencies to eschew and objectify creation examined above are accompanied by a hermeneutic that focuses almost exclusively upon the divine–human drama. This hermeneutic lens has left the interpretative question raised by Scriptural depictions of nature's voices 'woefully-neglected'.[88]

---

87. Kevin Vanhoozer, *Remythologizing Theology: Divine Action, Passion and Authorship* (Cambridge: Cambridge University Press, 2010), 183.

88. Mark Harris, ' "The Trees of the Field Shall Clap Their Hands" (Isaiah 55:12): What Does It Mean to Say That a Tree Praises God?', in *Knowing Creation: Perspectives from*

The interpretative question raised by these texts is the possibility that nature is 'a theological reality in its own right'.[89] When these passages are dismissed as 'poetic fancy', revealing an attitude of 'hasty anthropocentrism', the possibility of a richer theology of nature arising from these texts is ruled out *a priori*.[90]

Terrence Fretheim essay 'Nature's Praise of God in the Psalms' ignited a (now lively) debate of interpreting nature as a theological subject within the Hebrew Scriptures. Fretheim's article makes clear a panpsychist interpretation of these passages (particularly Ps. 148) has not been entirely absent from biblical scholarship.[91] These passages are certainly poetic, but they are not *merely* poetic; they are not without referent in the real world. Psalm 19:1–4, in particular, shows that the Psalmist recognized the interpretative problem of describing the very real praises of non-human creatures in anthropomorphic language:

> The heavens are telling the (*spr*) glory of God;
> and the firmament proclaims (*ngd*) his handiwork.
> Day to day pours forth speech (*nb'*),
> and night to night declares (*ḥwh*) knowledge.
> There is no speech, nor are there words;
> their voice is not heard;
> yet their voice goes out through all the earth,
> and their words to the end of the world. (NRSV[92])

This passage implies that the psalmist understood the theme of nature's praise both metaphorically *and* realistically.[93] Metaphor and realism are not mutually

Theology, Philosophy and Science, ed. Andrew B. Torrance and Thomas H. McCall (Grand Rapids, MI: Zondervan, 2018), 288. Santmire describes creation's praise of God as 'one of the least understood themes in the Old Testament'. Santmire, *Travail of Nature*, 198–99.

89. Harris, "'The Trees of the Field'", 287.

90. Terence E. Fretheim, 'Nature's Praise of God in the Psalms', *Ex Auditu* 3 (1987): 21. Fretheim, 'Nature's Praise', 21; Harris, "'The Trees of the Field'", 304.

91. Fretheim ('Nature's Praise', 20) cites the following realist interpretations: Hermann Gunkel, *Die Psalmen* (Göttingen: Vandenhoeck & Ruprecht, 1926); L. I. J. Stadelmann, *The Hebrew Conception of the World* (Rome: Pontifical Biblical Institute, 1970), 94, 7; H. W. Robinson, *Inspiration and Revelation in the Old Testament* (Oxford: Clarendon Press, 1946), 12, 15–16, 47; H. and H. A. Frankfort et al., *The Intellectual Adventure of Ancient Man: An Essay of Speculative Thought in Ancient Near East* (Chicago: University of Chicago Press, 1946), 4.

92. All Scripture quotations labelled NRSV are from New Revised Standard Version Bible, copyright © 1989 National Council of the Churches of Christ in the United States of America. Used by permission. All rights reserved worldwide.

93. Howard N. Wallace writes, 'The acceptance of the words of the psalmist as a metaphor does not allow us to dismiss them too quickly as simply a feature of the poetry … The metaphor points to a reality embodied within the physical world, one that our contemporary Western minds are not usually trained to comprehend.' Howard N. Wallace,

exclusive (indeed, theologians employ the two in conjunction all the time to speak of God). These passages realistically depict aspects of the natural world as subjects and describe the worship of these non-human creatures through metaphorical comparison to human worship.

It is unsurprising, therefore, that some of nature's illocution is depicted through non-anthropomorphic verbs such as 'quake' (*nût*; Ps. 99:1) for the earth and 'roar' (*r'm*; Ps. 98:7; Is. 42:10) for the seas and coastlands. Jeremiah 12:4 may be helpful here: 'How long will the land mourn, and the grass of every field wither?' Not only is mourning, the responsive act of a subject, parallel to a physical withering in this passage, but the verbal root of 'mourn' can imply 'dry up', although mourn is more common and it is paralleled with 'grown black'. It may be that drying up or growing black *is* the 'voice' of mourning. These descriptions are more in keeping with responses we would expect from these features of the natural world, but that is not to suggest that they do not constitute speech acts.

One of the most strikingly panpsychist discussions of the illocution of the non-human world is found in Rowan Williams's Gifford Lectures. Williams affirms that 'the bare fact is that the material world *speaks*'.[94] Williams extends the evolutionary grounds of human language deep into our embodied connection to the material world because 'material objects and the material world as such as always already "saturated" with the works of mind'.[95] The symbolic exchange that underpins causation in the natural world is, Williams suggests, more closely analogous to the cognition of human language than to the cogs of an inanimate machine. If the communication of the natural world, witnessed to in the Scriptural mythos, is to be realistically interpreted then the implied 'metaphysic' is a panpsychist ontology. Non-human creatures are communicating subjects, although the methods of communication are expected to be unique and appropriate to each creature. Rachel Muers has recently affirmed,

> Stones and trees cannot actually speak. It is not, however, very controversial to say that stones and trees can and do make sense, in all sorts of publically available ways (including ecological and theological ways) ... Specific natural phenomena, as we observe and interact with them, *tell* us things ... it is neither reasonable nor useful to reduce this 'telling' entirely to an act of meaning-making on the part of the observer.[96]

'"*Jubilate Deo omnis terra*": God and Earth in Psalm 65', in *The Earth Story in the Psalms and the Prophets*, ed. Norman C. Habel (Sheffield: Sheffield Academic Press, 2001), 62, 63.

94. Rowan Williams, *The Edge of Words: God and the Habits of Language* (London: Bloomsbury, 2014), 123.

95. Williams, *Edge of Words*, 101–3.

96. Rachel Muers, 'The Holy Spirit, the Voices of Nature and Environmental prophecy', *Scottish Journal of Theology* 67 (2010): 332.

Muers argues that the contemporary environmental crisis can be interpreted as a new narrative of prophecy – that the Spirit is gifting non-human nature with 'the miraculous extension of gifts of speech and hearing'.[97] This miracle need not be the creation of non-human subjects *ex nihilo* where there were none previously in the natural world. Instead, the miracle may take place, in accordance with the account of the inner presence of the Holy Spirit given in Chapter 4, as a transformation of humanity's recognition of the normative standing of the natural world, so that we can 'hear' the voices of creation that God has heard and loved since time began; 'Creation voices. It has never been silent.'[98]

What difference would it make for environmental ethics if we granted meaning-making voice to the non-human world? The importance of speech, auditory or otherwise, for animal rights is explored in Nicholas Wolterstorff's article 'Why Animals Don't Speak'. Building on his earlier work on *Divine Discourse*, Wolterstorff argues, 'To perform a speech action is to acquire a certain *normative standing* in one's society, a standing constituted in part by a certain complex of rights and/or responsibilities.'[99] It is not just that speech acts create or give moral standing to a speaker, but that noises or movements become speech acts only when the creature in question has moral standing in a community.[100] In order to hear a voice, we must first consider its owner to be a speaker – that is, figure of normative standing in a community. This is because 'speaking is a normative interaction' that includes the subject within a shared field of ethical consideration.[101]

Wolterstorff's argument serves to highlight how radical it is that the biblical authors frequently attribute illocutionary action to various non-human aspects of creation. Bauckham is right to refer to the Scriptural witness of creation's praise to God as 'the strongest antidote to anthropocentrism in the biblical and Christian tradition'.[102] Similarly, Northcott writes that 'humanity and the cosmos

97. Muers, 'Holy Spirit', 323.

98. Graham Ward, *Cities of God* (London: Routledge, 2000), 9.

99. Nicholas Wolterstorff, 'Why Animals Don't Speak', *Faith and Philosophy* 4, no. 4 (October 1987): 471; Nicholas Wolterstorff, *Divine Discourse: Philosophical Reflections on the Claim That God Speaks* (Cambridge: Cambridge University Press, 1995).

100. Wolterstorff, 'Why Animals Don't Speak', 474.

101. Wolterstorff, 'Why Animals Don't Speak', 478. Wolterstorff exemplifies the real power, and danger, of turning our ears away from the voices of nature and overlooking the passages of Scripture that give nature a normative standing in the divine economy, when he concludes that animals (nor non-human creation more widely) 'do not constitute a moral community' with either humanity or God (Wolterstorff, 'Why Animals Don't Speak', 475). The consequences of this conclusion for environmental ethics seem nothing sort of disastrous.

102. Bauckham, 'Joining Nature's Praise', 48. Bauckham rejects the panpsychist interpretation of these passages (which he misconstrues as attributing 'rational consciousness to all things') and argues instead that 'all creatures bring glory to God simply by being themselves' such that non-human creatures need only to exist to praise God. Bauckham, 'Joining Nature's Praise', 47. This is a neat and tidy solution which interprets

have moral significance, [because] both are required to make a moral response to the creator'.[103] The link between subject-to-subject illocutionary action and ethical standing underlines the significance of panpsychism for recovering a robustly biblical ecological ethic and remythologizing the Christian imagination.[104] Tying nature's voices, as depicted in Scripture, to a Christian ecology does not fall foul of the Augustinian problem of intrinsic values, discussed above. Fretheim affirms that non-human voices function as metaphors 'in terms of their intrinsic value rather than their instrumental value', but this intrinsic value is orientated towards God as its proper end.[105] Thus, the voices of creation – in so far as they witness to the Creator – are of sacramental value – a valuing of God through the signification, the 'voices' of creation.

Creation as community: One body, one spirit and one church

To speak of intrinsic values as sacramentally anchored, such that creation is a congregation that expresses praise and lament and groans in petition to God, is to speak of an ecclesia of creatures.[106] In a typically disorientating style, Simone Weil asks, 'How can the church call itself Catholic if the universe itself is left

these passages as little more than an affirmation of creation's protological goodness. The problem is that the Scriptural passages do not merely describe creation as praising God by virtue of their existence, but command or call creation to actively praise God (Dan. 3:52–90; Ps. 69:34; 89:5; 96:11–12; 98:7–8; 103:22; 148; 150:6; Isa. 42:10–11; Joel 2:21–2). Moreover, Scripture not only depicts creation praising but also as lamenting and groaning (Is. 24:4, 20–23; 33:9; Jer. 4:23–38; 11:23; 12:4, Hos. 4:3, Joel 1:10; 1:20; Hab. 2:11–12, and 'the mantra for Christian environmentalism', Rom. 8:19–22). Bauckham's 'just by being' interpretation of the voice of creation, that does not require subjectivity, fails to include the range of illocutionary acts and the invocative tense of these passages. This critique of Bauckham is made in David Horrell, *The Bible and the Environment: Towards a Critical Ecological Biblical Theology* (London: Equinox, 2010), 134; John Bolt, 'The Relation between Creation and Redemption in Romans 8:18–27', *Calvin Theological Journal* 30 (1995): 34. Quoted in Cherryl Hunt, David G. Horrell and Christopher Southgate, 'An Environmental Mantra? Ecological Interest in Romans 8.19–23 and a Modest Proposal for Its Narrative Interpretation', *Journal of Theological Studies* 59, no. 2 (2008): 546–79.

103. Northcott, *Environment*, 181. See Richard Cartwright Austin, *Hope for the Land: Nature in the Bible* (Atlanta, GA: John Knox Press, 1988), 49.

104. Moreover, the biblical instances of speech acts or symbolic utterance among non-human creatures can be taken as a minimal sort of evidence (but certainly not a proof) that panpsychism is compatible with a biblically shaped theology, influenced as much by Hebraic worship as Hellenistic philosophy.

105. Fretheim, 'Nature's Praise', 22, 26.

106. Margaret Baker has developed a rich exegetical reading of the priestly texts of the Hebrew Scriptures to argue that the temple and the creation mirror one another. The worship of the people of God in the temple is directly concerned with a theology of creation where God is in the midst of the created order and Adam (all humanity) plays a priestly

out?'[107] In this question catholicity connotes a universal breadth and inclusivity as wide as the indwelling action of God's Spirit. This is to imply that a Christian response to the ecological crisis is not only an important teaching *of* the church, but it must also be a teaching *about* the church, as a community of creatures existing in response to the Triune God.[108]

The idea of creation as a *community*, the 'earth community', is frequently spoken of as central to ecological theology, and yet the metaphysical implications of this metaphor are rarely examined.[109] Only subjects can form communities, for objects only form collections. Thus, to speak of creation as a community is to speak of creation as a diversity of subjects and for subjectivity to be a fundamental aspect of the universe. To speak of creation as a community is to invoke a panpsychist vision of the universe. If creation is a chorus, a community responding to and standing in relationship with God, then the creation may be properly considered a congregation, an *ecclesia* before the Creator.

The church is more than just a community of worshipers, however, for it has a Christological foundation. Here the humanity of Christ may appear to drive a wedge between the church as a human institution and the church as a cosmic chorus of praise. Yet, to posit any such wedge would be to forget the cosmic implications of the incarnation, death and resurrection realized by the presence of the Spirit. A cosmic Christology should neither be a cosmic (deep) incarnation such that the Logos is directly incarnate in all material existence, nor should it follow Teilhard de Chardin in anticipating a suprahuman consciousness engulfing and absorbing the subjects of creation. Instead, the presence of the Spirit of Christ that stretches across the whole panpsychist universe communicates Christ and transforms the universe into his ecclesial body; 'for in one Spirit we were all baptized into one body' (1 Cor. 12:13 NRSV). The presence of the Spirit, within even the most fundamental subjects of creation, is the Spirit of the risen Christ connecting creation to the One who sits at the right hand of the Father as the Great High Priest. This same, one, Spirit cries, 'Abba, Father!' and intercedes in the depths of creation with sighs too deep for human words (Rom. 8:15, 23–26).[110] Orthodox theologian John Chryssavgis expresses something of the implication

role in the natural order. Margaret Barker, *Creation: A Biblical Vision for the Environment* (London: T&T Clark, 2010), 18, 22, 122, 228.

107. Simone Weil, *Waiting for God* (New York: G. P. Putnam's Sons, 1951), 101.

108. Judith Gruber, 'Ec(o)clesiology: Ecology as Ecclesiology in *Laudato Si*', *Theological Studies* 78, no. 4 (2017): 808.

109. Examples of such language can be seen in Thomas Berry, *Befriending the Earth: A Theology of Reconciliation between Humans and the Earth* (Mystic: Twenty-Third, 1991), 13; Santmire, *Nature Reborn*, 116; Ernst M. Conradie, *An Ecological Christian Anthropology: At Home on Earth?* (Aldershot: Ashgate, 2005), 2; Leopold, *Sand County Almanac*, xix.

110. Moltmann advocates a similar proposal when he writes, 'The Creator, through the Spirit, *dwells* in his creation as a whole, and in every individual created being, by virtue of his Spirit holding them together and keeping them in life. The inner secret of the creation is this indwelling of God.' Moltmann, *God in Creation*, xii.

that this theology has for humanity's relationship to the environment when he writes,

> If one can visualize the activity of the Spirit in nature, then one can also perceive the consubstantiality between humanity and the created order; then one will no longer envisage humanity as the crown of a creation which it is able or called to subdue.[111]

To emphasize the work of the Holy Spirit within the interiority of the non-human world is to posit a continuity between human and other creatures, and to relinquish any claim that creation *needs* humanity as a mediator before God, to save it, to control or cultivate it. The boundaries of the church, as the body of Christ, are not limited by the incarnation of God to share a common nature with one species but are determined by the scope of the work of the Holy Spirit to transform the material subjects of this world into a Eucharistic extension of the Lamb who was slain. In a panpsychist creation, the boundaries of the church are cosmic.

The concept of a 'cosmic Eucharist' or 'cosmic liturgy' forms a central tenet of the response by Orthodox theologians to the ecological crisis.[112] This cosmic theological vision where the boundaries of the church encompass the entire universe is often expressed in panpsychist or quasi-panpsychist sentiments. The Metropolitan of Sourozh, Anthony Bloom, writes that

> there is not an atom in this world, from the meanest speck of dust to the greatest star, which does not hold in its core … the thrill, the tremor of its first movement

---

111. John Chryssavgis, 'The Earth as Sacrament: Insights from Orthodox Christian Theology and Spirituality', *The Oxford Handbook of Religion and Ecology*, ed. Roger S. Gottlieb (Oxford: Oxford University Press, 2006), 96.

112. Elizabeth Theokritoff, 'Creation and Priesthood in Modern Orthodox Thinking', *Ecotheology* 10, no. 3 (2005): 347; John Chryssavgis, 'New Heaven and a New Earth: Orthodox Christian Insights from Theology, Spirituality, and the Sacraments', in *Toward an Ecology of Transfiguration: Orthodox Christian Perspectives on Environment, Nature, and Creation*, ed. John Chryssavgis and Bruce V. Foltz (New York: Fordham University Press, 2013), 152–62; Olivier Clément, *On Human Being: A Spiritual Anthropology* (London: New City, 2000); Metropolitan Paulos mar Gregorios, *The Human Presence* (Madras: Christian Literature Society, 1980); Alexander Schmemann, *The World as Sacrament* (London: Darton, Longman & Todd, 1966); Philip Sherrard, *The Rape of Man and Nature* (Ipswich: Golgonooza Press, 1987). Theokritoff, 'Creation and Priesthood'; Kallistos Ware, *The Orthodox Church* (London: Penguin, 1993); Ware, 'Through Creation to the Creator'; John Zizioulas, 'Man in Priest of Creation', in *Living Orthodoxy in the Modern World*, ed. A. Walker and C. Carras (London: SPCK, 1996), 178–88.

of existence, of its coming to being, of its possessing infinite possibilities and of entering into the divine realm, so that it knows God, and rejoices in Him.[113]

Similarly, Bishop Kallistos Ware describes the Orthodox contribution to environmental ethics to lie in a sacramental, and subject-laden, view of the cosmos such that 'the environment consists not in dead matter but in living relationship [with God]'.[114]

The substantial continuity between all things, which resonates with the panpsychist argument from continuity, is expressed in the Eucharistic theology of the Orthodox church. Olivier Clément describes the 'great cosmic Eucharist' whereby we transform the universe 'from this dot of matter brought into the incandescence of the glorious Body, the fire spreads even to the rocks and the stars whose substance is present in the bread and wine'.[115] This sacramental view of the creation has the power to make every Sunday Eucharist an ecological parable, and a reflection of the importance of non-human matter within God's redemptive economy.[116] This is to reject any strong separation of the church as wholly sacred and the secular world as wholly profane, such that the promise of redemption applies only to the former at the expense of the latter. Instead, there is one reality, one comprehensive order, over which Christ is Lord, and although all things are not yet as they should be, we trust and hope that they will be when Christ returns.

What then is the role of humanity within a panpsychist universe whereby all creatures share in the dialogue between Creator and creation as an assembly of praise? Panpsychism, by counteracting the objectification of non-human creation from dead material to a community of subjects, offers a way to rehabilitate the various roles of leadership and responsibility discussed above. In particular, the Orthodox view of humanity as priests who mediate between God and creation can be transformed into a view of humanity as ministers, pastors or worship leaders, who join with non-human creatures leading them into closer relationship with God.[117] A comparative shift may also be possible in the depiction of human

113. Anthony Bloom, Metropolitan of Sourozh, 'Body and Matter in Spiritual Life', in *Sacrament and Image: Essays in the Christian Understanding of Man*, ed. A. M. Allchin (London: Fellowship of St Alban and St Sergius, 1987), 41.

114. Kallistos Ware, *Through the Creation to the Creator: Pallis Memorial Lecture 1995* (London: Friends of the Centre, 1996), 9; quoted in Theokritoff, 'Creation and Priesthood'.

115. Clément, *On Human Being*, 116.

116. John Habgood, 'A Sacramental Approach to Environmental Issues', in *Liberating Life: Contemporary Approaches to Ecological Theology*, ed. C. Birch, W. Eaken and J. B. McDaniel (Maryknoll, NY: Orbis Books, 1990), 46–53.

117. This idea emerges out of liturgical uses of the Scriptural passages that employ nature's voices. For example, the use of the Psalms in the daily offices and the Song of the Three Children (Dan. 3:28–65) on Holy Saturday in Orthodox churches where newly baptized Christians join the ranks of all creatures offering praise to God. Some orthodox theologians, contrary to John Zizioulas and Philip Sherrad critiqued above, emphasize that Orthodox theology of priesthood views the laity (and all creatures) *concelebrants* with the

stewardship, where humanity does not manage or control a material holding but is given temporary guardianship over God's non-human children, to care and raise them to flourish. Whichever metaphor is chosen the importance of panpsychism's contribution is the recognition of subjectivity to all creatures who stand in continuity with humanity in worship of the Creator.

Conclusion

This chapter explored the potential for panpsychism as an ontological resource for articulating the intrinsic and sacramental value of creation. The benefit of a panpsychist ontology for ecology is not as an alternative to Christian theology, but as a way to recover the richness within the Christian tradition for articulating humanity's shared creaturehood with the non-human world. It was argued that without panpsychism the objectification of creation – as the material for human worship, the empty household to be managed or the backdrop to the God–human drama – distorted the Christian imagination. A panpsychist metaphysic allows creation to be viewed as a congregation, a family and a chorus of praise in relationship with God. It was suggested that a cosmic Christology could be engaged at this point, with a pneumatic and ecclesial understanding of the body of Christ, extending throughout the subjects of creation by the indwelling Spirit. Humanity's vocation in the community may still be one of leadership (priesthood or guardianship) since this is congruent with the higher-order complexity of mind that humans possess, but this is a difference of degree and not an absolute difference in kind. Panpsychism may be counter-intuitive for many, but its benefits for constructing a Christian response to the ecological crisis are profound.

The articulation of an ecological doctrine of creation is one of the most significant challenges for the doctrine of creation today. As such the resource of panpsychism to this area, in addition to discussions of divine action, should not be dismissed lightly. Yet, what this investigation into ecological theology has uncovered is the Scriptural and liturgical basis to which panpsychism may also lay claim. Panpsychism is the metaphysic that is presupposed in the Scriptural depiction of the voices of nature, and these passages are prolific in the liturgies and

priests; John Chryssvgis, 'Ministry in the Orthodox Church', *Sourozh* 50 (199): 27–30. In the context of a cosmic liturgy, 'the place of the laity is taken by the rest of creation. Non-human creation is not merely passive material which is offered by humans in one way of another; it is also the community which provides the offering, each creature bringing its daily work – which is what the bread-making represents for human beings – to be transfigured into Christ.' Theokritoff, 'Creation and Priesthood', 354. If nothing else, this shows that there is a diversity of ways that Orthodox theologians conceive of the notion of a cosmic priesthood. Those variants, which invoke panpsychist imagery, do not fall foul of the ecologically critique offered by Bauckham and Northcott, as surveyed in the section 'How a mental monopoly distorts doctrine'.

hymns of many churches. Earlier chapters introduced panpsychism in a purely philosophical context and argued for an integration into Christian theology on this basis. What this chapter has shown is that this integration is not an imposition of dry rationalism, but already resounds within the context of worship. In response to the God who speaks creation into being from nothing and who continues the dialogue among and within all creatures, let the voices of creation give praise.

CONCLUSION

Far from providing final statements or definitive answers, this book has opened a line of enquiry into what I have called *theological panpsychism*. Panpsychism, as an ontological position regarding mind and matter within creation, cannot solely determine theological content and could be combined with any number of models of God. It is because panpsychism is, in and of itself, so theologically neutral that the version I have developed here requires the additional qualifier *theological*. The precarious partnership between panpsychism and naturalism was discussed, but I have not explicitly considered panpsychism's relationship to pantheism or panentheism here, although it could be employed within either model.[1]

This neutrality has been a guiding methodological principle of this book, and so central to both its constructive and critical argumentation. Constructively, the disentanglement of mentality from divinity has allowed me to consider the fecundity of panpsychism when the traditional affirmation of *creatio ex nihilo* is maintained. If this methodological principle or theological doctrine were compromised, then mentality would wrongly stand in metaphysical continuity with divinity, and we would have naturalized God. The subsumption of the divine being under a naturalistic framework was the critique levelled against both Process theology in the introduction and emergence theologies in Chapter 1. It was seen that while emergence theory does not necessitate such naturalization, the interdisciplinary aims of emergentism – as an overarching worldview used to unite all academic disciplines and all reality – made such an extension into theology difficult to avoid.

If a theologian employing emergence theory were to avoid such an error, however, she would still encounter the philosophical difficulties facing the emergence of mind as a repeated instance of *anima ex nihilo* for every new mind. While a theologian can certainly maintain that God inputs souls into the universe for every new ensouled creature (the traditional theory of creationism)

---

1. Joanna Leidenhag, 'Unity between God and Mind? A Study on the Relationship between Panpsychism and Pantheism', *Sophia: International Journal of Philosophy and Traditions* 58, no. 4 (2019): 543–61; Joanna Leidenhag, 'Can Panpsychism Help Make Sense of Panentheism?', in *Panpsychism and Panentheism*, ed. Ludwig Jaskolla and Benedikt Göcke (Leiden: Studies in Philosophy of Religion, Mentis Press, 2020), 65–90.

in conjunction with material complexity, this is perhaps not the most elegant story for the origin of souls. Traditional debates in theological anthropology over the origin of the soul, creationism and traducianism may well be parallel to some forms of emergent dualism and theological panpsychism, respectively. This antiquated question over how souls are created and how they relate to the body is in need of updating if dualistic positions in anthropology are to continue to regain prominence in academia and become successful paradigms for future research. It is not enough to assert the existence of the soul; theologians must also attempt to provide a compelling story regarding the soul's relationship to the body and the wider cosmos, and this is something panpsychism and emergence theory both try to do. While this book has laid important groundwork in considering the implications of panpsychism for the doctrine of creation, further research will need to consider the consequences of a panpsychist philosophy of mind for theological anthropology.

Following in the wake of leading philosophers who have become disgruntled with the theory of emergence, I turned to consider the recent revival of panpsychism as a serious philosophical articulation of the place of mind within our universe. Contemporary panpsychism can be characterized as the product of three commitments. The first is the rejection of emergence theory. Since emergence theory and panpsychism both fight for the sacred middle ground between reductive physicalism and Cartesian dualism, they stand as natural competitors. The second is the return to emphasizing the reality of mind and *qualia* in light of the so-called 'hard problem' of consciousness; here panpsychism stands as an ally for more dualistic philosophers. Yet, this alliance is challenged by the third commitment: an ontological continuity between all things, as implied by evolutionary science. The ability to hold these three commitments together has returned panpsychism to the academic stage as an attractive ontology. Of the problems currently facing panpsychism, the combination problem is by far the most serious. While more work needs to be done in this area, the current proposals indicate that, so far, this is not sufficient reason to abandon the panpsychist research project. Panpsychism, not a complete or finished theory, is as least as cogent as its main philosophical competitors.

Further reflection on the combination problem will be essential if research into theological panpsychism is to be continued in the area of anthropology. Questions of personal identity, unity and continuity over time, both in this life and in the intermediate state or resurrected body, will need to be addressed. For example, since panpsychism is committed to a view of subjects that are not closed off from one another, but can combine or unite, exploration into how this relational notion of subjectivity might parallel theological discussion of the ecclesial body of Christ could be a profitable line of investigation. This, in turn, could draw upon a panpsychist understanding of the Eucharist, which was very briefly touched upon at several points, to suggest a real unity with Christ as the ground for a Christological anthropology. While the combination problem remains a puzzle for panpsychist philosophers, it may yet contain great potential for theological anthropology.

After assessing the coherency of panpsychism as a philosophical position, I turned at the end of Chapter 2 to consider the relationship between panpsychism and Christian theology. It was first argued that if panpsychist philosophers were to consistently apply their argumentation to the universe as a whole, rather than just to individual creatures, then it would point them towards theism. While panpsychism does not strictly entail theism, it carries commitments and arguments that are strongly congruent with belief in a transcendent Creator. Further investigation into the apologetic advantages of panpsychism is an avenue of enquiry yet to be fully explored. If this argument rings alarm bells in the mind of secular panpsychists, it should be an encouragement to theistic philosophers and theologians to consider a future alliance between Christian theism and panpsychism.

A brief interlude considered the relationship between panpsychism and theology in the thought of Gottfried Wilhelm von Leibniz. This historical investigation served as a reconnaissance mission, to discover how panpsychism has been employed to serve theological ends previously, and so to learn what distinctive contributions panpsychism might make today. First, it was seen that panpsychism both arose out of and served to defend Leibniz's affirmation of the doctrine of creation *ex nihilo*. This was an important discovery, since the doctrine of creation *ex nihilo* is the theological commitment that underpins the methodological principle discussed above. The consequence of placing mentality firmly on the side of creation is that the initial act of creation becomes radically unique, such that no ontological additions or radically new features of the world need to be created at a later date. Second, therefore, the created order is to be considered comprehensive and complete, in the sense of being pregnant with all future developments. This does not lead to a cosmos that is closed off or emptied of divine presence and activity. Rather, the interior depth that panpsychism posits within all of creation provides a kind of ontological 'space' for God's indwelling Spirit. Thus, third, a panpsychist creation is sacramentally construed as open to the interactive experience of the Creator. As such, panpsychism offers Christian theology a truly distinctive way of maintaining the absolute and radical transcendence of God, while articulating a robust sense of the immanence of God as felt by creatures.

In many ways, this balance between transcendence and immanence has been the central problem for recent theologies of creation. The difficulty of holding together these two aspects of God's relationship with the world have been most keenly felt in discussions regarding divine action and eco-theology. These two areas of debate were employed as testing grounds for theological panpsychism. Chapter 4 examined how a shadow, characterized through the language of divine intervention, has been cast over theological claims for special divine action. This shadow has arisen in light of scientific assumptions, ethical concerns and theo-political tensions. Each of these issues have been separately responded to, with increasing degrees of success, in the work of Robert J. Russell, David Ray Griffin and Kathryn Tanner. This chapter furthered the idea that panpsychism is a flexible ontology by arguing that it would benefit each theological project separately. Overall, panpsychism provides an ontological space for articulating the interior presence of the Holy Spirit, not merely accompanying but also transforming the creation, without interrupting or injecting new entities into the comprehensive created order. It was argued that if the model of double agency, with which panpsychism is largely congruent, is to account for the variety and interactive nature of Christianity's central claims regarding divine action, then an account of the particular and internal presence of the Spirit is also required. Panpsychism's main contribution is to combine a theory of secondary powers with the felt internal presence of the Holy Spirit, by positing indwelling powers in continuity with consciousness within all things.

After exploring and critiquing the role that panpsychism already plays within eco-philosophy, Chapter 5 argued that panpsychism provides an ontological framework for realistically interpreting the voices and response of creation. This chapter draws upon the idea of panpsychism as a sacramental ontology, full of sacramental value, and offered a view of creation as a community of praise. While it is already clear that panpsychism excludes ontological depictions of human uniqueness, it may still be that human beings have a distinctive role to play as leaders, priests and stewards of this created community.

It was noted in the beginning of this book that panpsychism suffers from a cumbersome name, counter-intuitive content and its fair share of historical baggage. Yet, I have argued that if contemporary theologians can overlook these hindrances, then panpsychism has the potential to be of great benefit to Christian theology. A world in which mind is a fundamental property found throughout creation is a cosmos full of experience, open to God's presence, and responsive in giving God glory. A more enchanted and theologically rich ontology would be hard to come by. At the very least, the revival of panpsychism within philosophy of mind is not a development that theologians should fear and resist, but is a trend that theologians should welcome and may profitably employ within a doctrine of creation.

BIBLIOGRAPHY

Abraham, William J. *Divine Agency and Divine Action: Exploring and Evaluating the Debate*, vol. 1. Oxford: Oxford University Press, 2017.

Adams, Marilyn McCord. 'The Indwelling of the Holy Spirit: Some Alternative Models'. In *The Philosophy of Human Nature in Christian Perspective*, edited by Peter J. Weigel and Joseph G. Prud'homme, 83–99. New York: Peter Lang, 2005.

Adams, Robert. *Leibniz: Determinist, Theist, Idealist*. Oxford: Oxford University Press, 1994.

Albahari, Miri. 'Beyond Cosmopsychism and the Great I Am: How the World Might Be Grounded in Universal "Advaitic" Consciousness'. In *Routledge Handbook of Panpsychism*, edited by William Seager. London: Routledge, 2020.

Alexander, Samuel. *Space, Time and Deity: The Gifford Lectures, 1916–1918*, vol. 2. London: Macmillan, 1920.

Alston, William P. *Divine Nature and Human Language: Essays in Philosophical Theology*. Ithaca, NY: Cornell University Press, 1989.

Alston, William P. 'Divine Action, Human Freedom, and the Laws of Nature'. In *Quantum Cosmology and the Laws of Nature: Scientific Perspectives on Divine Action*, edited by Robert J. Russell, Nancey Murphy and C. J. Isham, 185–206. Vatican City State/Berkeley, CA: Vatican Observatory/Centre for Theology and the Natural Sciences, 1996.

Antognazza, Maria Rosa. *Leibniz on the Trinity and the Incarnation: Reason and Revelation in the Seventeenth Century*. New Haven, CT: Yale University Press, 2007.

Antognazza, Maria Rosa. 'Leibniz's Theory of Substance and His Metaphysics of the Incarnation'. In *Locke and Leibniz on Substance*, edited by Paul Lodge and Tom Stoneham, 231–53. London: Routledge, 2015.

Aquinas, Thomas. *Summa Theologiae, Questions on God*. Edited by Brian Davies and Brian Leftow. Cambridge: Cambridge University Press, 2006.

Aristotle. *De Anima*. Translated by J. A. Smith. Oxford: Clarendon Press, 1931.

Aristotle. *The Metaphysics*. In *The Complete Works of Aristotle*, edited by Jonathan Barnes. Princeton, NJ: Princeton University Press, 1998.

Armstrong, David. 'Naturalism, Materialism, and First Philosophy'. In *Contemporary Materialism*, edited by Paul Moser and J. D. Trout, 35–46. New York: Routledge, 1995.

Armstrong-Buck, Susan. 'Whitehead's Metaphysical System as a Foundation for Environmental Ethics', *Environmental Ethics* 8 (1986): 241–59.

Augustine. *The Works of Aurelius Augustine*. In *On Christian Doctrine; the Enchiridion; on Catechising; and on Faith and the Creed*, edited by Marcus Dods. Edinburgh: T&T Clark, 1873.

Austin, Richard Cartwright. *Hope for the Land: Nature in the Bible*. Atlanta, GA: John Knox Press, 1988.

Backus, Irena. *Leibniz: Protestant Theologian*. Oxford: Oxford University Press, 2016.

Baillie, Donald M. *God Was in Christ: An Essay on Incarnation and Atonement*. London: Faber & Faber, 1961.

Balthasar, Hans Urs von. *Presence and Thought: An Essay on the Religious Philosophy of Gregory of Nyssa*. Translated by Mark Sebanc. San Francisco, CA: Ignatius Press, 1995.

Barbour, Ian. 'Neuroscience, Artificial Intelligence, and Human Nature: Theological and Philosophical Reflections'. In *Neuroscience and the Person: Scientific Perspectives on Divine Action*, edited by Robert J. Russell, Nancey Murphy, Theo Meyering and Michael Arbib, 249–80. Vatican City State/Berkeley, CA: Vatican Observatory/Centre for Theology and the Natural Sciences, 1999.

Barker, Margaret. *Creation: A Biblical Vision for the Environment*. London: T&T Clark, 2010.

Barth, Karl. 'How My Mind Has Changed', *Christian Century* 56 (1939): 37–8.

Barth, Karl. *Church Dogmatics* III/1. Edited and translated by G. W. Bromiley and T. F. Torrance. London: T&T Clark, 2009.

Barth, Karl. *Church Dogmatics* III/2. Edited by G. W. Bromiley and T. F. Torrance, translated by Harold Knight et al. Edinburgh: T&T Clark, 1960.

Barth, Karl. *Church Dogmatics* IV/3.1. Edited and translated by G. W. Bromiley and T. F. Torrance. Edinburgh: T&T Clark, 2009.

Barth, Markus. 'Christ and All Things'. In *Paul and Paulinism: Essays in Honour of C. K. Barrett*, edited by M. D. Hooker and S. G. Wilson, 160–72. London: SPCK, 1982.

Basil. *Homelia Hexaemeron*. In *Nicene and Post-Nicene Fathers*, edited by Philip Schaff and Henry Wallace, 2nd series, vol. 8. Peabody, MA: Cosimo, 1995.

Batterman, Robert W. 'Emergence, Singularities, and Symmetry Breaking', *Foundations of Physics* 41, no. 6 (2010): 1031–50.

Bauckham, Richard. 'Joining Nature's Praise of God', *Ecotheology* 7 (2002): 45–59.

Bavel, Tarsicius J. van. 'The Creator and the Integrity of Creation', *Augustinian Studies* 21 (1990): 1–33.

Bedau, Mark A., and Paul Humphreys. 'Introduction'. In *Emergence: Contemporary Readings in Philosophy and Science*, edited by Mark A. Bedau and Paul Humphreys, 1–6. Cambridge, MA: MIT Press, 2008.

Berry, Thomas. *Befriending the Earth: A Theology of Reconciliation between Humans and the Earth*. Mystic, CT: Twenty-Third, 1991.

Birch, Charles, and John B. Cobb. *Liberation of Life: From the Cell to the Community*. Cambridge: Cambridge University Press, 1985.

Bloom, Anthony, Metropolitan of Sourozh. 'Body and Matter in Spiritual Life'. In *Sacrament and Image: Essays in the Christian Understanding of Man*, edited by A. M. Allchin, 36–46. London: Fellowship of St Alban and St Sergius, 1987.

Boersma, Hans. 'Sacramental Ontology: Nature and the Supernatural in the Ecclesiology of Henri de Lubac', *New Blackfriars* 88, no. 1015 (2007): 242–73.

Boersma, Hans. *Heavenly Participation: The Weaving of a Sacramental Tapestry*. Grand Rapids, MI: Eerdmans, 2011.

Bolt, John. 'The Relation between Creation and Redemption in Romans 8:18–27', *Calvin Theological Journal* 30 (1995): 34–51.

Bonaventura. *The Soul's Journey to God*. London: SPCK Classics of Western Spirituality, 1978.

Broad, C. D. *The Mind and Its Place in Nature*. New York: Routledge, [1925] 2013.

Broad, C. D. *Leibniz: An Introduction*. Edited by C. Lewy. Cambridge: Cambridge University Press, 1975.

Brown, Sam P., and Rufus A. Johnstone. 'Cooperation in the Dark: Signalling and Collective Action in Quorum-Sensing Bacteria', *Proceedings of the Royal Society Biological Sciences* 268, no. 1470 (2001): 961–5.

Brown, Stuart. 'Soul, Body and Natural Immortality', *The Monist* 81, no. 4 (1998): 573–90.

Brunner, Emil. *Revelation and Reason*. Philadelphia, PA: Westminster Press, 1946.

Brüntrup, Godehard. 'Emergent Panpsychism'. In *Panpsychism: Contemporary Perspectives*, edited by Godehard Brüntrup and Ludwig Jaskolla, 48–74. Oxford: Oxford University Press, 2017.

Brüntrup, Godehard, and Ludwig Jaskolla. 'Introduction'. In *Panpsychism: Contemporary Perspectives*, edited by Godehard Brüntrup and Ludwig Jaskolla, 1–16. Oxford: Oxford University Press, 2017.

Buber, Martin. *I and Thou*. Translated by Ronald Smith, 2nd edn. New York: Charles Scribner's Sons, 1958.

Bultmann, Rudolf. *Jesus Christ and Mythology*. New York: Charles Scribner's Sons, 1958.

Callicott, J. Baird. 'Intrinsic Value, Quantum Theory, and Environmental Ethics', *Environmental Ethics* 7 (1985): 257–75.

Calvin, Jean. *Institutes of the Christian Religion*. Translated by Henry Beveridge. Peabody, MA: Hendrickson, 2008.

Carroll, Sean. *The Big Picture: On the Origins of Life, Meaning, and the Universe Itself*. New York: Dutton, 2016.

Chalmers, David J. 'The Puzzle of Conscious Experience', *Scientific American* 273 (1995): 80–6.

Chalmers, David J. *The Conscious Mind: In Search of a Fundamental Theory*. Oxford: Oxford University Press, 1996.

Chalmers, David J. 'Facing Up to the Hard Problem of Consciousness'. In *Explaining Consciousness: The Hard Problem*, edited by Jonathan Shear, 9–33. Cambridge, MA: MIT Press, 1997.

Chalmers, David J. *The Character of Consciousness*. Oxford: Oxford University Press, 2010.

Chalmers, David J. 'Panpsychism and Panprotopsychism'. In *Panpsychism: Contemporary Perspectives*, edited by Godehard Brüntrup and Ludwig Jaskolla, 19–47. Oxford: Oxford University Press, 2017.

Chalmers, David J. 'The Combination Problem'. In *Panpsychism: Contemporary Perspectives*, edited by Godehard Brüntrup and Ludwig Jaskolla, 179–214. Oxford: Oxford University Press, 2017.

Chryssavgis, John. 'The Earth as Sacrament: Insights from Orthodox Christian Theology and Spirituality'. In *The Oxford Handbook of Religion and Ecology*, edited by Roger S. Gottlieb, 92–113. Oxford: Oxford University Press, 2006.

Chryssavgis, John. 'New Heaven and a New Earth: Orthodox Christian Insights from Theology, Spirituality, and the Sacraments'. In *Toward an Ecology of Transfiguration: Orthodox Christian Perspectives on Environment, Nature, and Creation*, edited by John Chryssavgis and Bruce V. Foltz, 152–62. New York: Fordham University Press, 2013.

Clark, Stephen R. L. 'Global Religion'. In *Philosophy and the Natural Environment*, edited by Robin Attfield and Andrew Belsey, 113–26. Cambridge: Cambridge University Press, 1994.

Clarke, D. S. *Panpsychism and the religious attitude*. New York: SUNY Press, 2003.

Clarke, Samuel. *A Demonstration of the Being and Attributes of God*. Edited by Ezio Vailati. Cambridge: Cambridge University Press, 1998.

Clayton, Philip. *God and Contemporary Science*. Edinburgh: Edinburgh University Press, 1997.

Clayton, Philip. *The Problem of God in Modern Thought*. Grand Rapids, MI: Eerdmans, 2000.

Clayton, Philip. *Mind and Emergence: From Quantum to Consciousness*. Oxford: Oxford University Press, 2004.

Clayton, Philip. 'Conceptual Foundations of Emergence Theory'. In *The Re-Emergence of Emergence: The Emergentist Hypothesis from Science to Religion*, edited by Philip Clayton and Paul Davies, 1–34. Oxford: Oxford University Press, 2006.

Clayton, Philip. *Adventures of the Spirit: God, World, Divine Action*. Minneapolis, MN: Fortress Press, 2008.

Clayton, Philip. 'Towards a Theory of Divine Action That Has Traction'. In *Scientific Perspectives on Divine Action: Twenty Years of Challenge and Progress*, edited by Robert J. Russell, Nancey Murphy and William R. Stoeger SJ, 85–110. Vatican State/Notre Dame, IN: Vatican State Observatory/Centre for Theology and the Natural Sciences, 2008.

Clayton, Philip, and Steven Knapp. *The Predicament of Belief: Science, Philosophy and Faith*. Oxford: Oxford University Press, 2011.

Clement, Olivier. *On Human Being: A Spiritual Anthropology*. London: New City, 2000.

Cleve, J. van. 'Mind-Dust or Magic? Panpsychism versus Emergence', *Philosophical Perspectives* 4 (1990): 215–26.

Clough, David L. *On Animals. Volume One: Systematic Theology*. London: T&T Clark, 2012.

Cobb, John B. Jr. *A Christian Natural Theology: Based on the Thought of Alfred North Whitehead*. London: Lutterworth Press, 1966.

Cobb, John B., Jr. 'All Things in Christ'. In *Animals on the Agenda: Questions about Animals for Theology and Ethics*, edited by Andrew Linzey and Dorothy Yamamoto, 173–80. London: SCM Press, 1998.

Cobb, John B., Jr, and David Ray Griffin. *Process Theology: An Introductory Exposition*. Louisville, KY: Westminster John Knox Press, 1976.

Coleman, Sam. 'Being Realistic: Why Physicalism May Entail Panexperientialism'. In Galen Strawson et al., *Consciousness and Its Place in Nature*, edited by Anthony Freeman, 40–52. Exeter: Imprint Academic, 2006.

Coleman, Sam. 'Mental Chemistry: Combination for Panpsychists', *Dialectica* 66 (2012): 137–66.

Coleman, Sam. 'The Real Combination Problem: Panpsychism, Micro-Subjects, and Emergence', *Erkenntnis* 79 (2014): 19–44.

Coleman, Sam. 'Panpsychism and Neutral Monism: How to Make Up One's Mind'. In *Panpsychism: Contemporary Perspectives*, edited by Godehard Brüntrup and Ludwig Jaskolla, 249–82. Oxford: Oxford University Press, 2017.

Coleman, Sam. 'The Evolution of Nagel's Panpsychism', *Klesis* 41 (2018): 180–202.

Conradie, Ernst. *An Ecological Christian Anthropology: At Home on Earth?* Aldershot: Ashgate, 2005.

Conradie, Ernst. 'The Whole Household of God (Oikos): Some Ecclesiological Perspectives (Part 1)', *Scriptura* 94 (2007): 1–9.

Conradie, Ernst. 'The Whole Household of God (Oikos): Some Ecclesiological Perspectives (Part 2)', *Scriptura* 94 (2007): 10–28.

Copan, Paul, and William Lane Craig. *Creation Out of Nothing: A Biblical, Philosophical, and Scientific Exploration*. Grand Rapids, MI: Baker Academic, 2004.

Copestake, David R. 'Emergent Evolution and the Incarnation of Jesus Christ', *Modern Believing* 36 (1995): 27–33.

Cornforth, Daniel M., et al. 'Combinatorial Quroum Sensing Allows Bacteri to Resolve Their Social and Physical Environment', *Proceedings of the National Academy of Science of the United States of America* 111, no. 11 (2014): 4280–4.

Cotes, Roger. 'Cotes' Preface to the Second Edition of the *Principia*'. In Isaac Newton, *Newton's Philosophy of Nature: Selections from His Writings*, edited by H. S. Thayer, 116–34. New York: Hafner Library of Classics, 1953.

Craig, William Lane. 'The Cosmological Argument'. In *The Rationality of Theism*, edited by Paul Copan and Paul K. Moser, 112–31. London: Routledge, 2003.

Crane, Tim. 'The Significance of Emergence'. In *Physicalism and Its Discontents*, edited by Carl Gillett and Barry Loewer, 207–24. Cambridge: Cambridge University Press, 2001.

Crisp, Oliver. 'Incarnation'. In *The Oxford Handbook of Systematic Theology*, edited by John Webster, Kathryn Tanner and Iain Torrance, 160–75. Oxford: Oxford University Press, 2007.

Crisp, Oliver. 'Multiple Incarnations'. In *Reason, Faith, and History: Philosophical Essays for Paul Helm*, edited by Martin Stone, 219–38. Aldershot: Ashgate, 2008.

Danto, Arthur. 'Naturalism'. In *The Encyclopaedia of Philosophy*, edited by Paul Edwards, vol. 5. New York: Macmillan and Free Press, 1967.

Darwin, Charles. *The Life and Letters of Charles Darwin*, edited by Francis Darwin. New York: D. Appleton, 1896.

Davies, Paul. 'Introduction: Toward an Emergentist Worldview'. In *From Complexity to Life: On Emergence of Life and Meaning*, edited by Niels Henrik Gregersen, 3–18. Oxford: Oxford University Press, 2003.

Davies, Paul. 'Complexity and the Arrow of Time'. In *From Complexity to Life: On Emergence of Life and Meaning*, edited by Niels Henrik Gregersen, 72–92. Oxford: Oxford University Press, 2003.

Davies, Paul. 'Teleology without Teleology: Purpose through Emergent Complexity'. In *In Whom We Live and Move and Have Our Being: Panentheistic Reflections on God's Presence in a Scientific World*, edited by Philip Clayton and Arthur Peacocke, 95–108. Grand Rapids, MI: Eerdmans, 2004.

Davison, Andrew. 'Looking Back toward the Origin: Scientific Cosmology as Creation *ex nihilo* Considered "from the Inside"'. In *Creation* ex nihilo: *Origins, Development, Contemporary Challenge*, edited by Gary A. Anderson and Markus Bockmuehl, 367–89. Notre Dame, IN: Notre Dame University Press, 2018.

Deacon, Terrence. 'The Hierarchic Logic of Emergence: Untangling the Interdependence of Evolution and Self-Organization'. In *Evolution and Learning: The Baldwin Effect Reconsidered*, edited by B. Weber and D. Depew, 273–308. Cambridge, MA: MIT Press, 2003.

Deacon, Terrence. *Incomplete Nature: How Mind Emerged from Matter*. New York: Norton, 2012.

Deacon, Terrence, and Ursula Goodenough. 'From Biology to Consciousness to Morality', *Zygon: Journal of Religion and Science* 36, no. 1 (2003): 801–19.

Deacon, Terrence, and Ursula Goodenough. 'The Sacred Emergence of Nature'. In *The Oxford Handbook of Religion and Science*, edited by Philip Clayton and Zachary Simpson, 853–71. Oxford: Oxford University Press, 2008.

Delafield-Butt, Jonathan T., et al. 'Prospective Guidance in a Free-Swimming Cell', *Biological Cybernetics* 106 (2012): 283–93.

Delio, Ilia. *The Emergent Christ: Exploring the Meaning of Catholic in an Evolutionary Universe*. Maryknoll, NY: Orbis Books, 2011.

Dennett, Daniel. *Consciousness Explained*. Boston, MA: Little, Brown, 1991.

Devitt, Michael. 'Naturalism and the A Priori', *Philosophical Studies* 92 (1998): 45–64.

Diamond, Irene, and Gloria F. Orenstein. *Reweaving the World: The Emergence of Ecofeminism*. San Francisco, CA: Sierra Club Books, 1990.

Dooyeweerd, Herman. *A New Critique of Theoretical Thought: The Necessary Presuppositions of Philosophy*. Translated by David H. Freeman and William S. Young, vol. 1. Jordon Station, Ontario: Paideia Press Ltd., 1984.

Drees, Willem B. *Religion and Science in Context: A Guide to the Debates*. New York: Routledge, 2010.

Dupré, Louis. *Passage to Modernity: An Essay on the Hermeneutics of Nature and Culture*. New Haven, CT: Yale University Press, 1993.

Duve, Christian de. *Vital Dust: Life as a Cosmic Imperative*. New York: Basic Books, 1995.

Edwards, Denis. *Breath of Life: A Theology of the Creator Spirit*. Maryknoll, NY: Orbis Books, 2004.

Edwards, Denis. *Jesus and the Cosmos*. Eugene, OR: Wipf and Stock, 2004.

Edwards, Denis. 'The Redemption of Animals in an Incarnational Theology'. In *Creaturely Theology: On God, Humans, and Other Animals*, edited by David Clough and Celica Deane-Drummond, 81–99. London: SCM Press, 2009.

Ellis, Fiona. *God, Value and Nature*. Oxford: Oxford University Press, 2014.

Ellis, George F. R. 'Ordinary and Extraordinary Divine Action'. In *Chaos and Complexity: Scientific Perspectives on Divine Action*, edited by Robert John Russell, Nancey Murphy, and William R. Stoeger, SJ, 359–96. Vatican City State/Berkeley, CA: Vatican Observatory/Centre for Theology and the Natural Sciences, 1997.

Ellis, George F. R. 'True Complexity and Its Associated Ontology'. In *Science and Ultimate Reality: Quantum Theory, Cosmology, and Complexity*, edited by John D. Barrow, Paul C. W. Davies and Charles L. Harper Jr, 607–36. Cambridge: Cambridge University Press, 2004.

Ellis, George F. R. 'Physics, Complexity, and the Science-Religion Dialogue'. In *The Oxford Handbook of Religion and Science*, edited by Philip Clayton and Zachary Simpson, 751–66. Oxford: Oxford University Press, 2008.

Epperson, Michael. *Quantum Mechanics and the Philosophy of Alfred North Whitehead*. New York: Fordham University Press, 2012.

Erickson, Millard J. *Christian Theology*. Grand Rapids, MI: Baker Book House, 1985.

Farrer, Austin. *Faith and Speculation: An Essay in Philosophical Theology*. New York: New York University Press, 1967.

Farris, Joshua R. *The Soul of Theological Anthropology: A Cartesian Exploration*. New York: Routledge, 2016.

Feigl, Herbert. 'The "Mental" and the "Physical"', *Minnesota Studies in the Philosophy of Science* 2 (1958): 370–497.

Feigl, Herbert. 'Some Crucial Issues of Mind-Body Monism', *Synthese* 3, no. 4 (1971): 295–312.

Feinberg, Joel. 'The Rights of Animals and Unborn Generations'. In *Philosophy and Environmental Crisis*, edited by W. T. Blackstone, 43–68. Athens: University of Georgia Press, 1974.

Fergusson, David A. S. *The Providence of God: A Polyphonic Approach*. Cambridge: Cambridge University Press, 2018.

Ferré, Frederick. 'Personalistic Organicism: Paradox or Paradigm?' In *Philosophy and the Natural Environment*, edited by Robert Attfield, 59–73. Oxford: Oxford University Press, 1994.

Feynman, Richard. *The Character of Physical Law*. Cambridge, MA: MIT Press, 1967.

Flanagan, Owen. 'Varieties of Naturalism'. In *The Oxford Handbook of Religion and Science*, edited by Philip Clayton and Zachary Simpson, 403–52. Oxford: Oxford University Press, 2008.

Fodor, Jerry A. 'The Big Idea: Can There Be a Science of the Mind?' *Times Literary Supplement* (3 July 1992): 5.

Ford, Lewis. *The Lure of God: A Biblical Background for Process Theism*. Minneapolis, MN: Fortress Press, 1978.

Forrest, Peter. *God without the Supernatural: A Defence of Scientific Theism*. Ithaca, NY: Cornell University Press, 1996.

Frankenberry, Nancey. 'The Emergent Paradigm and Divine Causation', *Process Studies* 13 (1983): 202–17.

Frankfort, H., H. A. Frankfort, John A. Wilson, Thorkild Jacobsen and William A. Irwin. *The Intellectual Advent of Ancient Man*. Chicago: University of Chicago Press, 1946.

Freeman, Anthony. 'God as an Emergent Property', *Journal of Consciousness Studies* 8, no. 9–10 (2001): 147–59.

Fretheim, Terence E. 'Nature's Praise of God in the Psalms', *Ex Auditu* 3 (1987): 16–30.

Gabora, Liane. 'Amplifying Phenomenal Information: Toward a Fundamental Theory of Consciousness', *Journal of Consciousness Studies* 9, no. 8 (2002): 3–29.

Gillett, Carl. 'The Hidden Battles over Emergence'. In *The Oxford Handbook of Religion and* Science, edited by Philip Clayton and Zachary Simpson, 801–18. Oxford: Oxford University Press, 2008.

Gilkey, Langdon. 'Cosmology, Ontology and the Travail of Biblical Language', *Journal of Religion* 41 (1961): 194–205.

Göcke, Benedikt Paul. 'The Many Problems of Special Divine Action', *European Journal for Philosophy of Religion* 7, no. 4 (Summer 2015): 23–36.

Goff, Philip. 'Why Panpsychism Doesn't Help Us Explain Consciousness', *Dialectica* 63, no. 3 (2009): 289–311.

Goff, Philip. 'Can the Panpsychist Get around the Combination Problem?' In *Mind That Abides*, edited by David Skrbina, 129–36. Amsterdam: John Benjamins, 2009.

Goff, Philip. 'There Is No Combination Problem'. In *The Mental as Fundamental*, edited by Michael Blamauer, 131–40. Frankfurt: Ontos Verlag, 2011.

Goff, Philip. *Consciousness and Fundamental Reality*. Oxford: Oxford University Press, 2017.

Goff, Philip. 'The Phenomenal Bonding Solution to the Combination Problem'. In *Panpsychism: Contemporary Perspectives*, edited by Godehard Brüntrup and Ludwig Jaskolla, 284–302. Oxford: Oxford University Press, 2017.

Goff, Philip, William Seager and Sean Allen-Hermanson. 'Panpsychism'. In *The Stanford Encyclopaedia of Philosophy*, edited by Edward N. Zalta, Winter 2017, accessed 11 August 2020, https://plato.stanford.edu/archives/win2017/entries/panpsychism/.

Goodwin, Brian. *How the Leopard Changed Its Spots: The Evolution of Complexity*. Princeton, NJ: Princeton University Press, 2001.

Graves, Mark. *Mind, Brain and the Elusive Soul: Human Systems of Cognitive Science and Religion*. London: Routledge, 2008.

Greco, Monica. 'On the Vitality of Vitalism', *Theory, Culture & Society* 22, no. 2 (2005): 15–27.

Gregersen, Niels Henrik. 'The Cross of Christ in an Evolutionary World', *Dialog: A Journal of Theology* 40, no. 3 (2001): 192–207.

Gregersen, Niels Henrik. 'From Anthropic Design to Self-Organized Complexity'. In *From Complexity to Life: On the Emergence of Life and Meaning*, edited by Niels Henrik Gregersen, 206–31. Oxford: Oxford University Press, 2003.

Gregersen, Niels Henrik. 'Emergence: What Is at Stake for Religious Reflection?' In *The Re-Emergence of Emergence: The Emergence Hypothesis from Science to Religion*, edited by Philip Clayton and Paul Davies, 279–302. Oxford: Oxford University Press, 2006.

Gregersen, Niels Henrik. 'Emergence in Theological Perspective: A Corollary to Professor Clayton's Boyle Lecture', *Theology & Science* 4, no. 3 (2006): 309–20.

Gregersen, Niels Henrik. 'Emergence and Complexity'. In *The Oxford Handbook of Religion and Science*, edited by Philip Clayton and Zachary Simpson, 768–83. Oxford: Oxford University Press, 2008.

Gregersen, Niels Henrik. '*Cur deus caro*: Jesus and the Cosmos Story', *Theology & Science* 11, no. 4 (2013): 370–93.

Gregersen, Niels Henrik. 'Deep Incarnation and *Kenosis*: In, with, under, and as: A Response to Ted Peters', *Dialog: A Journal of Theology* 52, no. 3 (2013): 251–62.

Gregorios, Metropolitan Paulos mar. *The Human Presence*. Madras: Christian Literature Society, 1980.

Gregory of Nyssa, *Patrologiae Cursus Completus, Series Graeca*. Edited by J. P. Migne. Paris: Migne, 1857–66.

Gregory of Nyssa. *De hominis opificio* (PG 44.124–256). English translation: *On the Making of Man Gregory of Nyssa: Dogmatic Treatises*, translated by William Moore and H. A. Wilson. In *Nicene and Post-Nicene Fathers*, series 2, vol. 5, 386–427, edited by Philip Schaff and Henry Wace (1893). Reprinted. Peabody, MA: Hendrickson, 1995.

Griffin, David Ray. *Unsnarling the World-Knot: Consciousness, Freedom, and the Mind-Body Problem*. Eugene, OR: Wipf and Stock, 1998.

Griffin, David Ray. *Reenchantment without Supernaturalism: A Process Philosophy of Religion*. Ithaca, NY: Cornell University Press, 2001.

Griffin, David Ray. *Religion and Scientific Naturalism: Overcoming the Conflicts*. Albany: State University of New York Press, 2000.

Griffin, David Ray. 'Creation out of Nothing, Creation out of Chaos, and the Problem of Evil'. In *Encountering Evil: Live Options in Theodicy*, edited by Stephen T. Davis, 108–25. Louisville, KY: Westminster John Knox Press, 2001.

Griffin, David Ray. *Two Great Truths: A New Synthesis of Scientific Naturalism and Christian Faith*. Louisville, KY: Westminster John Knox Press, 2004.

Griffin, David Ray. *God, Power, and Evil: A Process Theodicy*. Louisville, KY: Westminster John Knox Press, 2004.

Griffin, David Ray. *Panentheism and Scientific Naturalism: Rethinking Evil, Morality, Religious Experience, Religious Pluralism, and the Academic Study of Religion*. Claremont, CA: Process Century Press, 2014.

Griffin, Donald R. 'From Cognition to Consciousness'. In *A Communion of Subjects: Animals in Religion, Science, and Ethics*, edited by Paul Waldau and Kimberley Patton, 481–504. New York: Columbia University Press, 2006.

Gruber, Judith. 'Ec(o)clesiology: Ecology as Ecclesiology in *Laudato Si*', *Theological Studies* 78, no. 4 (2017): 807–24.

Grumett, David. 'Blondel, Modern Catholic Theology, and the Leibnizian Eucharistic Bond', *Modern Theology* 23, no. 4 (2007): 561–77.

Gunkel, Hermann. *Die Psalmen*. Göttingen: Vandenhoeck & Ruprecht, 1926.

Gunton, Colin E. 'Trinity, Ontology and Anthropology: Towards a Renewal of the Imago Dei'. In *Persons Divine and Human*, edited by Christoph Schwöbel and Colin E. Gunton, 47–61. Edinburgh: T&T Clark, 1991.

Gunton, Colin E. *The Triune Creator: A Historical and Systematic Study.* Grand Rapids, MI: Eerdmans, 1998.

Gunton, Colin E. *Being and Becoming: The Doctrine of God in Charles Hartshorne and Karl Barth.* London: SCM Press, 2001.

Habel, Norman C. 'The Challenge of Ecojustice Readings for Christian Theology', *Pacifica* 12 (2000): 125–41.

Habgood, John. 'A Sacramental Approach to Environmental Issues'. In *Liberating Life: Contemporary Approaches to Ecological Theology*, edited by Charles Birch, 46–53. Maryknoll, NY: Orbis Books, 1990.

Hall, John Douglas. *Imaging God: Dominion as Stewardship.* Eugene, OR: Wipf and Stock, 1986.

Hameroff, Stuart, and Roger Penrose. 'Conscious Events as Orchestrated Space-Time Selections', *Journal of Consciousness Studies* 3, no. 1 (1996): 36–53.

Hameroff, Stuart, and Roger Penrose. 'Consciousness in the Universe: A Review of the "Orch OR" Theory', *Physics of Life Review* 11, no. 1 (2014): 39–78.

Hampton, Jean. *The Authority of Reason.* Cambridge: Cambridge University Press, 1998.

Harré, Rom. *Laws of Nature.* London: Duckworth, 1993.

Harris, Mark. '"The Trees of the Field Shall Clap Their Hands" (Isaiah 55:12): What Does It Mean to Say That a Tree Praises God?' In *Knowing Creation: Perspectives from Theology, Philosophy, and Science*, edited by Andrews. B. Torrance and Thomas H. McCall, 287–304. Grand Rapids, MI: Zondervan, 2018.

Harrison, Peter. 'Newtonian Science, Miracles, and the Laws of Nature', *Journal of the History of Ideas* 56, no. 4 (1995): 531–53.

Hartshorne, Charles. 'The Rights of the Subhuman World', *Environmental Ethics* 1 (1979): 49–60.

Hartshorne, Charles. 'A Reply to My Critics'. In *The Philosophy of Charles Hartshorne*, edited by Lewis Edwin Hahn, 569–731. Library of Living Philosophers, 20. LaSalle, IL: Open Court, 1991.

Hasker, William. *The Emergent Self.* Ithaca, NY: Cornell University Press, 1999.

Hasker, William. 'On Behalf of Emergent Dualism'. In *In Search of the Soul: Perspectives on the Mind-Body Problem*, edited by Joel B. Green, 75–114. Eugene, OR: Wipf and Stock, 2005.

Haught, John F. 'Religious and Cosmic Homelessness: Some Environmental Implications'. In *Liberating Life: Contemporary Approaches to Ecological Theology*, edited by C. Birch, W. Eakin and J. B. McDaniel, 159–81. Maryknoll, NY: Orbis Books, 1990.

Hebblethwaite, Brain. *Evil, Suffering, and Religion.* London: SPCK, 2000.

Hebblethwaite, Brain. 'The Impossibility of Multiple Incarnations', *Theology* 104 (2001): 323–34.

Hebblethwaite, Brian, and Edward Henderson. *Divine Action: Studies Inspired by the Philosophical Theology of Austin Farrer.* Edinburgh: T&T Clark, 1990.

Hefner, Philip. 'Is Theodicy a Question of Power? Review of *God, Power and Evil: A Process Theodicy* by David Ray Griffin', *Journal of Religion* 59, no. 1 (January 1979): 87–93.

Heim, Karl. *Transformation of the Scientific World View.* London: SCM Press, 1953.

Hempel, C. G., and P. Oppenheimer. 'Studies in the Logic of Explanation', *Philosophy of Science* 15 (1948): 567–79.

Hick, John. *The Metaphor of God Incarnate*. London: SCM Press, 1993.

Hill, William J., OP. 'The Two Gods of Love: Aquinas and Whitehead', *Listening* 14 (1976): 249–64.

Holland, John. *Emergence: From Chaos to Order*. Reading, MA: Addison-Wesley, 1998.

Horrell, David. *The Bible and the Environment: Towards a Critical Ecological Biblical Theology*. London: Equinox, 2010.

Hume, David. *An Enquiry Concerning Human Understanding and Concerning the Principles of Morals*, edited by L. A. Selby-Bigge. Oxford: Clarendon Press, 1902.

Humphreys, Paul. 'Computation and Conceptual Emergence', *Philosophy of Science* 75, no. 5 (December 2008): 584–94.

Hunt, Cherryl, David G. Horrell and Christopher Southgate. 'An Environmental Mantra? Ecological Interest in Romans 8.19–23 and a Modest Proposal for Its Narrative Interpretation', *Journal of Theological Studies* 59, no. 2 (2008): 546–79.

Inwood, B., and L. Gerson. *Hellenistic Philosophy*. Indianapolis, IN: Hackett, 1997.

Jackelén, Antje. 'Emergence Everywhere?! Reflections on Philip Clayton's *Mind and Emergence*', *Zygon: Journal of Religion and Science* 41, no. 3 (September 2006): 623–32.

Jackson, Frank. 'Epiphenomenal Qualia', *Philosophical Quarterly* 32 (1982): 127–36.

James, William. *Principles of Psychology* (New York: Dover, [1890] 1950).

Jaskolla, Ludwig, and Alexander Buck. 'Does Panexperiential Holism Solve the Combination Problem?' *Journal of Consciousness Studies* 19, nos. 9–10 (2012): 190–9.

Jenson, Robert. *Systematic Theology*, vol. 2: *The Works of God*. New York: Oxford University Press, 1999.

Jolley, Nicholas. *Leibniz and Locke: A Study on 'New Essays on Human Understanding'*. Oxford: Clarendon Press, 1984.

Juarrero, Alicia. *Dynamics in Action: Intentional Behaviour as a Complex System*. Cambridge, MA: MIT Press, 1999.

Kärkkäinen, Veli-Matti. *Creation and Humanity: A Constructive Christian Theology for a Pluralistic World*, vol. 3. Grand Rapids, MI: Eerdmans, 2015.

Käsemann, Ernst. 'Geist und Geistesgaben im NT'. In *Die Religion in Geschichte und Gegenwart*, edited by H. F. von Campenhausen et al., 3rd edn. Tübingen: J.C.B. Mohr, 1958.

Kauffman, Stuart. *At Home in the Universe: The Search for Laws of Self-Organization and Complexity*. New York: Oxford University Press, 1996.

Kauffman, Stuart. *Investigations*. New York: Oxford University Press, 2000.

Keller, Catherine. *The Face of the Deep: A Theology of Becoming*. New York: Routledge, 2003.

Keller, James A. *Problems of Evil and the Power of God*. Aldershot: Ashgate, 2007.

Kim, Jaegwon. *Supervenience and the Mind: Selected Philosophical Essays*. Cambridge: Cambridge University Press, 1993.

Kim, Jaegwon. 'Mental Causation and Two Concepts of Mental Properties', *American Philosophical Association Eastern Division Meeting* (December 1993): 2–23.

Kim, Jaegwon. 'From Naturalism to Physicalism: Supervenience Redux', *Proceedings and Addresses of the American Philosophical Association* 85, no. 2 (2011): 109–34.

King, Jeffry. 'Can Propositions Be Naturalistically Acceptable?' *Midwest Studies in Philosophy* 19 (1994): 53–75.

Kirkpatrick, Frank G. *The Mystery and Agency of God: Divine Being and Action in the World*. Minneapolis, MN: Fortress Press, 2014.

Knight, Christopher. 'Theistic Naturalism and "Special" Divine Providence', *Zygon: Journal of Religion and Science* 44, no. 3 (2009): 533–42.

Kooi, Cornelis van der. 'Calvin's Theology of Creation and Providence: God's Care and Human Fragility', *International Journal of Systematic Theology* 18, no. 1 (January 2016): 47–65.

Koons, Robert C. 'Knowing Nature: Aristotle, God, and the Quantum'. In *Knowing Creation: Perspectives from Theology, Philosophy, and Science*, edited by Andrew B. Torrance and Thomas H. McCall, 215–36. Grand Rapids, MI: Zondervan, 2018.

Koperski, Jeffrey. 'Divine Action and the Quantum Amplification Problem', *Theology and Science* 13, no. 4 (2015): 379–94.

Lampe, Geoffrey. *God the Spirit: The Bampton Lectures 1976*. Oxford: Clarendon Press, 1977.

Langton, Rae, and David Lewis. 'Defining Intrinsic', *Philosophical and Phenomenological Research* 58 (1998): 333–45.

Larvor, Brendan. 'Naturalism'. In *The Wiley Blackwell Handbook of Humanism*, edited by Andrew Copson and A. C. Grayling, 37–54. Oxford: Wiley-Blackwell, 2015.

Laughlin, Robert B., and David Pines. 'The Theory of Everything', *Proceedings of the National Academy of Sciences of the United States of America* 97, no. 1 (2000): 28–31.

Leibniz, Gottfried Wilhelm von. *Correspondence with John Bernoulli*. In *Leibnizens Mathematische Schriften*, 7 vols., edited by G. I. von Gerhardt. Berlin/Halle: A. Asher/W. H. Schmidt, 1849–63.

Leibniz, Gottfried Wilhelm von. *The Monadology and Other Philosophical Writings*. Translated by Robert Latta. Oxford: Clarendon Press, 1899.

Leibniz, Gottfried Wilhelm von. 'The Monadology'. In *Leibniz Selections*, edited by P. Wiener. New York: Charles Scribner's Sons, 1951.

Leibniz, Gottfried Wilhelm von . *Theodicy*. Translated by E. M. Huggard, edited by Austin Farrer. London: Routledge & Kegan Paul, 1951.

Leibniz, Gottfried Wilhelm von. 'The Controversy between Leibniz and Clarke'. In *Philosophical Papers and Letters*, 2 vols, edited by Leroy Loemker. Chicago: University of Chicago Press, 1956.

Leibniz, Gottfried Wilhelm von. *Gottfried Wilhelm Leibniz: Philosophical Papers and Letters*, 2nd edn. Edited and translated by Leroy E. Loemker. Dordrecht: D. Reidel, 1969.

Leibniz, Gottfried Wilhelm von. *New Essays on Human Understanding*. Translated by P. Remnant and J. Bennett. Cambridge: Cambridge University Press, 1982.

Leibniz, Gottfried Wilhelm von. *G. W. Leibniz: Philosophical Essays*. Edited and translated by Roger Ariew and Daniel Garber. Indianapolis, IN: Hackett, 1989.

Leibniz, Gottfried Wilhelm von. *Nature Itself*. In *Philosophical Texts*, edited by R. S. Woodhouse and Richard Francks. Oxford: Oxford University Press, 1998.

Leibniz, Gottfried Wilhelm von. *The Leibniz-Des Bosses Correspondence*. Edited by Brandon C. Look and Donald Rutherford. New Haven, CT: Yale University Press, 2007.

Leidenhag, Joanna. 'Critique of Emergent Theologies', *Zygon: Journal of Religion and Science* 51, no. 4 (December 2016): 867–82.

Leidenhag, Joanna. 'Saving Panpsychism: A Panpsychist Ontology and Christian Soteriology'. In *Being Saved: Explorations in Soteriology and Human Ontology*, edited by Marc Cortez, Joshua R. Farris and S. Mark Hamilton, 303–25. London: SCM Press, 2018.

Leidenhag, Joanna. 'The Revival of Panpsychism and Its Relevance for the Science-Religion Dialogue', *Theology & Science* 17, no. 1 (2019): 90–106.

Leidenhag, Joanna. 'Unity between God and Mind? A Study on the Relationship between Panpsychism and Pantheism', *Sophia: International Journal of Philosophy and Traditions* 58, no. 4 (2019): 543–61.

Leidenhag, Joanna. 'Can Panpsychism Help Make Sense of Panentheism?' In *Panpsychism and Panentheism: Philosophy of Religion Meets Philosophy of Mind*, edited by Ludwig Jaskolla and Benedikt Göcke, 65–90. Innsbruck Studies in Philsophy of Religion, vol. 2. Leiden: Mentis, 2020.

Leidenhag, Mikael. 'From Emergence Theory to Panpsychism – A Philosophical Evaluation of Nancey Murphy's Non-Reductive Physicalism', *Sophia: International Journal of Philosophy and Traditions* 55 (2016): 381–94.

Leidenhag, Mikael. *Naturalizing God? A Critical Evaluation of Religious Naturalism.* New York: SUNY Press, forthcoming.

Leiter, Brian. 'Naturalism and Naturalized Jurisprudence'. In *Analyzing Natural Law: New Essays in Legal Theory*, edited by Brian Bix, 79–104. Oxford: Clarendon Press, 1998.

Leopold, Aldo. *A Sand County Almanac.* New York: Oxford University Press, 1966.

Levine, J. 'Materialism and Qualia: The Explanatory Gap', *Pacific Philosophical Quarterly* 64 (1983): 354–61.

Lewes, George Henry. *Problems in Life and Mind.* 1874–9 five volumes. Volume II. New York: Houghton, Osgood, 1875.

Lewis, C. S. *Miracles: A Preliminary Study.* London: Centenary Press, 1947.

Lewtas, Patrick. 'Russellian Panpsychism: Too Good to Be True?' *American Philosophical Quarterly* 52, no. 1 (2015): 57–71.

Lewtas, Patrick. 'Panpsychism, Emergentism and the Metaphysics of Causation', *Pacific Philosophical Quarterly* 99, no. 3 (September 2018): 392–416.

Linzey, Andrew. 'The Neglected Creature. The Doctrine of the Non-Human Creation and Its Relationship with the Human in the Thought of Karl Barth'. PhD diss., University of London, 1986.

Linzey, Andrew. 'Is Christianity Irredeemably Speciesist?' In *Animals on the Agenda: Questions about Animals for Theology and Ethics*, edited by Andrew Linzey and Dorothy Yamamoto, xi–xx. London: SCM Press, 1998.

Locke, John. *An Essay Concerning Human Understanding.* Dent: Dutton, [1689] 1964.

Lockwood, M. *Mind, Brain and the Quantum.* Oxford: Blackwell, 1989.

Lockwood, M. 'The "Many Minds" Interpretation of Quantum Mechanics', *British Journal for the Philosophy of Science* 47, no. 3 (1996): 159–88.

Long, A. A. *Hellenistic Philosophy: Stoics, Epicureans and Sceptics.* Berkley: University of California Press, 1974.

Look, Brandon C. 'Gottfried Wilhelm Leibniz'. In *The Stanford Encyclopaedia of Philosophy*, edited by Edward N. Zalta, Spring 2014 Edition, accessed 11 August 2020, https://plato.stanford.edu/archives/spr2014/entries/leibniz/.

Louth, Andrews. *Maximus the Confessor.* New York: Routledge, 1996.

Macquarrie, John. *Principles of Christian Theology*, 2nd edn. New York: Scribner's Sons, 1977.

Macquarrie, John. *In Search of Deity.* London: SCM Press, 1984.

Madell, Geoffrey. *Mind and Materialism.* Edinburgh: Edinburgh University Press, 1988.

Mathew, Gervase. 'The Material Becomes Articulate', from *Byzantine Aesthetics*. In *The Creation Spirit: An Anthropology*, edited by Robert van de Weyter and Pat Saunders, 18. London: Darton, Longman, and Todd, 1990.

Mathews, Freya. *The Ecological Self.* London: Routledge, 1991.

Mathews, Freya. *For Love of Matter: A Contemporary Panpsychism*. New York: SUNY Press, 2003.

Mathews, Freya. 'Why the West Failed to Embrace Panpsychism?' In *Mind That Abides: Panpsychism in the New Millennium*, edited by David Skrbina, 341–60. Amsterdam: John Benjamins, 2009.

May, Gerhard. *Creation ex Nihilo: The Doctrine of 'Creation out of Nothing' in Early Christian Thought*. Translated by A. S. Worrall. Edinburgh: T&T Clark, 1994.

McDaniel, Jay. 'Physical Matter as Creative and Sentient', *Environmental Ethics* 5, no. 4 (1983): 291–317.

McFague, Sallie. *Super, Natural Christians: How We Should Love Nature*. London: SCM Press, 1997.

McFarland, Ian A. *From Nothing: A Theology of Creation*. Louisville, KY: Westminster John Knox Press, 2014.

McGinn, Colin. *The Character of Mind*. Oxford: Oxford University Press, 1982.

McGinn, Colin. *The Problem of Consciousness: Essays toward a Resolution*. Oxford: Basil Blackwell, 1991.

McHenry, Leemon B., and George W. Shields. 'Analytic Critiques of Whitehead's Metaphysics', *Journal of the American Philosophical Association* 2, no. 3 (2016): 483–503.

Meixner, Uwe. 'Idealism and Panpsychism'. In *Panpsychism: Contemporary Perspectives*, edited by Godehard Brüntrup and Ludwig Jaskolla, 387–406. Oxford: Oxford University Press, 2017.

Mercer, Christia. *Leibniz's Metaphysics: Its Origins and Development*. Cambridge: Cambridge University Press, 2001.

Midgley, Mary. *Beast and Man: The Roots of Human Nature*. Hassocks: Harvester Press, 1978.

Midgley, Mary. 'The End of Anthropocentrism?' In *Philosophy and the Natural Environment*, edited by Robin Attfield and Andrew Belsey, 103–22. Cambridge: Cambridge University Press, 1994.

Milbank, John. 'Materialism and Transcendence'. In *Theology and the Political: The New Debate*, edited by Creston Davis, John Milbank and Slavoj Žižek, 393–426. Durham, NC: Duke University Press, 2005.

Milbank, John. 'The Grandeur of Reason and the Perversity of Rationalism: Radical Orthodoxy's First Decade'. In *The Radical Orthodoxy Reader*, edited by John Milbank and Simon Oliver, 367–404. London: Routledge, 2009.

Mill, John Stuart. *System of Logic*. London: Longmans, Green, Reader, and Dyer, 1843.

Moltmann, Jürgen. *God in Creation: An Ecological Doctrine of Creation*. London: SCM Press, 1985.

Moreland, J. P. 'An Enduring Self: The Achilles' Heel of Process Philosophy', *Process Studies* 17 (1988): 193–9.

Moreland, J. P. *Consciousness and the Existence of God*. New York: Routledge, 2008.

Moreland, J. P. 'A Critique of and Alternative to Nancey Murphy's Christian Physicalism', *European Journal for Philosophy of Religion* 8, no. 2 (2016): 107–28.

Morgan, C. Lloyd. *Emergent Evolution*. New York: Henry Holt, 1923.

Morowitz, Harold J. 'Emergence of Transcendence'. In *From Complexity to Life: On the Emergence of Life and Meaning*, edited by Niels Henrik Gregersen, 177–86. Oxford: Oxford University, 2003.

Morowitz, Harold J. 'The "Trinitarian" World of Neo-Pantheism: On Panentheism and Epistemology'. In *In Whom We Live and Move and Have Our Being: Panentheistic*

Reflections on God's Presence in a Scientific World, edited by Arthur Peacocke and Philip Clayton, 131–6. Grand Rapids, MI: Eerdmans, 2004.

Morowitz, Harold J. *The Emergence of Everything: How the World Became Complex.* Oxford: Oxford University Press, 2004.

Morris, Simon Conway. *Life's Solution: Inevitable Humans in a Lonely Universe.* Cambridge: Cambridge University Press, 2003.

Morris, Simon Conway. *The Runes of Evolution: How the Universe Became Self-Aware.* West Conshohocken, PA: Templeton Press, 2015.

Muers, Rachel. 'The Holy Spirit, the Voices of Nature and Environmental Prophecy', *Scottish Journal of Theology* 67 (2014): 323–39.

Mulgan, Tim. 'What Is Good for the Distant Future? The Challenge of Climate Change for Utilitarianism'. In *God, the Good, and Utilitarianism: Perspectives on Peter Singer*, edited by John Perry, 141–59. Cambridge: Cambridge University Press, 2014.

Murphy, Nancey. 'Divine Action in the Natural Order: Buridan's Ass and Schrödinger's Cat'. In *Chaos and Complexity: Scientific Perspectives on Divine Action*, edited by Robert John Russell, Nancey Murphy and William R. Stoeger, SJ, 325–58. Vatican City State/Berkeley, CA: Vatican Observatory/Centre for Theology and the Natural Sciences, 1997.

Murphy, Nancey. 'Nonreductive Physicalism: Philosophical Issues'. In *Whatever Happened to the Soul? Scientific and Theological Portraits of Human Nature*, edited by Warren S. Brown, Nancey Murphy and H. Newton Malony, 127–48. Minneapolis, MN: Fortress Press, 1998.

Murphy, Nancey. 'Nonreductive Physicalism'. In *In Search of the Soul: Perspectives on the Mind-Body Problem*, edited by Joel B. Green, 115–38. Eugene, OR: Wipf and Stock, 2005.

Murphy, Nancey. *Bodies and Souls, or Spirited Bodies?* Cambridge: Cambridge University Press, 2006.

Murphy, Nancey. 'Emergence, Downward Causation and Divine Action'. In *Scientific Perspectives on Divine Action: Twenty Years of Challenge and Progress*, edited by Robert J. Russell, Nancey Murphy and William R. Stoeger, SJ, 111–31. Vatican State/Notre Dame, IN: Vatican Observatory/Centre for Theology and the Natural Sciences, 2008.

Murphy, Nancey, and Warren Brown. *Did My Neurons Make Me Do It? Philosophical and Neurobiological Perspectives on Moral Responsibility and Free Will.* New York: Oxford University Press, 2007.

Mørch, Hedda Hassel. *Panpsychism and Causation: A New Argument and a Solution to the Combination Problem.* PhD thesis, University of Oslo, 2014.

Nachtomy, Ohad. 'Leibniz's View of Living Beings: Embodied or Nested Individuals'. In *Embodiment: A History*, edited by Justin E. H. Smith, 189–215. Oxford: Oxford University Press, 2017.

Naess, Arne. 'The shadow of the Deep, Long-Range Ecology Movement: A Summary', *Inquiry* 16 (1973): 95–100.

Nagasawa, Yujin, and Khai Wager. 'Panpsychism and Priority Cosmopsychism'. In *Panpsychism: Contemporary Perspectives*, edited by Godehard Brüntrup and Ludwig Jaskolla, 113–130. Oxford: Oxford University Press, 2017.

Nagel, Thomas. *Mortal Questions.* Cambridge: Cambridge University Press, 1979.

Nagel, Thomas. 'The Mind Wins!' *New York Review* (4 March 1993): 37–41.

Nagel, Thomas. *The Last Word.* New York: Oxford University Press, 1997.

Nagel, Thomas. *Secular Philosophy and the Religious Temperament: Essays 2002–2008.* Oxford: Oxford University Press, 2010.

Nagel, Thomas. *Mind and Cosmos: Why the Materialist Neo-Darwinian Conception of Nature Is Almost Certainly False.* Oxford: Oxford University Press, 2012.

Nash, Roderick. *The Rights of Nature: A History of Environmental Ethics.* Madison: University of Wisconsin Press, 1989.

Nino el-Hani, Charbel, and Antonio Marcos Pereira. 'Higher-Level Descriptions: Why Should We Preserve Them?' In *Downward Causation: Minds, Bodies and Matter,* edited by Peter Bøgh Andersen, Claus Emmeche, Niels Ole Finnemann and Peder Voetmann Christiansen, 118–42. Aarhus: Aarhus University Press, 2000.

Northcott, Michael S. *The Environment & Christian Ethics.* Cambridge: Cambridge University Press, 1996.

O'Donovan, Oliver. *The Problem of Self-Love in Augustine.* New Haven, CT: Yale University Press, 1980.

O'Donovan, Oliver. '*Usus* and *Fruito* in Augustine *De Doctrina Christiana I.*', *Journal of Theological Studies* 33, no. 2 (October 1982): 361–97.

O'Donovan, Oliver. *Resurrection and Moral Order: An Outline for Evangelical Ethics.* Grand Rapids, MI: Eerdmans, [1986] 1994.

Oord, Thomas Jay. *Theologies of Creation: Creatio ex Nihilo and Its New Rivals.* New York: Routledge, 2015.

Ortner, Sherry. 'Is Female to Male as Nature Is to Culture?' In *Woman, Culture and Society,* edited by M. Z. Rosaldo and L. Lamphere, 67–87. Stanford, CA: Stanford University Press, 1974.

Osborn, Laurence. *Guardians of Creation: Nature in Theology and the Christian Life.* Leicester: Apollos, 1993.

Papineau, David. *Philosophical Naturalism.* Oxford: Basil Blackwell, 1993.

Peacocke, Arthur R. *Creation and the World of Science.* Oxford: Clarendon Press, 1979.

Peacocke, Arthur R. *God and the New Biology.* London: Dent, 1986.

Peacocke, Arthur R. *Theology for a Scientific Age: Being and Becoming – Natural, Divine, and Human.* Minneapolis, MN: Fortress Press, 1993.

Peacocke, Arthur R. *Paths from Science Towards God: The End of All Our Exploring.* Oxford: OneWorld, 2001.

Peacocke, Arthur R. *All That Is: A Naturalistic Faith for the Twenty-First Century.* Minneapolis, MN: Fortress Press. 2009.

Phemister, Pauline. *Leibniz and the Environment.* Oxford: Routledge, 2016.

Philo. *The Words of Philo.* Translated by C. D. Yonge. Peabody, MA: Hendrickson, 1993.

Pickstock, Catherine. 'Thomas Aquinas and the Quest for the Eucharist'. In *The Radical Orthodoxy Reader,* edited by John Milbank and Simon Oliver, 265–84. London: Routledge, 2009.

Pittenger, Norman. *The Lure of Divine Love: Human Experience and Christian Faith in a Process Perspective.* Edinburgh: Pilgrim Press, 1979.

Plant, Judith. *Healing the Wounds: The Promise of Ecofeminism.* Philadelphia, PA: New Society, 1989.

Plantinga, Alvin. 'What Is 'Intervention'?' *Theology and Science* 6, no. 4 (2008): 369–401.

Plantinga, Alvin. *Where the Conflict Really Lies: Science, Religion, and Naturalism.* Oxford: Oxford University Press, 2012.

Plantinga, Alvin, and Michael Tooley. *Knowledge of God.* Oxford: Blackwell, 2008.

Plato, *Laws.* Translated by Trevor J. Saunders. In *Plato Complete Works,* edited by John M. Cooper, 1318–1616. Indianapolis, IN: Hackett, 1997.

Plumwood, Val. *Feminism and the Mastery of Nature.* London: Routledge, 1993.

Poe, Harry Lee, and Chelsea Rose Mytyk. 'From Scientific Method to Methodological Naturalism: The Evolution of an Idea', *Perspectives on Science and Christian Faith* 59, no. 3 (September 2007): 213–19.

Polkinghorne, John. *Science and Creation: The Search for Understanding*. London: SPCK, 1988.

Polkinghorne, John. 'The Laws of Nature and the Laws of Physics'. In *Quantum Cosmology and the Laws of Nature: Scientific Perspectives on Divine Action*, edited by Robert J. Russell, Nancey Murphy and C. J. Isham, 429–40. Vatican City State/Berkeley, CA: Vatican Observatory/Centre for Theology and the Natural Sciences, 1996.

Polkinghorne, John. *Science and Providence: God's Interaction with the World*. West Conshohocken, PA: Templeton Press, 2005.

Polkinghorne, John. *Reason and Reality: The Relationship between Science and Theology*. London: SPCK Classics, 2011.

Pollard, William G. *Chance and Providence: God's Action in the World Governed by Scientific Laws*. New York: Charles Scribner's Sons, 1958.

Popper, Karl R., and John C. Eccles. *The Self and Its Brain*. Berlin: Springer, 1977.

Pringle-Pattison, Andrew Seth. *The Idea of God in the Light of Recent Philosophy: The Gifford Lectures, University of Aberdeen, 1912–1913*. New York: Oxford University Press, 1920.

Pruss, Alexander. 'The Leibnizian Cosmological Argument'. In *The Blackwell Companion to Natural Theology*, edited by William Lane Craig and J. P. Moreland, 24–100. Malden, MA: Blackwell, 2012.

Rad, Gerhard von, *Genesis: A Commentary*. Translated by John H. Marks. Philadelphia, PA: Westminster, 1961.

Ramsey, Ian T. *Models for Divine Activity*. London: SCM Press, 1973.

Rasmussen, Larry L. 'Theology of Life and Ecumenical Ethics'. In *Ecotheology: Voices from South and North*, edited by D. G. Hallman, 112–29. Geneva: World Council of Churches, 1994.

Reagan, Tom. *The Case for Animal Rights*. Berkeley: University of California Press, 1983.

Reagan, Tom. 'Does Environmental Ethics Rest on a Mistake?', *The Monist* 75, no. 2 (April 1992): 161–82.

Richardson, Alan. *An Introduction to the Theology of the New Testament*. New York: Harper & Row, 1958.

Ricoeur, Paul. *History and Truth*. Translated by Charles A. Kelby. Evanston, IL: Northwestern University Press, 1965.

Rist, John. *The Mind of Aristotle*. Toronto: University of Toronto Press, 1989.

Ritchie, Jack. *Understanding Naturalism: Supervenience*. New York: Routledge, 2014.

Robinson, H. W. *Inspiration and Revelation in the Old Testament*. Oxford: Clarendon Press, 1946.

Rolston III, Holmes. *Philosophy Gone Wild: Essays in Environmental Ethics*. Amherst, NY: Prometheus Books, 1986.

Rolston III, Holmes. *Environmental Ethics: Duties to and Value in the Natural World*. Philadelphia, PA: Temple University Press, 1988.

Rolston III, Holmes. 'Values in Nature and the Nature of Value', *Royal Institute of Philosophy Supplement* 36 (1994): 13–30.

Rolston III, Holmes. 'Divine Presence – Causal, Cybernetic, Caring, Cruciform: From Information to Incarnation'. In *Incarnation: On the Scope and Depth of Christology*, edited by Niels Henrik Gregersen, 255–88. Minneapolis, MN: Fortress Press, 2015.

Rorty, Richard. 'Religion as Conversation-Stopper', *Common Knowledge* 3, no. 1 (1994): 1–6.

Rorty, Richard. 'Religion in the Public Square: A Reconsideration', *Journal of Religious Ethics* 31, no. 1 (2003): 141–9.

Rosenberg, Gregg. *A Place for Consciousness: Probing the Deep Structure of the Natural World*. Oxford: Oxford University Press, 2004.

Rosenberg, Gregg. 'Land Ho? We Are Close to a Synoptic Understanding of Consciousness'. In *Panpsychism: Contemporary Perspectives*, edited by Godehard Brüntrup and Ludwig Jaskolla, 153–76. Oxford: Oxford University Press, 2017.

Ruether, Rosemary Radford. *Sexism and God-Talk: Toward a Feminist Theology*. London: SCM Press, 1983.

Russell, Bertrand. *The Analysis of Matter*. London: Routledge, [1927] 1992.

Russell, Bertrand. *A Critical Exposition of the Philosophy of Leibniz*. Cambridge: Cambridge University Press, [1935] 1990.

Russell, Bertrand. *Portraits from Memory*. Nottingham: Spokesman, [1956] 1995.

Russell, Robert J. 'Christian Discipleship and the Challenge of Physics: Formation, Flux, and Focus', *Perspectives on Science and Christian Faith* 42, no. 3 (1990): 139–54.

Russell, Robert J. 'Cosmology from Alpha to Omega', *Zygon: Journal of Religion and Science* 29, no. 4 (December 1994): 567–8.

Russell, Robert J. 'Introduction'. In *Chaos and Complexity: Scientific Perspectives on Divine Action*, edited by Robert John Russell, Nancey Murphy and William R. Stoeger, SJ, 1–31. Vatican City State/Berkeley, CA: Vatican Observatory/Centre for Theology and the Natural Sciences, 1997.

Russell, Robert J. 'Does "The God Who Acts" Really Act?' *Theology Today* 54 (1997): 44–65.

Russell, Robert J. 'Quantum Physics and the Theology of Non-Interventionist Objective Divine Action'. In *The Oxford Handbook of Religion and Science*, edited by Philip Clayton and Zachary Simpson, 579–95. Oxford: Oxford University Press, 2006.

Russell, Robert J. 'Challenge and Progress in "Theology and Science"'. In *Scientific Perspectives on Divine Action: Twenty Years of Challenge and Progress*, edited by Robert J. Russell, Nancey Murphy and William R. Stoeger SJ, 9–17. Vatican State/Notre Dame, IN: Vatican State Observatory/Centre for Theology and the Natural Sciences, 2008.

Russell, Robert J. *Cosmology. From Alpha to Omega: The Creative Mutual Interaction of Theology and Science*. Minneapolis, MN: Fortress Press, 2008.

Sansbury, Timothy. 'The False Promise of Quantum Mechanics', *Zygon: Journal of Religion and Science* 42 (2007): 111–21.

Santmire, H. Paul. *The Travail of Nature: The Ambiguous Ecological Promise of Christian Theology*. Minneapolis, MN: Fortress Press, 1985.

Santmire, H. Paul. *Nature Reborn: The Ecological and Cosmic Promise of Christian Theology*. Minneapolis, MN: Fortress Press, 2000.

Saunders, Nicholas. 'Does God Cheat at Dice? Divine Action and Quantum Possibilities', *Zygon: Journal of Religion and Science* 35, no. 3 (2000): 517–44.

Saunders, Nicholas. *Divine Action & Modern Science*. Cambridge: Cambridge University Press, 2002.

Schaeffer, Jonathan. 'Monism: The Priority of the Whole', *Philosophical Review* 119, no. 1 (2010): 31–76.

Schaeffer, Jonathan. 'The Internal Relatedness of All Things'. *Mind* 119, no. 474 (2010): 341–76.

Schaeffer, Jonathan. 'The Action of the Whole', *Aristotelian Society: Proceedings of the Aristotelian Society Supplementary* 87 (2013): 67–87.

Schmemann, Alexander. *The World as Sacrament*. London: Darton, Longman & Todd, 1966.

Schneider, Susan. 'Idealism, or Something Near Enough'. In *Idealism: New Essays in Metaphysics*, edited by Tyron Goldschmidt and Kenneth L. Peace, 275–89. Oxford: Oxford University Press, 2017.

Scott, Peter. *A Political Theology of Nature*. Cambridge: Cambridge University Press, 2003.

Seager, William E. *Metaphysics of Consciousness*. London: Routledge, 1991.

Seager, William E. 'Consciousness, Information, and Panpsychism', *Journal of Consciousness Studies* 2, no. 3 (1995): 272–88.

Seager, William E. 'Panpsychism'. In *The Oxford Handbook of Philosophy of Mind*, edited by Ansgar Beckermann, Brian P. McLaughlin and Sven Walter, 206–20. Oxford: Oxford University Press, 2009.

Seager, William E. 'Panpsychism, Aggregation and Combinatorial Infusion', *Mind and Matter* 8, no. 2 (2010): 167–84.

Seager, William E., ed. *Routledge Handbook of Panpsychism*. New York: Routledge, 2017.

Seager, William E. 'Panpsychist Infusion'. In *Panpsychism: Contemporary Perspectives*, edited by Godehard Brüntrup and Ludwig Jaskolla, 229–48. Oxford: Oxford University Press, 2017.

Searle, John R. 'The Mind-Body Problem'. In *John Searle and His Critics*, edited by Ernest Lepore and Robert van Gulick, 141–6. Cambridge, MA: Basil Blackwell, 1991.

Searle, John R. *The Rediscovery of the Mind*. Cambridge, MA: MIT Press, 1992.

Sellars, Roy Wood. 'Panpsychism or Evolutionary Materialism', *Philosophy of Science* 27, no. 4 (October 1960): 329–50.

Sellars, Wilfrid. 'Empiricism and the Philosophy of Mind'. In *Science, Perception and Reality*, 127–96. London: Routledge & Kegan Paul, 1963.

Shani, Itay. 'Cosmopsychism: A Holistic Approach to the Metaphysics of Experience', *Philosophical Papers* 44, no. 3 (2015): 389–437.

Sheldrake, Rupert. *The Rebirth of Nature: The Greening of the Science of God*. London: Rider, 1990.

Sherrard, Philip. *Rape of Man and Nature: An Enquiry into the Origins and Consequences of Modern Science*. Ipswich: Golgonooza Press, 1987.

Shults, F. LeRon. *Christology and Science*. Aldershot: Ashgate, 2008.

Shuttle, Augustine. 'Evolution and Emergence: A Paradigm Shift for Theology', *Philosophy & Theology* 22, nos. 1–2 (2010): 235–64.

Silberstein, Michael. 'Emergence, Theology, and the Manifest Image'. In *The Oxford Handbook of Religion and Science*, edited by Philip Clayton and Zachary Simpson, 784–800. Oxford: Oxford University Press, 2008.

Singer, Peter. *Animal Liberation*, 2nd edn. London: Cape, 1990.

Skrbina, David. *Panpsychism in the West*. Cambridge, MA: MIT Press, [2005] 2017.

Skrbina, David. 'Realistic Panpsychism: Commentary on Strawson'. In Galen Strawson et al., *Consciousness and Its Place in Nature*, edited by Anthony Freeman, 151–7. Exeter: Imprint Academic, 2006.

Skrbina, David. 'Panpsychism in History: An Overview'. In *Mind That Abides*, edited by David Skrbina, 1–29. Amsterdam: John Benjamins, 2009.

Skrbina, David. 'Ethics, Eco-Philosophy, and Universal Sympathy', *Dialogue and Universalism* 4 (2013): 59–74.

Smith, James K. A. *Introducing Radical Orthodoxy: Mapping a Post-Secular Theology*. Grand Rapids, MI: Baker Academic, 2004.

Smith, Justin. *Divine Machines: Leibniz and the Sciences of Life*. Princeton, NJ: Princeton University Press, 2011.

Sonderegger, Kathryn. *Systematic Theology: The Doctrine of God*. Minneapolis, MN: Augsburg Fortress, 2015.

Soskice, Janet. 'Why *Creatio ex nihilo* for Theology Today?' In *Creation* ex nihilo: *Origins, Development, Contemporary Challenges*, edited by Gary A. Anderson and Markus Bockmuehl, 36–54. Notre Dame, IN: Notre Dame University Press, 2018.

Sperry, Roger W. 'Consciousness and Causality'. In *The Oxford Companion to the Mind*, edited by Richard L. Gregory, 164–6. Oxford: Oxford University Press, 1987.

Sperry, Roger W. 'In Defense of Mentalism and Emergent Interaction', *Journal of Mind and Behaviour* 12, no. 2 (1991): 221–46.

Spinoza, Baruch. *Ethics*. Translated by R. H. M. Elwes. New York: Dover Press, 1951.

Sprigge, Timothy L. S. 'Are There Intrinsic Values in Nature?' In *Applied Philosophy*, edited by B. Almond and D. Hill, 37–44. New York: Routledge, 1991.

Sprigge, Timothy L. S. 'Panpsychism'. In *Routledge Encyclopedia of Philosophy*. Abingdon: Taylor and Francis, 1998, viewed 8 August 2018, https://www.rep.routledge.com/articles/thematic/panpsychism/v-1.

Stadelmann, L. I. J. *The Hebrew Conception of the World*. Rome: Pontifical Biblical Institute, 1970.

Stapp, Henry. *Mindful Universe: Quantum Mechanics and the Participating Observer*. Berlin: Springer, 2007.

Stephan, Achim. 'Emergence and Panpsychism'. In *Panpsychism: Contemporary Perspectives*, edited by Godehard Brüntrup and Ludwig Jaskolla, 334–48. Oxford: Oxford University Press, 2017.

Stoeger, William R. 'Contemporary Physics and the Ontological Status of the Laws of Nature'. In *Quantum Cosmology and the Laws of Nature: Scientific Perspectives on Divine Action*, edited by Robert J. Russell, Nancey Murphy and C. J. Isham, 207–34. Vatican City State/Berkeley, CA: Vatican Observatory/Centre for Theology and the Natural Sciences, 1996.

Strawson, Galen. 'Realistic Monism: Why Physicalism Entails Panpsychism', *Journal of Consciousness Studies* 13, nos. 10–11 (2006): 3–31.

Strawson, Galen. 'Realistic Monism: Why Physicalism Entails Panpsychism'. In *Consciousness and Its Place in Nature: Does Physicalism Entail Panpsychism?*, edited by Anthony Freeman, 3–32. Exeter: Imprint Academic, 2006.

Strawson, Galen. *Real Materialism and Other Essays*. Oxford: Oxford University Press, 2008.

Stroud, Barry. 'The Charm of Naturalism', *Proceedings and Addresses of the American Philosophical Association* 70, no. 2 (1996): 43–5.

Studebaker, Steven M. 'The Spirit in Creation: A Unified Theology of Grace and Creation Care', *Zygon: Journal of Religion and Science* 43, no. 4 (2008): 943–60.

Stump, Eleonore. 'Omnipresence, Indwelling, and the Second-Personal', *European Journal for Philosophy of Religion* 5, no. 4 (Winter 2013): 29–53.

Taliaferro, Charles. 'Dualism and Panpsychism'. In *Panpsychism: Contemporary Perspectives*, edited by Godehard Brüntrup and Ludwig Jaskolla, 369–86. Oxford: Oxford University Press, 2017.

Tanner, Kathryn. *God and Creation in Christian Theology: Tyranny or Empowerment?* Oxford: Blackwell, 1988.

Tanner, Kathryn. *The Politics of God: Christian Theologies and Social Justice*. Minneapolis, MN: Augsburg Fortress, 1992.

Tanner, Kathryn. *Jesus, Humanity and Trinity: A Brief Systematic Theology*. Minneapolis, MN: Fortress Press, 2001.

Tanner, Kathryn. *Christ the Key*. Cambridge: Cambridge University Press, 2010, 274.

Tanner, Kathryn. 'Creation *Ex Nihilo* as Mixed Metaphor', *Modern Theology* 29, no. 2 (April 2013): 138–55.

Taylor, Charles. *Sources of the Self: The Making of the Modern Identity*. Cambridge: Cambridge University Press, 1989.

Taylor, Paul. *Respect for Nature: A Theory of Environmental Ethics*. Princeton, NJ: Princeton University Press, 1986.

TeSelle, Eugene. 'Divine Action: The Doctrinal Tradition'. In *Divine Action: Studies Inspired by the Philosophical Theology of Austin Farrer*, edited by Brian Hebblethwaite and Edward Henderson, 71–92. Edinburgh: T&T Clark, 1990.

Theokritoff, Elizabeth. 'Creation and Priesthood in Modern Orthodox Thinking', *Ecotheology* 10, no. 3 (2005): 344–63.

Thiselton, Anthony C. *The Holy Spirit – in Biblical Teaching, through the Centuries, and Today*. Grand Rapids, MI: Eerdmans, 2013.

Thomas, Emily. 'Samuel Alexander's Space-Time God: A Naturalist Rival to Current Emergentist Theologies'. In *Alternative Concepts of God: Essays on the Metaphysics of the Divine*, edited by Yujin Nagasawa and Andrei A. Buckareff, 255–73. Oxford: Oxford University Press, 2016.

Thomas, Owen. 'Recent Thought on Divine Agency'. In *Divine Action: Studies Inspired by the Philosophical Theology of Austin Farrer*, edited by Brian Hebblethwaite and Edward Henderson, 35–50. Edinburgh: T&T Clark, 1983.

Thunberg, Lars. *Microcosm and Mediator: The Theological Anthropology of Maximus the Confessor*. Lund: Håkan Ohlssons Boktrycheri, 1965.

Tillich, Paul. *Systematic Theology*, vol. 2: *Existence and the Christ*. Chicago: University of Chicago Press, 1957.

Tononi, Giulio. 'Consciousness as Integrated Information: A Provisional Manifesto', *Biological Bulletin* 215, no. 3 (2008): 216–42.

Tracy, Thomas. 'Particular Providence and the God of the Gaps'. In *Chaos and Complexity: Scientific Perspectives on Divine Action*, edited by Robert John Russell, Nancey Murphy and William R. Stoeger, SJ, 289–324. Vatican City State/Berkeley, CA: Vatican Observatory/Centre for Theology and the Natural Sciences, 1997.

Vanhoozer, Kevin. 'Human Being, Individual and Social'. In *The Cambridge Companion to Christian Doctrine*, edited by Colin E. Gunton, 158–88. Cambridge: Cambridge University Press, 1997.

Vanhoozer, Kevin. *Remythologizing Theology: Divine Action, Passion and Authorship*. Cambridge: Cambridge University Press, 2010.

Wallace, Howard N. ' "*Jubilate Deo omnis terra*": God and Earth in Psalm 65'. In *The Earth Story in the Psalms and the Prophets*, edited by Norman C. Habel, 51–64. Sheffield: Sheffield Academic Press, 2001.

Ward, Graham. *Cities of God*. London: Routledge, 2000.

Ward, Keith. *More Than Matter? Is There More to Life Than Molecules?* Grand Rapids, MI: Eerdmans, 2010.

Ware, Kallistos. *The Orthodox Church*. London: Penguin, 1993.

Ware, Kallistos. *Through the Creation to the Creator*. Pallis Memorial Lecture 1995. London: Friends of the Centre, 1996.

Ware, Kallistos. 'Through Creation to the Creator'. In *Toward an Ecology of Transfiguration: Orthodox Christian Perspectives on Environment, Nature, and Creation*, edited by John Chryssavgis and Bruce V. Foltz, 86–105. New York: Fordham University Press, 2013.

Webster, John. ' "Love Is Also a Lover of Life": *Creatio ex nihilo* and Creaturely Goodness', *Modern Theology* 29, no. 2 (April 2013): 156–71.

Weil, Simone. *Waiting for God*. New York: G. P. Putnam's Sons, 1951.

Weston, Anthony. 'Beyond Intrinsic Values: Pragmatism in Environmental Ethics', *Environmental Ethics* 7 (1985): 321–39.

White, Lynn, Jr. 'The Historical Roots of Our Ecologic Crisis', *Science* 155, no. 3767 (10 March 1967): 1203–7.

White, Lynn, Jr. 'Continuing the Conversation'. In *Western Man and Environmental Ethics: Attitudes toward Nature and Technology*, edited by Ian G. Barbour, 55–64. Reading, MA: Addison-Wesley, 1973.

Whitehead, Alfred North. *Science and the Modern World*. New York: Free Press, [1925] 1967.

Whitehead, Alfred North. *Religion in the Making: Lowell Lectures, 1926*. Cambridge: Cambridge University Press, 1926.

Whitehead, Alfred North. *Process and Reality*. Edited by David Ray Griffin and Donald W. Sherburne, cor. edn. New York: Free Press, [1928] 1978.

Whitehead, Alfred North. *Adventures of Ideas*. New York: Free Press, [1933] 1967.

Whitehead, Alfred North. *Modes of Thought*. New York: Capricorn Books, 1938.

Wildman, Wesley. 'The Divine Action Project, 1988–2003', *Theology and Science* 2 (2004): 31–75.

Williams, Rowan. *The Edge of Words: God and the Habits of Language*. London: Bloomsbury, 2014.

Williams, Rowan. *Christ the Heart of Creation*. London: Bloomsbury, 2018.

Wimsatt, William C. 'The Ontology of Complex Systems: Levels of Organization, Perspectives, and Causal Thickets', *Canadian Journal of Philosophy* supplementary 20 (1994): 207–74.

Wimsatt, William C. *Re-Engineering Philosophy of Limited Beings: Piecewise Approximations to Reality*. Boston, MA: Harvard University Press, 2007.

Wimsatt, William C. 'Aggregativity: Reductive Heuristics for Finding Emergence'. In *Emergence: Contemporary Readings in Philosophy and Science*, edited by Mark A. Bedau and Paul Humphreys, 99–110. Cambridge, MA: MIT Press, 2008.

Wirzba, Norman. *From Nature to Creation: A Christian Vision for Understanding and Loving Our World*. Grand Rapids, MI: Baker Academic, 2015.

Wolff, Hans Walter. *Anthropology of the Old Testament*. Edited and Translated by Margaret Kohl. London: SCM Press, 1974.

Wolterstorff, Nicholas. 'Why Animals Don't Speak', *Faith and Philosophy* 4, no. 4 (October 1987): 463–85.

Wolterstorff, Nicholas. *Divine Discourse: Philosophical Reflections on the Claim That God Speaks*. Cambridge: Cambridge University Press, 1995.

Wolterstorff, Nicholas. 'An Engagement with Rorty', *Journal of Religious Ethics* 31, no. 1 (2003): 129–39.

Wright, N. T. 'Mind, Spirit, Soul and Body: All for One and One for All; Reflections on Paul's Anthropology in His Complex Contexts', 26 November 2013, http://www.ntwrightpage.com/Wright_SCP_MindSpiritSoulBody.htm.

Wright, Sewall. 'Panpsychism in Science'. In *Mind in Nature: The Interface of Science and Philosophy*, edited by John B. Cobb, Jr and David R. Griffin. Lanham, MD: University Press of America, 1977. PDF file, accessed 11 August 2020, http://www.religion-online.org/cgi-bin/relsearchd.dll/showchapter?chapter_id=1852.

Wuketits, Franz M. 'Organisms, Vital Forces, and Machines'. In *Reductionism and Systems Theory in Life Sciences: Some Problems and Perspectives*, edited by Paul Hoyningen-Huene and Franz M. Wuketits, 3–28. Dordrecht, NL: Kluwer Academic Press, 1989.

Yong, Amos. *The Spirit of Creation: Modern Science and Divine Action in the Pentecostal-Charismatic Imagination*. Grand Rapids, MI: Eerdmans, 2011.

Yong, Amos. *The Cosmic Breath: Spirit and Nature in the Christianity-Buddhism-Science Trialogue*. Leiden: Brill, 2012.

Zizioulas, John. 'Man, the Priest of Creation'. In *Living Orthodoxy in the Modern World*, edited by A. Walker and C. Carras, 178–88. London: SPCK, 1996.

Zizioulas, John. 'Priest of Creation'. In *Environmental Stewardship: Critical Perspectives-Past and Present*, edited by R. J. Berry, 273–90. London: T&T Clark, 2006.

Zizioulas, John. 'Proprietors or Priests of Creation?' In *Toward an Ecology of Transfiguration: Orthodox Christian Perspectives on Environment, Nature and Creation*, edited by John Chryssavgis and Bruce V. Foltz, 163–72. Fordham Scholarship Online, 2014.

INDEX

Lightning Source UK Ltd.
Milton Keynes UK
UKHW022301250121
377657UK00003B/144